DATE DUE			

X

Philosophers in Conversation

Interviews from
The Harvard Review of Philosophy

WITH A FOREWORD BY
Thomas Scanlon

EDITED BY
S. Phineas Upham

IN CONSULTATION WITH HRP FOUNDER
Joshua Harlan

Routledge
New York and London

Published in 2002 by
Routledge
29 West 35th Street
New York, NY 10001

Published in Great Britain by
Routledge
11 New Fetter Lane
London EC4P 4EE

Routledge is an imprint of the Taylor & Francis Group.

Cover and interior photographs: Stanley Cavell, Alan Dershowitz, Harvey C. Mansfield, Hilary Putnam, W. V. Quine, John Rawls, Michael Sandel, Cornel West: courtesy Harvard News Archives; Umberto Eco: photo by Nancy Crampton, courtesy Harcourt, Inc.; Richard Rorty: courtesy University of Virginia; Henry Allison: courtesy The Harvard Review of Philosophy; Alexander Nehamas: courtesy Princeton University; Cora Diamond: courtesy photographer Mary Bernard; Peter Unger: courtesy Peter Unger.

Printed in the United States of America on acid-free paper.
10 9 8 7 6 5 4 3 2 1

Library of Congress Cataloging-in-Publication Data is available from the Library of Congress.

Philosophers in Conversation: Interviews from The Harvard Review of Philosophy / edited by S. Phineas Upham

ISBN 0-415-93778-7 (pbk.) – ISBN 0-415-93779-5

Philosophers in Conversation

Michael Travers
on *Philosophy*
the philosophical life

Contents

Foreword
by Thomas Scanlon of Harvard University

The Harvard Review of Philosophy, in which these interviews first appeared, is a remarkable phenomenon. A journal started and run entirely by undergraduate students, it has maintained a consistently high level of quality for ten years, publishing articles by well-known philosophers as well as by students, and attracting a wide readership. The interviews collected here have been a prominent feature of the *Review* since the beginning. (The interview with John Rawls appeared in its very first issue.) They were conducted entirely by students, usually, although not invariably, by undergraduates. (Steven Gross, who interviewed Henry Allison, and Leif Wenar, who participated in the interview with Michael Sandel, were graduate students in philosophy at Harvard at the time the interviews were conducted.)

The interviews deal with the ideas expressed in their subjects' published writings, but go far beyond merely asking them to explain their well-known views and to respond to criticisms. As Josh Harlan, one of the founding editors, wrote in his introductory note to the first issue of the *Review*, students are curious about larger questions, such as "What is philosophy?" "What is its relevance?" and "Why pursue it?" Accordingly, the interviewees are asked not only "What did you mean by such-and-such?" and "How would you respond to Professor so-and-so's objection?" but also, in almost every case, "How did you come to be interested in philosophy in the first place?" "What are your aims in doing philosophy?" and "Why do you think it is important?"

Two other questions figure prominently in the interviews. One of these is the relation between "analytic" philosophy, which is the main focus of attention in most of the leading departments in North America and Great Britain, and "Continental" philosophy of the kind that has, at least until recently, been dominant in France and Germany. Diverse perspectives on this question are reflected in the interviews with Umberto Eco, Stanley Cavell, Hilary Putnam, Richard Rorty, and W. V. Quine. A second question that comes up in many interviews is the relation between study of the history of philosophy and work on particular philosophical problems, such as epistemological skepticism or the foundations of morality. Training in philosophy, at both undergraduate and graduate levels, standardly involves studying the works of great figures in the history of the subject, going back more than two thousand years, as well as the latest developments. But, why, it might be asked, should the history of philosophy have more relevance to someone studying philosophy than the history of chemistry does to someone learning chemistry? For me, one of the most interesting things in reading the interviews was the wide variety of answers that interviewees gave to this question. (The interview with Henry Allison contains a particularly sustained and probing discussion.)

The interviews deal with many different areas of philosophy. Political philosophy is strongly represented: the interviews with Harvey C. Mansfield, John Rawls, Richard Rorty, and Michael Sandel explore their diverse views not only about justice but also about the relation between political philosophy and everyday politics. Philosophy of mind, philosophy of language and logic, as well as the philosophies of Socrates, Kant, Nietzsche, Heidegger, and Wittgenstein. The relation between philosophy and literature is explored by Cavell, Eco, Alexander Nehamas, and Cornel West; and the relation between philosophy and religion is also discussed in a number of these interviews. As this list indicates, the writers interviewed form an eclectic mix that reflects the interests and enthusiasms of the students who have, at various times, worked on the *Review*, rather than any particular conception of the current state of philosophy.

In the early years of the *Review*, students interviewed professors whose courses they had taken, in the philosophy department or outside of it; later they also interviewed people outside of Harvard whose works they had read. This history accounts for the heavy representation of Harvard professors among the interviewees. There is a benefit here for the reader, since teachers are willing to talk with their students in a way that they might not with just any interviewer. So readers have the rare opportunity of listening in on conversations in which eager, intelligent, and sophisticated students press their distinguished professors with questions about their views of philosophy and its role in their lives. These philosophers' differing views as well as their distinct personalities come across clearly in the way they respond to the students' questions. No single reader is likely to find all of the interviews equally interesting or appealing. But anyone interested in, or curious about, contemporary philosophy is sure to enjoy many of these candid encounters with eminent thinkers.

Thomas Scanlon is Alford Professor of Natural Religion, Moral Philosophy, and Civil Polity at Harvard University. His primary areas of work have been in moral and political philosophy. His book *What We Owe to Each Other* was published by Harvard University Press in 1998.

Editor's Note

My thanks to the people who have made this book possible, especially Mr. William Roberts, *The Harvard Review of Philosophy*'s (*HRP*) lead trustee. Mr. Roberts's encouragement and support are an invaluable part of *HRP*. We are pleased to be publishing at Routledge, where the help of editors Damian Treffs, Damon Zucca, and Robert Byrne has been wonderful. Within the Harvard philosophy department our advisors Thomas Scanlon and Robert Nozick have been a constant resource. Thank you to Joshua Harlan who founded *HRP* in 1991 and has been a help to me throughout the editing of this book.

The interviews in this book were done by *HRP* staff members, mostly undergraduates, between 1991 and 2001. Thanks to John Maier, Berislav Marusic, Ben Wikler, Nicolaus Petri, Christine Telyan, Tian Mayimin, and Ari Weinstein for their unstinting contributions to the introductions of the interviews. My special thanks to John and Beri for their generous help in preparing this book, and to Simon Dedeo who has been such an important part of *HRP*.

As Editor-In-Chief of *HRP* from 1998 to 2000, as well as working to prepare these interviews for this publication, I have come to appreciate even more than before the dedication and excellence of *HRP* in all of its activities. These interviews, always simultaneously accessible and demanding, playful and serious, satisfying and thought-provoking, provide not only an insight into great philosophers, but also an insight into what makes philosophy great.

—*S. Phineas Upham*

Why do Philosophy?

Can Philosophy help us to live a better life?

~~How has~~

Which philosophy has had the greatest impact on your & why?

You enjoy reading novels which have philosophical ideas within them, which & often has had the greatest impact?

In terms of current events, how could philosophy be used to better understand a situation?

John Rawls

Asked to describe John Rawls, his old friend and fellow philosopher Rogers Albritton said, "My principal sense of Jack is of a man who has an incredibly fine moral sense in his dealings with other human beings. He is not just the author of a great book, he is a very admirable man. He is the best of us."[1] John Rawls's *A Theory of Justice* published in 1971 has been described as a watershed moment in modern political philosophy, restoring it as an important area for philosophical concern. It is also one of the most comprehensive and influential works of modern liberalism. More than 200,000 copies have been sold worldwide and more than 5,000 books or articles have discussed it, which is especially noteworthy because *A Theory of Justice* is such a serious, theoretical, and dense work.

In his books and articles, Rawls keeps famously private about his life except to lavish credit on others for their help and ideas. He refuses most interviews, has only accepted honorary degrees from universities with which he has personal ties (Oxford, Princeton, Harvard), and has long since removed himself from *Who's Who*. The following interview granted to *The Harvard Review of Philosophy* in 1991 is the first of only three interviews Rawls has ever given, and all three were with students or former students. Rawls's adult life has been almost exclusively devoted to thinking, teaching, and writing about the problems of social justice, cooperation, and individual rights.

John Bordley Rawls was born in 1921, the second of five sons in a well-to-do and well-respected Baltimore family. He went to Kent prep school in Connecticut, and took both his undergraduate and doctoral philosophy degrees from Princeton University, entering as a freshman in 1939. After college and before graduate school, Rawls joined the army. He served with the 32nd Infantry Division during World War II in New Guinea and the Philippines in some of the bloodiest fighting of the war and was with the occupation army in Japan. After teaching at Cornell and MIT Rawls settled at Harvard, where he is now James Bryant Conant University Professor Emeritus, living in Lexington, Massachusetts. He has spent time as a visiting scholar at Oxford, Stanford's Institute for advanced Study in the Behavioral Sciences, the University of Michigan, and the Institute for Advanced Study at Princeton. He has received numerous awards for his work, the most recent being the National Humanities Award presented by President Clinton and the Rolf Schock Prize in Philosophy from the Royal Swedish Academy—both in 1999.

---

1. Quoted in Ben Rogers, "Behind the Veil: John Rawls and the Revival of Liberalism," *Lingua Franca* 9 (5) (1999).

Rawls holds civil and political rights at the center of his philosophy. He takes our freedom to choose our own ends to be the distinctive feature of human nature. His opus on justice revived what was a neglected liberal tradition of the rights-based social contract. In this work he rejects utilitarianism, which advocates the maximization of the aggregate well-being of a society, as not sufficiently respecting the rights of individuals. In the spirit of Kant, whom he admires greatly, Rawls insists that people ought to be treated as ends, not as means. Rawls also criticizes libertarianism, which advocates that an individual's rights ought never be infringed upon, by arguing that taking rights seriously implies taking social equality seriously. He feels that it is not enough to avoid having civil and political rights infringed, one must have the meaningful use of these rights in a society.

Famously, Rawls developed the idea of the "original position," a thought experiment in which people are placed behind what he calls the "veil of ignorance." They are denied all knowledge about everything that makes them the particular individuals they are: wealth, age, talents, race, religion, skill, sex, and any conception of the good life. Rawls believes that what people in this position would choose for their society could be considered the principles of justice. He argues that in this position people would choose a low-risk strategy in which liberties and the highest minimum levels of wealth, opportunity, and power are promoted even at the expense of lowering average levels of one or another. Rawls's related idea, the "difference principle," is perhaps his most controversial and often-challenged argument. Here he argues that social and economic differences are acceptable only if these differences benefit the least advantaged in society.

Throughout Rawls's career he has dedicated himself to writing articles and giving lectures, elaborating his theory of justice, and responding to the numerous criticisms raised by others. He is famous not only for illuminating the misunderstandings of his critics, but for being willing to rethink his arguments and incorporate changes. In 1993 he published his second book, *Political Liberalism*, which is his most comprehensive response to more than thirty years of critics. When the paperback edition came out in 1996 it contained an important second introduction and included a "Reply to Habermas," making it, in effect, a second edition of this work. Despite suffering from several strokes, the first in 1995, which affected his ability to work, Rawls completed his *Law of Peoples* in 1998–perhaps his most emotionally explicit work. This was published together with "The Idea of Public Reason Revisited" in 1999. Most recently, in 2001, after decades of work, he has published *Justice as Fairness: A Restatement*, about which he speaks in our interview. In this short volume, edited by Erin Kelly, he attempts to reformulate and put in compact form his lifelong work on justice. His *Collected Papers*, edited by Samuel Freedman, was published in 1999, and his *Lectures on the History of Moral Philosophy*, edited by Barbara Herman, appeared in 2000.

A story still repeated about Rawls among philosophy students in Emerson Hall at Harvard University seems particularly telling. Once, when attending a dissertation defense, Rawls noticed that the sun was shining in the eyes of the candidate. He rose and positioned himself, standing uncomfortably, between the candidate and the sunlight for the rest of the session. Emanating from Rawls's work, ideas, and life, despite his inclination toward privacy, is the image of a man who cares intensely about justice, social welfare, and individual happiness. φ

John Rawls
For the Record

Interview by
Samuel R. Aybar,
Joshua D. Harlan, and
Won J. Lee in 1991

HRP: Tell us about yourself. How did you become interested in philosophy?

Rawls: Well, I don't think we know really how we become interested in something, or why. We can only say what happened when. I went to Princeton and eventually became a philosophy major. In September of my freshman year Hitler invaded Poland and the war in Europe overshadowed everything. I spent a great deal of time reading about the First World War and about the question of war itself. Of course, in that generation we all knew we were going to be in the war sooner or later. It made that generation, in terms of its experience of war, very different from recent generations. I was in the army for three years, from the beginning of '43 to the beginning of '46, spending some time in the Pacific, in New Guinea, the Philippines, and Japan. I can't say how that affected me exactly, but it must have had an influence. When the war was over I went back to Princeton as a graduate student for the spring term of 1946.

HRP: Did you expect to be a philosophy student when you entered Princeton?

Rawls: I didn't know what I was going to do. I had gone to Kent School in Kent, Connecticut, a private school. But I had not yet developed any well-formed intellectual interest and I thought of several different majors, including chemistry and mathematics, but I soon found they were beyond me, and settled down finally in philosophy.

HRP: Tell us more about your formative experiences in the army. Were your later ideas about justice more influenced by your thoughts about the societies our nation was confronting, or by your feelings about the structure of military society?

Rawls: Well, as I have said, I think we don't know why we come to do things, or what exactly influences us this way or that. My being in the war for three years must have had some important affect, but I wouldn't say those years were particularly formative. When I think about the views in philosophy I

3

came to hold, I don't see that their content is traceable to my experiences in those years. I have often thought there must surely be some connection but I've not been able to pin it down. Perhaps that's a failure of reflection on my part. Of course, like a lot of people, I came out of the army firmly disliking it and thinking it is of first importance that the military be subordinate to civilian government. Nothing new in that.

HRP: Was it as a graduate student that you became interested in the area of philosophy in which you eventually became well known?

Rawls: Well, I was always interested in moral philosophy, from the beginning. I was also for a long time interested in religion. The Kent School was a church school. It was founded by Father Sill, who belonged to the Episcopal Order of the Holy Cross and there were usually several other members of the order at the school. We went to chapel every day and twice on Sunday. I wouldn't say it was an especially religious-minded student body. But you couldn't avoid religion altogether. You had to have some reaction to it.

HRP: Where are you originally from?

Rawls: I grew up in Baltimore and spent all my youth there, except for summers in Maine, and of course much of the year at boarding school in my teens. My father was from North Carolina, my mother from an old Maryland family. Most of my family was there and so was my wife's mother's family. Many of my oldest friends are still there.

HRP: When did you start doing the actual thinking and writing that led to *A Theory of Justice*?

Rawls: I began to collect notes around the fall of 1950 after I had completed my thesis. By then I had been reading some economics on my own and that fall I attended a seminar given by W. J. Baumol—he's a well-known economist now. I tried to do all the work. We read *Value and Capital* by J. R. Hicks, and I attempted to master that book, and also parts of Samuelson's *Foundations*, its chapter of welfare economics leading me to articles in the so-called new welfare economics. This was going on while I was a graduate student, and continued when I was an instructor at Princeton for two years, 1950 to 1952. I also read some of Walras's *Elements* and studied a little bit of game theory. Von Neumann's book with Morgenstern had just come out in 1944; that was the big work on game theory that founded the subject. Several essays by Frank Knight in his *Ethics of Competition* I found highly instructive; he was as much interested in social philosophy as economics. As a result of all these things, somehow—don't ask me how—plus the stuff on moral theory which I wrote my thesis on—it was out of that, in 1950 to 1951, that I got the idea that eventually turned into the original position.

The idea was to design a constitution of discussion out of which would come reasonable principles of justice. At that time I had a more complicated procedure than what I finally came up with. During this whole time I had to teach classes in philosophy, but I kept up my interest in economics as best I could. Then my wife and I went to England with our two-year-old daughter for a year on a Fulbright Fellowship.

HRP: Did you publish that original, more complicated formula?

Rawls: No, I couldn't work it out. It's all in notes on old paper somewhere at home turning brown.

HRP: Could you tell us a little bit about that formula?

Rawls: As I mentioned, it was an attempt to formulate a constitution of discussion among people that would make them agree—given their circumstances—to what we would think of as reasonable principles of justice. They had to make proposals to a central referee in ignorance of what others were proposing, and there was a limit to the time in which argument could go on, so some kind of agreement would be reached. There were lots of other details. You can imagine. Eventually, I cut through all of that by imposing the veil of ignorance and greatly limited what people knew; I also made the agreement binding in perpetuity. All that was an enormous simplifying device. The original way was just too complicated. There were certain seemingly insoluble problems; for example, how great to make the pressure for people to agree, how much time do we allow, and things of that sort. Remember, we need[ed] some philosophical justification for any answer. The later formulation of the original position has the virtue of avoiding the issues that got me interested in the idea in the first place, [such as] game theory and general equilibrium as used by economists, things I never knew much about. It then occurred to me, "Well, I have to get rid of all this." I think it was, in retrospect, the thing to have done. Although I think there are other ways it might have been done, and indeed can be done. For example, Professor Scanlon [T. M. Scanlon, Harvard University] doesn't use anything like the veil of ignorance; there is some resemblance [in his argument] to the original position, but his idea is actually quite different. So his view is another possibility. Also, for all I know you might design a constitution of discussion, which might be more realistic and succeed where I failed to see how to go. I wouldn't exclude other possibilities.

HRP: What are some of the significant changes that have taken place between *A Theory of Justice* and *A Briefer Restatement*?

Rawls: I want the *Restatement* to be compact and to convey everything, even if in outline, in one place. Incidentally, I don't like that title but haven't a better one now, so in default I'll call it that. I want it to be more accessible and more readable than *Theory*. I'd like it to come out soon, but I have a few more parts to go. I try to do three things: one is to recast the argument from the original position and put in it a simpler form, improving faults in the book's exposition; another is to reply to various objections, explaining why I reject some but incorporating changes others seem to require; and finally, I try to combine the view of the book with what I have written in articles since.

HRP: Are most of those articles responses to criticism from other people?

Rawls: Well, I don't think so really. I have responded to people, certainly, so there are responses; but what I am mainly doing in these articles, as I now understand having written them—you don't always understand what you're doing until after it has happened—is to work out my view so that it is no longer internally inconsistent. To explain: to work out justice as fairness the book uses throughout an idea of a well-ordered society, which supposes that everybody in that society accepts the same comprehensive view, as I say now. I came to think that that simply can never be the case in a democratic society, the kind of society the principles of the book itself require. That's the internal inconsistency. So I had to change the account of the well-ordered society and this led to the idea of overlapping consensus and related ideas. That is really what the later articles are about. Beginning with the three lectures in the *Journal of Philosophy*, that's what they are doing.

So I don't see these articles mainly as replies to other people's objections, although I do make replies to important objections here and there, and in footnotes. People deserve to be answered if their objections make valuable points and can be dealt with reasonably. That's part of one's obligation when one engages in these things. But the main aim is to develop this other part of the view and then to bring it together with the view of *A Theory of Justice*. As I see it, the development is from within—that is, I came to see there was something wrong; therefore, I had to correct it. When I first began to work out the idea of overlapping consensus and the ideas that go along with it, I thought it would be simple, even trivial. I thought the idea of such a consensus is so obvious, it wouldn't be a problem; but it turned out to be more complicated than I had anticipated; and I'm still not quite done with it. Also, in the *Restatement*, as I have indicated, I wanted to make certain improvements in the argument. In some cases there were things that were unclear; in other cases, there were just plain errors.

HRP: You said that you feel that it is somehow your "duty" to reply to criticism, if you can reasonably do so. What role do you see yourself playing as a writer that makes you incur that responsibility?

Rawls: Well, there are a number of things. I think that first of all, you have an obligation as a member of an academic community to reply to people if it can be done reasonably, and in a way that advances discussion. You want to avoid quarrels and fruitless wrangles. There are people whose criticisms are very good and they deserve an answer. That's all part of academic life. In a democratic society, as ours is, although it distressingly falls short of what it should be, I see political philosophy as addressing the citizenry—not government, that's not who you are addressing—[but] other people like you who comprise the electorate. It's important to carry on political discussion at the deepest level, and to do it as clearly as possible so that it is accessible to people generally. In that indirect way, if they find your ideas convincing, you might change society for the better, or more realistically perhaps, you might prevent it from getting worse. In a democratic society, political philosophy doesn't, of course, have any authority; but it can try to win the authority of human reason. There is no institutional judge of whether you succeed in that, any more than there is in science, or in any other rational inquiry. Yet that it is the only authority political philosophy can recognize.

HRP: Supposedly your theories have influenced democratic movements in Eastern Europe. Do you know anything about that?

Rawls: I don't, really. *A Theory of Justice* has been translated into all major European languages. But I don't know how widely it is known among the Eastern Europeans. I was told that certain parts of *A Theory of Justice* were in Russian, but I haven't seen it. Parts of it have been translated, I'm also told, into Hungarian. I haven't heard of a Polish translation, but there may be one in part. It has been translated some time ago into Chinese, Korean, and Japanese. Someone told me he heard copies of the book were seen in Tiananmen Square.

HRP: Did you expect that *A Theory of Justice* would receive the kind of response that it did?

Rawls: No. I certainly didn't expect it, and it's probably a good thing I didn't. Otherwise I wouldn't have been able to write it. I mean, you would feel people were looking over your shoulder, and you'd have to be too careful.

HRP: How did it become so famous? It was published in 1971. Did it immediately become well known?

Rawls: That's an interesting question. I'm not the best person to answer it. My own view, to answer your question, is to grant that *A Theory of Justice* has some merit. I don't know how much, and that is not for me to say. Granting that, I think it gained attention from a conjunction of circumstances. You have to remember [the historical context.] It was a long time ago, so you probably don't remember. Why should you? I wouldn't remember in your place. It was during the Vietnam War and soon after the Civil Rights movement. They dominated the politics of the day. And yet there was no recent book, no systematic treatise, you might say, on a conception of political justice. For a long time there had been a relative dearth of political philosophy—both in political science and moral philosophy. Very good things, some of permanent importance, had been done. I am thinking, for example, of H. L. A. Hart's *Concept of Law* and his other writings, Isaiah Berlin's *Four Essays on Liberty* and his many essays, and Brian Barry's *Political Argument*, all these in the 1960s. But there was no book of the scope and extent of the book on the idea of justice that touched upon so many questions of the time. Its size and scope was a little mad, actually. In writing it I guessed it was about 350 pages; when it was put in galleys and the Press told me it was nearly 600 pages (587 to be exact) I was astounded. Anyway, so you had this, I would say "political-intellectual," need for a book of this sort. For example, the issues discussed in chapter six about conscientious objection and civil disobedience were much discussed topics then. Yet there was no systematic contemporary book that dealt with them. Of course, there were older books, and there were contemporary essays. I am thinking of the splendid essays of Michael Walzer collected in his *Obligations*. So *Theory* was the first large work coming after this period of serious political conflict. And serious political conflict shows the need for political philosophy and normally calls it forth. So *Theory* captured attention fairly quickly. But, you know, I can't really take an objective view about all this. Yet that's my explanation. It was a matter of coincidence. Fifteen years earlier or later its status would be entirely different. Of course, you know, it's been criticized severely and much of it is quite just criticism. Yet somehow the book continues to be read. I'm not one to say that it survives the criticism.

HRP: How do you feel when you are criticized?

Rawls: One has to learn to accept criticisms. Often they are not well founded and based on misunderstanding. Those I try to ignore. But there are criticisms that are very good. While I'm not overjoyed by those, I do appreciate them, eventually, and I try to incorporate them into what I write later. I'll give you an example. H. L. A. Hart in 1973 raised fundamental criticisms of my views on the basic liberties and he was absolutely right. I was stuck about what to reply but eight years later I decided what the answer should be. I wrote it out and it was published in 1982. That was of enormous value to me. It caused some pain, certainly, but now I can state the view in a much stronger form.

HRP: What about having some of your more illustrious critics right here in the Harvard Philosophy Department? Does that make things more tense, or do you also appreciate that?

Rawls: Well, actually, there are two sides to it. A certain amount of tension goes with it. For example, Nozick [Professor Robert Nozick, Harvard University] had interesting and important objections. In part they were based on misunderstandings, though in part they were very good points. Although I haven't done a whole article replying to him, I have replied to him at several points (although not by name) in an article I [wrote] in 1978. I now see things more clearly. There is a part of the *Restatement,* the section on viewing the distribution of native endowments as a common asset. It is an attempt to cope with some of his objections. So even if you think an objection is not entirely right, it may raise a real question that enables you to understand things better.

HRP: When you have a critical give and take with someone like Robert Nozick, does that go on only in the pages of major philosophy journals, or will you sit down together in your office and argue about it?

Rawls: It all depends. But in the case of a colleague, we try first to talk about it. In the case of Hart, who is in England, we correspond a bit, and occasionally he comes into town and we have a talk. It varies from case to case. I have always viewed philosophy as a conversational subject. One learns best by talk and writing should be subjected to talk and criticism, sometimes it seems almost endlessly, before it gets printed up.

HRP: How does it feel to be so well known?

Rawls: I try to ignore it, though I probably don't succeed. It shows up in how people treat me, for example, when they are introduced to me and see me for the first time. It wouldn't be good for anybody to think about that, as it would badly affect their work. So I try not to walk around thinking about it.

HRP: So you have found that the most rewarding part of engaging with critics is that it straightens out your thoughts?

Rawls: Yes, I like to think that, yes. The straightening out of my thoughts. It would be dishonest to say that I don't care about the response. Sure I care about the response and I care about how accepting it is. I thought I would publish *A Theory of Justice* and some friends might read it. I had been writing it for a long time, so I would finally get it off my desk and then do something else. There were times in writing the book when I said to myself, "This is really pretty good." I put that aside as building morale to keep going. Had it been regarded as a decent enough work, that would, I think, have been enough to satisfy me. But [being accepted] is very important in that had the book fallen flat, that would have been upsetting. Since no attention is without criticisms, the criticisms I've gotten, however painful temporarily, have been important to me.

HRP: So you expected, when you published originally, that you would then move on to some new topic?

Rawls: Yes, I had planned on doing some other things mainly connected with the third part of the book, which was the part I liked best, the part on moral psychology. That would not be exactly a new but a related topic. I have never gotten around to that and never will. I thought the way things have turned out that it would be better if I spent my time trying to state justice as fairness more convincingly and to reply to people and remove their objections. I'm not sure that's the best thing to have done, but that's what I have done. I'm a monomaniac really. I'd like to get something right. But in philosophy one can't do that, not with any confidence. Real difficulties always remain.

HRP: What can we expect from you in the near future in terms of publications and teaching?

Rawls: I just turned 70, so I have to take that into account. Some time soon, I hope I can get the *Restatement* in shape. It will be about the size it is now, less than 200 pages. I don't want it to get longer. There are no surprises in it. What you have seen is what you get. I also have some lectures I'm working on which are based on the lectures I gave at Columbia in 1980. From my later articles I am adding three more to those three, so eventually they may come out too. Both books are about the same length. After that, I have no plans. There comes a time when you should stop writing and that may be it.

HRP: Has using the *Restatement* in class been useful in its development?

Rawls: Yes, definitely. It began as handouts for the course and I have used it a number of times now and each time it gets bigger. Actually, I wrote the book in much the same way and there were versions of it that existed as early as 1963. I don't know that I could do this anywhere but at Harvard. The class has never complained about this and I am very appreciative of that.

HRP: How did you select the authors, other than yourself, that you ask students in your class on political philosophy to read?

Rawls: Well, we did four last year. I'm trying to indicate the tradition of democratic thought that's been in our political culture for a long time. One way to do that is to read a few important historical texts in political philosophy.

One studies how a present day restatement tries to use ideas in these texts in a serious way. The ideas are changed in certain ways, but nevertheless they are there. That's one way to do political philosophy. As you read these older texts, and read them seriously, you come to see how a tradition of thought can evolve over time. Of course, you could equally well read contemporary writers, and in some ways that might be better. But I haven't often done that. I might do that next year. I don't know how the historical approach that I have most often followed appeals to students, but that is one way to do it. The four I picked last year [Locke, Rousseau, Mill, and Marx] are obviously important, but another four might do just as well. I pick Marx because now he tends not to be taken seriously and it's good to know his thought. His criticism of capitalism is an important part of the democratic tradition and I try to present him as sympathetically as I can. I don't know if that comes across or not, but I try to do that. I try to treat them all seriously. They are well worth studying.

HRP: Were you ever interested in going into politics yourself?

Rawls: No. I've never been interested. Well, I'm interested in politics, but not in having a political career. I think I'd be very bad at it.

HRP: You seem far too honest.

Rawls: I don't know if that is it, because I might learn to be dishonest. There are different skills that one has. It's not suited to my temperament.

HRP: When you look at current events, in general, do you think of them with the *A Theory of Justice* framework in mind?

Rawls: Not really. Well, like anyone else, I react to current events and present problems in a certain way. I'm sure that my view must affect in some manner how I see them, but I don't just ask what justice as fairness would say. That would be limiting. I don't see a political conception of justice as something that will tell me what to think. It's a great mistake to think of it as a device that will give you answers, which will deliver the answers to all sorts of questions when you want them. That is one reason I am reluctant to answer questions about specific political topics. It suggests the wrong idea: that we could [have] some theoretical way of doing that, which is usually not so at all. I think of justice as fairness as trying to answer certain specific though basic questions. Its scope is limited. In any case, a reasonable view is important but it doesn't begin to be enough by itself. Judgment, informed opinion, due consideration, and much, much else are required. Usually if a question interests me, I may form an opinion on its merits. That's probably the best thing to do—and then see whether the opinion is reasonable, and what other people think. Except for special cases, I wouldn't ask whether the opinion fits with *A Theory of Justice*. Besides, it would be a mistake to apply one's principles all the time. You need to examine things apart from them, else you risk becoming an ideologue. People who have opinions on everything derived from their so-called principles are not to be trusted.

HRP: What has been your reaction to the campus controversy surrounding the hanging of a Confederate flag in a dormitory window?

Rawls: I don't know that I have a useful opinion on that. I'm not acquainted with the circumstances. But it would be highly offensive to black students. The southern secession that caused the Civil War was totally unjustified. It was unjustified because it was secession to preserve slavery. There are some circumstances under which secession is permissible; but it has to be done for a reasonable cause. The preservation of slavery is plainly not such a cause. That fact dominates the picture. Also, we have to ask what kinds of symbols are appropriate for undergraduates to display. I would try to encourage southern students to find another symbol of their southern culture. Because whatever they say to themselves, the meaning of the Confederate flag is already fixed by our history, by secession as a way to preserve slavery; and that as late as the last century and even then as secession from the oldest democracy in the world. It is impossible now to change the meaning of the flag.

HRP: If you were an administrator of the university, would you hold President Bok's position ("I don't approve of this, but I'm not going to compel anyone to take it down,") or would you feel that a student engaging in offensive behavior should be compelled to stop?

Rawls: I haven't thought about the matter from the president's point of view. One might make a distinction between free discussion of ideas, which is especially important in the university, and forms of behavior that might be properly thought [of as] offensive to other students and then penalized in some way. But suppose that displaying the flag is a form of verbal behavior, or speech, then you have to decide when forms of behavior become legitimate speech, where that line is. And that is very difficult. I think I would try to persuade southern students to find another symbol. In a student body, itself viewed as a democratic society in the small, there are forms of speech that, for historical or other good reasons, certain groups find offensive or demeaning or hostile, and therefore out of decency and mutual civility ought not to be said. But I would probably do the same thing Bok did, when all things were considered. While there ought to be a tacitly understood code of decent and civil conduct among undergraduates, one would hope it could be affirmed by students themselves, without administrative enforcement. One hopes they could have a shared sense of what is appropriate to other people's legitimate feelings.

HRP: What would you say to a student now who is interested in philosophy? Would you say to make it a career?

Rawls: I rarely, if ever, encourage people to go into philosophy. I impress upon them the drawbacks. If you very strongly want to do it, that's one thing. Otherwise, you probably shouldn't go into philosophy, because it does have its hardships and trials, and most who would be good at it would be much better off—at least by society's standards—in doing something else. The real rewards of philosophy are personal and private and you should understand that. I think philosophy is a very special subject, particularly in our society, which pays very little attention to most serious philosophy, even when it is very well done. However, this is not a complaint, and it may be a good thing.

HRP: Why do philosophy?

Rawls: In every civilization there should be people thinking about these questions. It's not just that this kind of inquiry is good in itself. But a society in which nobody thinks seriously about questions of metaphysics and epistemology, moral and political philosophy, is really lacking as a society. Part of being civilized is being aware of these questions and the possible answers to them. They affect how you see your place in the world, and part of what philosophy does if it is done well is to make reasonable answers to these questions accessible to thoughtful people generally, and so available as part of culture. It's the same thing as art and music—if you're a good composer, or if you're a good painter, you contribute to people's understanding. Don't ask me exactly how.

In particular, political philosophy takes various forms. Society often has very deep problems that need to be thought about seriously. In a democratic society you are always having conflicts between liberty and equality. Moreover, it is a still an unsettled question, I think, as to what are the most appropriate grounds of toleration and of the fundamental pluralism that characterizes our society. It is vital to have views about these matters. It's important also to have a conception of one's society as a whole. I believe people, or at least many people, have a need of such conceptions and it makes a difference in preserving democratic institutions [as] what they are. Political philosophy may address that need. φ

Hilary Putnam

Hilary Putnam is a prominent figure in twentieth-century Anglo-American philosophy and has made significant contributions to many discussions in the discipline. He has written on, among other subjects, the philosophy of mind, philosophy of mathematics, philosophy of language, metaphysics, value theory, philosophy of religion, as well as artificial intelligence, and quantum mechanics. He has put forward many proposals and theories that have found wide acclaim. It is a characteristic mark of his thinking that he scrutinizes his own views thoroughly and sometimes finds problems with them. Thus Putnam is also famous for renouncing his philosophical positions— often at the great dismay of his disciples and colleagues who continue to work on those projects. When he was once criticized for often changing his views, he replied, "What do *you* do when you find that you are wrong?" Putnam's willingness to reexamine his position and change his mind is a testimony to his intellectual integrity.

There are two well-known turns in Putnam's thinking that should be mentioned here. The first is his proposal and subsequent criticism of functionalism. This is the view, according to Putnam's version, that the mental properties of the brain can be described in terms of properties that are definable without recourse to chemistry or physics but can be represented with Turing Machines. Putnam's critique of this view comes out of his deeper reflections on the nature of reference. The second turn in Putnam's thinking is his proposal of a position called internal realism, which he presented as an alternative to a prominent view of truth and justification known as metaphysical realism. Internal realism is the view that to say of a statement that it is true in the conditions in which it is considered (say in the context) is to say that it could be justified if the epistemic conditions were good enough. Later, Putnam concluded that this view ran into various problems. He now maintains, first, that some empirical statements can be true even though they could not be verified (the statement that there aren't any intelligent extraterrestrials might be an example, he points out!); and, second, there is no one single vocabulary in which all true statements can be formulated. In particular, he denies that the vocabulary of science is such a vocabulary. Putnam also claims that value judgments, descriptions of fact, and linguistic conventions all "interpenetrate." The question "Is that a fact or a value judgment?" is often a bad question; the right answer may be "both." (Putnam calls this "pragmatic realism.")

In identifying views like functionalism, metaphysical realism, and internal realism as laden with philosophical temptations, Putnam finally turns to thinkers like Wittgenstein on the one hand, and William James and John Dewey on the other. Putnam's current writings thus center around American pragmatism, skepticism, and the work of Stanley Cavell. Very recently, Putnam has also written an introduction to Franz Rosenzweig's *Understanding the Sick and the Healthy* thus extending his reflections on Jewish thought. Even after his retirement, Putnam remains a prolific and widely interested writer.

Hilary Putnam was born in Chicago in 1926, received his AB from the University of Pennsylvania in mathematics and philosophy, and took his Ph.D. in philosophy from UCLA in 1951 after studying with Hans Reichenbach. He taught at Northwestern, Princeton, and MIT, before coming to Harvard in 1976. Putnam has served as Walter Beverley Pearson Professor of Mathematical Logic and later as Cogan University Professor. He retired in June of 2000. His books include *Realism with a Human Face* (1990), *Pragmatism: An Open Question* (1995), and *The Threefold Cord: Mind, Body, and World* (1999). His last lecture at Harvard was published in Volume VIII of *The Harvard Review of Philosophy*. φ

Hilary Putnam
On Mind, Meaning, and Reality

Interview by
Josh Harlan
in 1992

HRP: What are the ultimate goals of the philosophy of mind? What distinguishes the philosophy of mind from such fields as neuroscience, cognitive science, and psychology?

Putnam: Like all branches of philosophy, philosophy of mind is the discussion of a loose cluster of problems, to which problems get added (and sometimes subtracted) in the course of time. To make things more complicated, the notion of the "mind" is itself one which has changed a great deal through the millenia. Aristotle, for example, has no notion which exactly corresponds to our notion of "mind." The *psyche*, or soul, in Aristotle's philosophy is not the same as our "mind" because its functions include such "non-mental" functions as digestion and reproduction. (This is so because the "soul" is simply the form of the organized living body in Aristotle's philosophy. Is this obviously a worse notion than our present-day notion of mind?) And the *nous*, or reason, in Aristotle's philosophy, excludes many functions which we regard as mental (some of which are taken over by the *thumos*, the integrative center which Aristotle locates in the heart).

Even in my lifetime I have seen two very different ways of conceiving the mind: one, which descended from British empiricism, conceived of the mental as primarily composed of sensations. "Are sensations (or *qualia*, as philosophers sometimes say) identical with brain processes?" was *the* "mind-body problem" for this tradition. (The mind conceived of as a "bundle of sensations" might be called "the English mind.") The other way conceived of the mind as primarily characterized by reason and intentionality—by the ability to judge, and to refer. (This might be called "the German mind.")

Interestingly, the rise of the computer, and of computer models for cognition, lead to a decline in talk about "sensations" and to an increase in talk about thinking and referring in English language philosophical literature. But the concern of materialistically inclined English-speaking philosophers with "mind body identity" did not decline. Instead, the question got reformulated as, "Are thinking and referring identical with computational states of the brain?"

In my present view, these "identity" questions are misguided, although it took me many years to come to this conclusion (which I defend at length in *Representation and Reality*). I think the search for an "identity" between properties having to do with the description of thought and reference and physical, or at least computational, properties is driven by a *fear*—the fear that the only alternative is to return to dualism, to the picture of a ghost in a machine. But that is not the only alternative. The right alternative—an alternative defended, in different ways, not only by myself but earlier by Wittgenstein, by Austin, by Strawson, by Donald Davidson (and even much earlier in a peculiar way, by William James)—is to see the natural scientific description of the living human organism (a description which systematically abstracts from purpose and meaning) and the "mentalistic" description in terms of purpose and meaning as complementary.

Neither is reducible to the other but that does not mean that they are in any sense competitors. Of course, this involves rejecting the claim that the scientific description is the only "first-class" description of reality, i.e., that it is the "perspective-free" description of the whole of reality. And that claim has deep roots in the Western way of thinking since the seventeenth century. Thus the discussion in philosophy of mind today has become uncontainable discussions in philosophy of mind become discussions in metaphysics, in epistemology, in metaphilosophy, etc.

Coming back to the question as you posed it, the question of the "ultimate goals" of philosophy of mind, one might say that there are two competing answers today. The answer of traditional philosophy is that the goal is to answer the identity questions I listed, that is, either to tell us in materialistic terms exactly what is constitutive of thinking, referring, perceiving, etc.—in short, to squeeze the conceptual scheme of purpose and meaning inside the scientific scheme—or, failing that, to establish that dualism is correct, that we have immaterial souls over and above our bodies and brains. The answer of the competing current I described, in which I include myself, is that the goal should be to render philosophy of mind, as traditionally conceived, obsolete. The first current, in its reductionist form, does expect answers to the problems of philosophy of mind (as it conceives them) to come from neuroscience, cognitive science, and psychology). The second current thinks that these subjects give us information that constrains what we can say about human beings in the language of purpose and meaning, but that the project of reducing our mentalistic concepts to "scientific" ones is misguided.

HRP: When discussing certain issues, you occasionally have referred to fictional creations such as "Isaac Asimov's robots." What role can science fiction play in philosophy?

Putnam: Philosophy, almost by definition, is interested in exploring the bounds of the possible (*The Bounds of Sense* is the title of a famous work by Peter Strawson). Science fiction is a fertile source of scenarios, of possibilities that we might be tempted to overlook. Or at least I have found it so.

HRP: You are credited with modeling Cartesian skepticism with the notion of a world in which all sentient beings are "brains in a vat." What does this thought experiment show us? Could our notion of reality be an illusion?

Putnam: My discussion of the "brain in a vat" model of Cartesian skepticism is too long to summarize here, but I can say what my purpose was: my purpose was to argue that concepts and world involve each other, that the concepts you have depend on the world you inhabit and how you are related to it. The idea that we first have concepts in some purely "private" medium and we must *then* proceed to see if anything corresponds to them has had a powerful grip on our thinking ever since Descartes, but it is at bottom completely incoherent. Or that, at least, is what I claim to show. Our notion of reality is necessarily subject to correction (that is part of what makes it a notion of *reality*), but the thought that it could be an "illusion" has only the appearance of making sense.

HRP: Please tell us about your book *Realism with a Human Face* (Harvard University Press, 1990). How does it reflect a change in your earlier views?

Putnam: *Realism with a Human Face* does not reflect a change in my views as compared to, say, *Reason, Truth and History* written about ten years earlier, but it does reflect a development of them in several directions. For one thing, the sorts of criticisms I made of metaphysical realism in *Reason, Truth and History* are now being used by Rorty and others to defend relativism, and I regard relativism as a bogus alternative. So I have had to examine Rortian relativism in some detail. In addition, I have had to try to show that the philosophical view I proposed under the name "internal realism" really is a *realism* that giving up the idea that there is just one true and complete description of reality, say the scientific description, does not mean abandoning the notion of an objective world to which our descriptions must conform.

Perhaps most important, I try to defend the idea that the theoretical and practical aspects of philosophy depend on each other. Dewey wrote (in *Reconstruction in Philosophy*) that "philosophy recovers itself when it ceases to be a device for dealing with the problems of philosophy and becomes a method, cultivated by philosophers, for dealing with the problems of men"; I think that the problems of philosophers and the problems of men and women are connected, and that it is a part of the task of a responsible philosophy to bring out the connection.

HRP: Can you illustrate the connection you are thinking of?

Putnam: Quite easily. Doubts as to whether normative judgments, and particularly ethical judgments, can be "objective" are almost universal nowadays and clearly connected with the view that there is a fundamental dichotomy between "facts" and "values"—a view that is the product of the philosophy shop. I see the task of undermining this dichotomy as one of the central points at which one can address a real world malaise and a set of issues in theoretic philosophy at the same time.

HRP: Harvard's philosophy department seems little concerned with modern Continental philosophy; why is this so?

Putnam: I know that is how it seems to many undergraduates, but in fact in our graduate teaching we are much more involved in Continental philosophy than are most main-line philosophy departments. I have taught Habermas's philosophy more than once and also dealt with some of Derrida's views; Stanley Cavell has taught the work of Heidegger and Lacan among other Continental philosophers, and Fred Neuhouser and Charles Parsons both teach German philosophy including that of Marx and Husserl.

It is, however, very difficult to do justice to this work at the undergraduate level. Remember that European students have three years of philosophy at the *Lycée* (high school) level. A Continental philosopher takes this background completely for granted. One cannot discuss his work responsibly unless one can assume a substantial preparation in the history of Western philosophy. I know that there are people who parrot Derrida's words without having studied what Derrida has studied, but that is not the kind of student this department wants to produce.

HRP: Jacques Derrida's philosophical positions have been described by Hazard Adams as "a radical challenge to prevailing notions of 'meaning' or 'rationality.'" What is your view on Derrida?

Putnam: Although Derrida's position may seem to support irrationalism, that is certainly not how Derrida wants to be seen. Nor, I think, is his challenge to the notions you mention wholly without parallel in our tradition. In my book *Renewing Philosophy* I compare Derrida's and Nelson Goodman's positions—there is, in fact, a significant overlap. Incidentally, Derrida's challenge to the notion of meaning is not claimed by him to be wholly original; he repeatedly gives credit to Saussure, especially to the *Cours de Linguistique Générale*. What is most novel in Derrida is a way of *reading*, characterized by the discovery of fatal contradictions between the official "meaning" of a text and the tropes used in the text. That way of reading has, I think, value, but not as a way of reading *every* text. It is striking to me that a philosopher who claims to be "deconstructionist" and who deplores "asser-toric tone" is himself relentlessly assetoric and a relentless generalizer. The problem that remains open after one has read Derrida is this: granted that Jacques Derrida is horrified when people see him as an irrationalist, has he, in fact, left himself the resources to *answer* the charge? I won't try to answer *that* question today!

HRP: On a more personal note, can you make any generalizations about your work habits? What is the process by which you choose areas to explore and develop new ideas?

Putnam: I find two things that help me to develop new ideas: self-criticism, that is, criticism of whatever I have previously published, and reading great philosophers. With regard to the first, I am *always* dissatisfied with some-thing or other about what I have previously written, and locating that some-thing, and trying to think why I am dissatisfied and what to do about it, often sets the agenda for my next piece of work. But that way of proceeding can also lead to going in circles, and I find that reading—Kant or Aristotle or Wittgenstein, or John Dewey, or William James, or Habermas, or one of my colleagues here at Harvard—always opens new possibilities. As I get smarter, Kant, Aristotle, etc. all get smarter as well. As far as work habits goes, I am a pacer. I have to walk many miles to write a paper, and I prefer to do it out of doors. For me, philosophy is a healthy life! φ

Umberto Eco

Umberto Eco, whose most famous fictional work, *Il nome della rosa* (*The Name of the Rose*, 1980) ends with the burning of a medieval library containing among other classical texts Aristotle's now lost volume on comedy, is, in a sense, an intellectual librarian.

Photo by Nancy Crampton

Umberto Eco was born in 1932 in a small Piedmontese town called Allessandria. He first studied law, and then medieval philosophy and literature at the University of Turin, and in 1954 he wrote his doctoral dissertation on Thomas Aquinas. His first job—strange for a medievalist—was with a local television station. In 1959 he switched jobs to *Case Editrice di Bompiani*, a publisher of print magazines. Since that time, Eco has always continued his journalistic activities alongside his varied academic and literary career. For the next fifteen years or so, his articles appeared regularly in the cultural sections of most of the better known Italian magazines and newspapers. Concurrently he published his first works on medieval aesthetics and the interpretation of medieval texts, most notably the *Opera Aperta* (*The Open Work*, 1962). In 1963 *Diario Minimo* (*Misinterpretations*, 1963), a collection of his spoofs on interpretation and exegesis, was published under the title of the editorial column in which it had first appeared.

A year later Eco began teaching in Milan and soon thereafter in Florence. His first professorship for semiotics was with the Architectural Faculty of the Polytechnical Institute, in Milan. During this time he published his first major work on semiotics, *La struttura assente* (*The Absent Structure*, 1968), which prefigured many of the themes of his most influential book on that subject, the *Theory of Semiotics* (original English version, 1976).

In 1975 Eco received tenure as the first professor of semiotics at the University of Bologna, a position that he holds to this day. Meanwhile he has also taught at a half-dozen American universities, at Cambridge University in England, and at the Collège de France. He is a *Chevalier de la Légion d'Honneur* as well as a *Cavaliere di Gran Croce al Merito della Repubblica Italiana*. His most recent work on semiotics is *Kant e l'ornitorinco* (*Kant and the Platypus*, 1999), which revisits the notion of conceptual schemata, and discusses the way language adjusts to newly discovered objects and phenomena.

Eco's career as a novelist began soon after his appointment at Bologna, and in 1980 he published *Il nome della rosa* (*The Name of the Rose*) to tremendous public and critical acclaim. He has penned three further novels, *Il pendolo di Foucault* (*Foucault's Pendulum*, 1988), *L'isola del giorno prima* (*The Island of the Day Before*, 1994) and most recently *Bendolino* (2001). Parallel to his activity as a fiction writer and semiotitian, Eco published two collections of essays: one on the interpretation of fiction and the other on the task of writing it. Also, he continued to develop his semiotic theories in *Semiotica e filosophia del linguaggio* (*Semiotics and the Philosophy of Language*, 1984) and *La ricerca della lingua perfetta nella cultura europea* (*The Search for the Perfect Language*, 1994). In the latter of these two volumes Eco provides an overview of the debate concerning the origins of language. He takes a critical look at the attempt to transfer the conclusions of that debate to a program for the perfection of the languages we speak.

Coming from the background of medieval thought and theology, Umberto Eco has brought his erudition to the study of writing and signs, to the theoretical examination of the art of textual interpretation, and to the question of how great works develop. His fiction and his non-fiction alike are (with the exception perhaps of *L'isola del giorno prima*) about books. He writes about books, he talks about books, and he collects books—his personal library in Milan contains more than 30,000 volumes. In his spare time he engages in civic projects, such as the planning of the *Biblioteca Multimediale Sala Borsa*, a public multimedia library. According to Eco, "libraries can take the place of God." And with his reach to both the ancient and the modern, the tragic and the tragically funny, Eco has perhaps done more than anyone alive today to remind us of the joys of reading and the treasures to be lifted from the crumbling pages of old books.

In the following interview, we see that Eco has abandoned his earlier attempts to define or summarize the theory of semiotics. In 1996 he said, "I don't think it's possible to try a general overview of the theory of semiotics [anymore]." What's more, he always refuses to venture any kind of interpretation of his own texts. In his postscript to *Il nome della rosa* (*The Name of the Rose*), Eco writes, "the author may not interpret. But he must tell why and how he wrote his book." In this vein, Eco says in this interview what he has said so often: that he regards his fictional writings as so many riddles, each with as many potential solutions as it has readers. As such, they are different from his philosophical writings, which aspire to present definitive answers to definite questions. He likens this difference to the one between Wittgenstein's *Philosophical Investigations* and *Tractatus*. It is interesting to compare Eco's comments on riddles and philosophy with Cora Diamond's discussion (also in this volume) of the *Tractatus* as itself a riddle. φ

Umberto Eco
On Semiotics and Pragmatism

Interview by
Chong-Min Hong,
David Lurie, and
Jiro Tanaka in 1993

HRP: Most of your academic work has centered around the field of semiotics. What exactly is semiotics? What, in your view, are its goals?

Eco: The technical answer should be that it is the study of semiosis in all of its aspects—but at this point I should define semiosis. And since I have written several books on this subject it probably would not be appropriate or adequate to answer in a few sentences (otherwise all these books would have been unnecessary, which I cannot admit). In academic terms I do not consider semiotics as a discipline, not even a department, but perhaps as a school, as an interdisciplinary network, studying human beings in so far as they reproduce signs, and not only the verbal ones.

The study of a specific system of signs is usually called "semiotics of ___." For instance, linguistics is a semiotics of verbal language; there is, as well, a semiotics of traffic lights. The difference between a language like English and the system of traffic lights is that the latter is simpler than the former. Then there is a general approach to the whole of the semiotic behavior, and I call this study general semiotics. In this sense semiotics asks some fundamental philosophical questions.

Try to imagine a philosophy of language that, instead of analyzing only our verbal behavior, analyzes every kind of sign production and interpretation. General semiotics is for me a form of philosophy—to be honest; I think it is the only acceptable form of philosophy, today. After all, when Aristotle says that Being can be told in various ways he characterizes philosophy as a semiotic inquiry.

HRP: Clearly, you have found that fiction enables you to accomplish something other than what you have accomplished in your philosophical and critical work. When you write your novels, in what sense do you approach philosophical questions differently than you do as a theorist?

Eco: Your question permits two different answers since it, in fact, concerns two different problems, namely, (a) the psychology of literary creation; and

(b) the role of literature in the philosophical debate, especially today. As for the first point I would say that when beginning a novel I do not think of any specific philosophical question. I start from an image, a situation, and I do not know where I am going. Only afterwards I realize that in some way I dealt with philosophical problems, which is not so inexplicable because they are *my* problems. At this point I realize that, when dealing with philosophical problems in an essayistic way, I try to reach a conclusion, a univocal one, ready to defend it—even though I am aware that in order to reach that conclusion I had to cut off some other possible ways of looking at the same problem.

On the contrary, when writing a novel I have an impression to stage and I try to represent the fact that the conclusions can be many. In other words I offer the readers a series of questions, not answers. To translate all this in terms of a "philosophical" metaphor to write scholarly work is like writing the *Tractatus*, whereas writing a novel is more like [writing] the *Philosophical Investigations*.

This leads us to the second part of your question. A consistent number of philosophers of our time have used literary creations as a playground for dealing with philosophical problems. There are philosophers reflecting on Kafka, on Mann, on Proust. They use literature as some Greek philosopher used myth, as an open-ended and problematic representation of human problems—just because poetic or narrative discourses are not to be accepted or refused (pass or fail) but can be explored as a source of unending questions.

HRP: Your writings, and especially your fiction, will be interpreted by various readers in numerous different ways. What is the difference between interpretation and misinterpretation?

Eco: I was largely influenced, at the beginning of my philosophical career, by Luigi Pareyson, whose philosophy of interpretation was in fact a form of hermeneutics. It is for that reason that decades later I met the thought of C. S. Peirce, and I was conquered by his theory of interpretation as the unifying category able to explain how Mind and languages (and even nature) work. But a central feature to Pareyson's philosophy was that every act of interpretation involved both freedom and fidelity (or respect). You are free because you are looking at something from your own perspective, but you are looking at *something*. Such a dialectic between freedom and loyalty still remains central in my thought and in the way I elaborated on Peirce's notion of unlimited semiosis (see, for instance, the recent essays in my book, *The Limits of Interpretation*).

To put the whole thing in a rude way, I still believe that there is a literal level in language, a zero degree. Interpretation starts from that level and cannot ignore it. Can you read *Finnegan's Wake* as a free interpretation of *Gone with the Wind*? If the answer is, "No" (and it is "No"—don't be silly), this means that some interpretations of a text simply cannot be accepted as an interpretation of that text. Then, if you ask me (and I did something like this in my literary parodies now published in English as *Misreadings*), I am able to write an essay in which I read Joyce as if he were Margaret Mitchell. You can say—and I agree—that even this is a way to interpret a text. But you would admit that there are, in the job of interpretation, degrees of fidelity. I can play Chopin with an ocarina and such an exercise can be hermeneutically fruitful, but generally people admit that a good performance by Cortot is closer to Chopin, and I think people are right.

HRP: The literary figures of St. Thomas Aquinas and James Joyce have figured prominently in your writings. What is it about Aquinas and Joyce that attracts you?

Eco: One meets an author for many reasons, and there is no previous program. It is like falling in love: it happens, and it is stupid to ask, "why with X rather than with Y?" Then, later in life, you might think that there was something like a project, but of course it is only a teleological illusion. To play the game of the teleological illusion, I see those two guys (Aquinas and Joyce) as very complementary for my education: one seems to work in order to produce Order, but his ordered world conceals a subtle way of putting out of joint the whole of the previous tradition; the other one seems to play on Chance and Disorder, but to do so he needs underlying ordered structures. Nice "fearful symmetry," isn't it? Certainly it did not depend on an intentional plot. But who knows?

HRP: Why has American pragmatism in general and the Harvard philosopher and pragmatist C. S. Peirce attracted so much attention on the Continent?

Eco: Apropos of American pragmatism, I would distinguish between the pragmatism of James or Dewey, and the philosophy of Peirce—you know that he was irritated by the Jamesian version of his ideas and he decided to call his philosophy "pragmaticism" so to distinguish it from pragmatism (he said that no one would have stolen such an ugly word). American pragmatism in the sense of James and Dewey had many followers in Italy in the first half of this century, and it happened as a reaction to the idealism of Croce and Gentile. Peirce was mainly rediscovered in the second half of the century, and it is his semiotic aspect that fascinated Europeans (by the way, such an aspect was the less-considered one among the happy few that studies Peirce in the U.S.–until recently). Peirce was studied because the structuralist semiotic approach had privileged the linguistic model, and Peirce was aware of the enormous variety of signs that we produce and use.

HRP: How do you distinguish Continental and analytic philosophy?

Eco: Every attempt to distinguish Continental from analytic philosophy according to their problems, questions, and answers is misleading. At every step one can discover that there is more in common than people usually believe. Nevertheless, what is in common is concealed, as if from both parts one worked in order to render both universes mutually impenetrable.

In order to explain the real difference, let me use an analogy concerning the difference between medieval and modern philosophy: The Schoolmen were continually innovat[ive] but they tried to disguise any innovation presenting it as a gloss, as a commentary of a unified tradition. On the contrary, modern philosophers like Descartes, were pretending to start from a "tabla rasa," by putting the previous traditions upside down and polemically casting it in doubt. Well, I think that analytical philosophy still has a medieval attitude: it seems that every discourse is expected to start from a previous one, everybody recognizing a sort of canon, let us say the Fregean one. In this line of thought one has to respect a common philosophical jargon, to start from a set of canonical questions, and any new proposal must stem from that corpus of questions and answers. Continental philosophers try to show that they have nothing to do with the previous philosophical discourses, even when they are only translating old problems into a new philosophical language. I know that there are other differences, but let me stress this one, which is most based on a difference of philosophical style than on a differing set of contents or methods.

HRP: The seventeenth-century English philosopher John Locke famously claimed in his *Essay Concerning Human Understanding* that "even ideas are signs," and Peirce seems to have held this position as well. Can the mind truly be structured as a signed process? If not, what then is the actual subject of semiotics?

Eco: The idea that concepts or ideas are signs is older than that–think of Ockham, for instance. But it can be found even before. Let us assume that something happens in the so-called Mind. If Mind = Brain, then what happens are certain physical states; if not I set you free to decide what the hell it can be. Certainly they are not things. But through the Mind we are able to think of things. Thus what happens in Mind, whatever it can be, even a dance of little gnomes, stands for something else. This (*aliquid stat pro aliquo*) is the definition of the sign, or of the semiotic process since the ancient times. Thus Mind is a semiotic business.

HRP: In recent years, intellectual life in the United States has centered around a furious debate over the political nature of knowledge. As a European and an intellectual grounded in the Western tradition, how do you view this controversy?

Eco: In European high schools you start reading Homer and Virgil at the age of twelve and at the age of sixteen you are supposed to know everything about Plato and Aristotle but you never read the Bible, not to speak of the Koran; the principles of Buddhism are quotes only when speaking of certain Western philosophers, and only those who study cultural anthropology at the university hear about African myths. This is a wrong curriculum, for it is Eurocentric. But likewise it would be wrong (and racist) to give black students access only to non-Western culture, keeping them afar from Plato or Aristotle. It is true that, as Benjamin Lee Whorf suggested, contemporary nuclear physics can probably be better expressed in Hopi than in English, but a great part of modern science can be understood only if one understands certain fundamental principles of the Western legacy; to know them is a right for every human being. The problem for the curricula of tomorrow is how to provide a complete culture (what the Greeks call an *enkyklios paideia*, a circular education), which will be "enkyklios" just because it will not only be Eurocentric. ϕ

Harvey C. Mansfield

Harvey C. Mansfield is known as a political philosopher and as a scholar of past thinkers, including Burke, Machiavelli, and Tocqueville. He is also renowned among his academic colleagues, as well as his students, for challenging or adding sophistication to widely accepted assumptions. Mansfield has often been called a conservative, but he rejects this label and, in our interview, calls it "merely political in the sense of temporary."

Harvey Mansfield received his undergraduate degree from Harvard in 1953 and has been on the faculty, where he is now the William R. Kenan, Jr., Professor of Government, since 1962. He has published a dozen books, including some that have significantly affected the modern political debate. His books sometimes grapple with great thinkers of the past, either critically or by translation. In his first book, *Statesmanship and Party Government: A Study of Burke and Bolingbroke*, published in 1965, Mansfield challenged the popular view of Burke as a Christian natural law theorist and instead emphasized Burke's prudence and innovation. Through such arguments he transformed the perception of Burke from being a traditional thinker to being a modern conservative. He has also written *Machiavelli's New Modes and Orders: A Study of the Discourses on Livy* in 1979, translated Machiavelli's *The Prince* in 1998, and, most recently in 2000, he translated Alexis de Tocqueville's *Democracy in America*. Often Mansfield's work incorporates great thinkers of the past to shed light on our present political condition. His 1978 *The Spirit of Liberalism* as well as *Taming the Prince: The Ambivalence of Modern Executive Power* distills lessons from past thinkers and applies them to our current conditions. Mansfield finds that Machiavelli's views, which he sees as most fully and attractively displaying modern political science, show how liberal constitutionalism allows for active and ambitious politicians, while preserving room for the realms of the economy and the intellectual life. It tames princes without repressing them. Mansfield sees Machiavelli as central to the ideas and successes of the American experiment.

Although long an admirer of the U.S. Constitution as a phenomenally successful document, Mansfield, in the spirit of Leo Strauss, sees conservatives as making a fundamental mistake when they impose a consistent conservative tradition on their thought. Instead, he argues, deeply cherished traditions often rise from the very discontinuities, revolutions, and sacrileges that are antithetical to orthodox conservatism.

In a festschrift for Mansfield this year, essays of his past and present graduate students were collected into a book called *Educating the Prince*. The project seeks to celebrate Harvey Mansfield through reflection, by collecting works of his former students and hoping that they cast light on the teacher. Indeed, the range and quality of the essays speaks to the prolific interests and celebrated pedagogy of Mansfield. His most recent project is to study the topic of manliness. He hopes to rediscover the underlying intrinsic meaning of the term from beneath the political and historical confusion. As usual, his ideas are unorthodox and challenging and, as usual, they are sure to be central to the debate. φ

Harvey C. Mansfield
On the Philosophy of Politics

Interview by
Josh Harlan and
Christopher Kagay
in 1993

HRP: How did you come to be a political philosopher?

Mansfield: I grew into it. It wasn't a decision. My hero as an undergraduate was Sam Beer, a wonderful man, now retired. My father was also a professor of political science. My first notion was to be a Soviet expert—know thy enemy. I came to realize that I would be spending my life, if I did this, reading things with a five-hundred–word vocabulary put out by apparatchiks. It was in my sophomore year that I met Sam Beer, who was interested in asking questions while studying comparative government that came out of political philosophy. Then I got more interested in those questions than in applications and it wasn't until after I graduated that I got caught up in Strauss. His book *Natural Right and History* came out the year that I graduated [from Harvard], 1953. I had, by then, also met a couple of his students. I was never a student of Strauss's. I met him at Berkeley. He was at the Institute for Behavioral Studies of all places in Palo Alto. He was running an informal reading seminar.

HRP: What, in your view, is political philosophy and why should students and others care about it?

Mansfield: Let me answer from the standpoint of philosophy. I would say that political philosophy is about self-knowledge. You cannot think comprehensively without thinking about the conditions of thought, without thinking about what makes it possible to live the life of a thinker. The answer to that question is political because politics determines the conditions under which thinkers can think. Simply from the standpoint of a thinker or philosopher I think political philosophy is a necessary pursuit, not accidental. It isn't an option for him to be or not to be interested in politics. Political philosophy tells of the connection between philosophers or thinkers and non-philosophers, between what is intelligible in thought and what is not, or what is specific or highest in the human and what is shared more generally with the lowest in the human and even with other creatures, the rest of nature, that is, the need to stay alive. If you reflect on this, political philosophy appears as the crucial field of philosophy—not the highest, but the crucial. It is at the crux where thinking meets non-thinking.

HRP: What does it mean to be a conservative? Are you comfortable with that label?

Mansfield: I'm not comfortable with that label because it's merely political in the sense of temporary. In other circumstances I can well imagine being a liberal, and anyway there are difficulties with being a conservative. I think of two, especially. One is that if conservative means holding to tradition, tradition often contains contradictory elements so that one has to be selective and no longer simply conservative. Another difficulty is a question of tactics. Should you go slow or go back? Going slow means keeping what has been done and slowing down the rate at which it is being done. It means maintaining a connection between the past and the present. Going back means making a break between the present and the past and so no longer keeping that connection. You see this on the Supreme Court today. Scalia wants to go back and this moderate couple of Kennedy and O'Conner in the middle wants to go slow. I think that there is no way of saying which of those two is always the better conservative tradition.

HRP: Is there a point of view that would identify conservative as valuing social practices that have emerged from the bottom up as the result of tradition over ideas, which have come from the top down, as it were—attempts to design social practices on a rational basis? Is that a different view of conservatism?

Mansfield: No, I think that's a reasonable view of conservatism and it's another reason why conservatism is questionable as a uniform, universal position. Clearly it's often better to be rational, and rational seems necessarily, as you suggest, to come from the top because what is rational comes from what is most reasonable and that one would find with those who have the most reason. Conservatives are in the habit of revering the founders, quite rightly, but a founding is an unconservative action.

HRP: That seems like a fundamental paradox.

Mansfield: It is. Therefore it's impossible always and with reason to be a conservative.

HRP: Is a Straussian a certain kind of conservative?

Mansfield: No, not essentially. Strauss himself once said that there is an odor of conservative politics about those who follow his way of thinking. Although most of the Straussians are conservative, there are some liberals. It is essentially about reviving political philosophy and not about changing

America. To be a Straussian may be to be a conservative but that isn't what one is principally.

HRP: What attracted you to the work of Strauss?

Mansfield: What first grabbed me was his solitary courage in raising again the question of classical, political philosophy as possibly true. Also, I was looking for an understanding of morals and politics which was in between relativism and absolutism and this seemed to offer a reasonable middle. That is what initially attracted me. Another point was just his marvelous way with texts, his interpretations of texts, his ability to see things—and not just to make up things or to imagine them—but to see things and show that they were there to be seen, in texts that I had read quickly and superficially. Then later on I met him and he was, by a very long shot, the most intelligent person I had ever met.

HRP: Do your political beliefs derive from your study of political philosophy?

Mansfield: The study of political philosophy provides at most an atmosphere of one's political thinking, not a set of principles from which one easily derives policies. Policies are too specific to the situation. But perhaps one learns that from political philosophy, say, from Aristotle's notion of the regime, that every regime has a certain character to which one must adopt one's political thinking. It makes no sense to be an anti-democrat in an established democracy; so one takes one's political premises as much from the situation as from the merely desirable. This is not to say that one should overlook alternative possibilities. It's a much better citizen of democracy who's aware of an anti-democratic regime, even of the advantages of such a regime, but that awareness has to be used with a view to the improvement of democracy and not with a view to some imaginary, and perhaps worse, alternative to our circumstances.

HRP: There almost seems to be a note of wistfulness in your voice when you said that it makes no sense to be anti-democratic in a democratic society. Do you think that in some way we could be better off in a less democratic society, or is that not a coherent question because then we wouldn't be we, we'd be someone else?

Mansfield: Well, it's a difficult question. I didn't mean to be wistful or nostalgic but realistic. I am not sure that this is the best political arrangement of all time. One should reserve in one's mind an allegiance to the best regime.

HRP: Along the lines of your saying that this is not necessarily the best possible political arrangement, what is your view of those who claim that this is the last political arrangement, that somehow there is a logic to history, and the political evolution of society is moving toward this type of government inexorably?

Mansfield: That's Francis Fukuyama and his famous thesis, borrowed from Hegel and Kojève. It isn't so much inexorable as it is looking at the trends which have actually occurred and the possibilities that presently exist. Somehow democracy has outlasted its totalitarian rivals in an impressive fashion and there doesn't seem to be on the scene presently an alternative that looks viable.

HRP: What about the emergence of Islamic fundamentalism?

Mansfield: I don't know about that. Fukuyama claims that this is not a viable alternative, that such regimes lose their faith very rapidly, that they depend on science and Western industrial economics and that those dependencies will necessarily have an effect.

HRP: Do you think that the importance of the political philosopher withers away as the world becomes more similar politically?

Mansfield: No, I think that we have not yet seen the last of chance events and that some powerful form of anti-democracy could easily spring up, unforeseen, unforeseeable. It could be some kind of fascism. There are two main objections to liberal democracy which were made, one by communism, the other by fascism. Those two objections have some validity to them, even if communism and fascism don't. Communism objected that liberal democracy is too selfish and unconcerned with the whole and fascism claimed that liberal democracy is base and unconcerned with the noble. Both of those are to some extent true. That's why I would say that liberal democracy is not a complete fulfillment of human nature or the perfection of human nature. One could always imagine a challenge to it, a better regime. In practice this might turn out worse as happened with communism and fascism, but people may well be tempted to try.

HRP: You have been identified as a critic of liberalism. What do you think is wrong with liberalism?

Mansfield: I published a book in 1987, *The Spirit of Liberalism,* in which I present myself as a friend of liberalism but it was the kind of friend who was subjecting to criticism the beliefs and practices of those who call themselves liberals, so I never really made it into their hearts. I suppose I have become expressly conservative since then, but I think that one could define the main task of conservatism today as trying to make liberalism live up to its own principles, in many respects: in economics, to the market and private property, in culture, to the high standards of our universities, in constitutional law, to the rights of the constitution and the institutions it established, etc. That's not just a rhetorical tactic used to shame liberals, but I think it's true that they've gotten away from the things that make liberalism attractive. This happened especially in the late '60s, a very powerful epoch which has done infinite mischief.

HRP: But liberals would claim in response that many of the social changes that occurred brought rights and equalities to segments of the population that did not enjoy them in the past. It seems as if there has to be something to be said for that.

Mansfield: You're probably thinking of the Civil Rights movement. That was the early and middle '60s, culminating in the passage of the first civil rights act, which was not subject to filibuster from southern senators—the first civil rights act represented a genuine consensus. This was 1964.

HRP: You're not referring to that when you suggest that mischief was done in the 1960s.

Mansfield: Not that, or not that mainly. An interpretation of the Civil Rights Act of 1964 came out the next year, which first began affirmative action, and which I think is a perversion of liberalism. It transforms our politics from a constitutional politics to a result-oriented politics. It makes a very big difference how minorities or less-advantaged groups get their rights—that they get them by their own efforts and through means which provide equality under the law. Simply to give them an equal result denies their pride, gives them no sense of achievement, and builds too much government.

HRP: Some would contend that affirmative action is not result-oriented in that sense, that affirmative action would not seek to take those who are of less merit on a particular scale and promote them equally along with those who have greater merits, but that it diversifies the available criteria of merit such that it provides different standards for evaluating people of different backgrounds. Do you take issue with that?

Mansfield: That's a possibility, but in practice I don't think it happens. In practice, people have been given things that they do not deserve on the basis of any reasonable criterion which is not result-oriented. The practice of affirmative action is much worse than the principle. If you listen to those who make the argument on principle you would think that if there's a small difference you would give them a push over the top as a sign that we are now a community and don't wish to despise any group within it. In fact what happens is that the advantage given by affirmative action is enormous. It goes as much to a black who comes from Scarsdale as one from Harlem.

This happens not only in admissions but even more in hiring. I am very upset at what is happening on the job market for graduate students in this department. Major injustices are being done to white males, which we will all be ashamed of in the next generation. The result has not been any improvement in our university community in race relations.

HRP: How does your criticism of liberalism apply to your Harvard colleague, John Rawls?

Mansfield: I did an article on him, which was published in the book that I mentioned. I forget what's in it. Essentially I think he tried to have his liberalism both ways. He prefers Kant to Locke because Kant has a certain moral elevation and Kant does not base his argument on the preservation of property. But Rawls does not go anywhere near all the way with Kant's moral sternness, an attitude which follows strictly from his premises, as everything in Kant does, and he does not comment on the political and moral politics actually proposed by Kant in his *Metaphysics of Morals*. So, he goes back in the direction of Locke in order to free himself from Kant's moral strictness. It's an inconsistent alternation, I think, between the desire to be moral and the desire to be compassionate. That would be a general summing up of his book that has, of course, many arguments in it.

HRP: You might be implying, then, that Rawls calls for a degree of redistribution that does not take sufficient account of merit.

Mansfield: Or of morality, but that looks towards the preservation of the community or the self-preservation of the community—his so-called thin theory of the good, which is a terrific qualification of Kantianism.

HRP: Does the original position seem to you to be an effective mechanism for modeling a fair decision-making process for principles of justice?

Mansfield: Very ineffective, because it takes away the knowledge you need to know. You would decide one thing if you didn't know what sex you were going to be and another if you did. There's really no reason to be bound by your sexless position once you've got a sex. He can't give a reason for being bound.

HRP: But isn't that just the point? Then people would be more willing to choose a basic structure for society that was more equal in its treatment of different genders.

Mansfield: They would be more likely to choose a sexless structure at the time that they don't know their sex. But why should they hold to that decision? It was, after all, a decision made in ignorance. The original position differs from the state of nature in Hobbes and Locke in that the latter is supposed to tell you what your true nature is. It's supposed to be a statement of what you really are. In the state of nature, where there's an equal ability to kill, you can see that men and women would be roughly equal because women, although somewhat weaker in brachial strength, can make up for it in cunning. There's some truth in the notion of equality. In the case of the original position, it's simply a counterfactual assumption which begs you to posit something which you know isn't the case, namely, that you have no sex. It begins by assuming that sex doesn't matter. How do you know that?

HRP: Which philosophers do you think have affected your thinking the most?

Mansfield: I think Locke has the most wisdom for us regarding principles. But the most beautiful book to read is Tocqueville's *Democracy in America,* by far. It's the best thing ever done about our country. It's not a book of principles like Locke's *Two Treatises.* The principles are there, they are just not thematic. Aristotle I like. It's always worth your while to find out what Aristotle has to say on any subject.

HRP: How consistent do you seek to be to some set of principles?

Mansfield: To repeat myself a little bit, here I take my bearing from Aristotle and his notion of the regime, which is, I think, the fundamental concept for all political scientists. It tells you that it's wrong to make abstract judgments on policy questions without relating them to the regime, that is, to the politics of a particular society at a particular time. So, you might want to adopt policies which are wrong abstractly but which are right for our type of democracy. For example, reliance on rights one can question abstractly. After all, aren't duties as important or more important than rights? But that isn't us. We have a different premise. It doesn't make sense to adopt a policy which doesn't derive from a premise which is ours or forseeably ours. That, I think, is the beauty of Tocqueville's new political science. It accepts this new democratic revolution as a fact. It also has some good things and some bad things. One can try to promote the good and prevent the bad but not with a view to some abstract situation. Usually the philosophers who spend their time with policies reason much too abstractly, as if what they were saying were good for Persia or Egypt in ancient times. It's a bit ridiculous because they're comfortable suburban liberals and their abstractions are much more narrowly founded than they realize. One should be self-conscious about the fact that we live in a liberal democracy of a certain kind, which can be moved in a good direction but can't fundamentally be altered. Prudence dictates that one not seek the abstract best out of some philosopher's book but using these principles and thinking about your own situation [one should] try to find some useful improvement.

HRP: Where do your views on social issues part way with those viewed as libertarians?

Mansfield: I am not 100 percent against big government. Certainly during the Cold War we needed a big military. And I also think that government necessarily and rightly plays a formative role in society. I do agree with the libertarians that limited government is the best for us now. But limited government had to be established by a founding which was not itself a stroke of limited government, but rather one which set up character, gave a tone to our whole society. Sometimes that tone and that character need to be recalled. Impressive actions like the Civil Rights movement or speeches which appeal to our patriotism—to the good things we share as Americans. So I don't think one should always be belittling the government. I do agree that government in recent times, and especially since the New Deal, has attempted to do too much and we need less of it. So my favorite figure in recent American politics is Reagan.

HRP: Which actions rising from the New Deal, which functions of government, do you see as the most pernicious? And considering that most of the big government changes that you might view as pernicious were in response to at least what some Americans thought was a necessary wave of change, how better to bring about change than through government, through the increase in size of government?

Mansfield: Well, the New Deal made economic mistakes by attempting to establish what it called "freedom from want." It made structural mistakes in the government by attacking American federalism, by immensely increasing government bureaucracy, and by setting in motion policies that have made us more dependent on government, which means we are less independent as citizens of a republic. And I think that is the meaning of the New Deal as a whole, and so I think as a whole it was mistaken, though parts of it may be valuable and lots of it may now be impossible to repeal. I think government is often needed for making big changes, but it should make these changes in such a way as to leave space for free citizens to exercise their freedom on their own responsibility.

HRP: One of the changes of the New Deal was to legitimize the role of government in everyday life in a more active way, for instance, in macroeconomic stabilization by providing, say, social security, and I think many would claim that those policies have been a tremendous success. You no longer see the tremendous cycle of depression that had ravished America in the 1870s and in the 1920s, and the elderly have gone from being an incredibly impoverished population to one which no longer suffers from poverty to such a great extent. Do you think that either of those programs in themselves and the precedent and philosophical change that they represent is something that we should be concerned about or be sorry about?

Mansfield: Well, it's hard to speak except on the whole. Certainly there are amenities which come from the New Deal as you say. But one must be careful to accept uncritically the New Deal version of past history. Also, the New Deal itself was not very successful economically until World War II and not even then so successful, nor have we succeeded in abolishing the business cycle. Nor do we have the same kind of virtue which people used to have that enables them to live through good times and bad. As we get richer and more secure, it seems we get more concerned with security and less tolerant of insecurity. This is the dependency I'm speaking of. What was the other thing you mentioned?

HRP: Social security.

Mansfield: Oh yes, social security and the old. Well that's good, except that most people do not have to look ahead to take care of themselves in their old age. This is a bad idea for the family because it means that children don't have to take care of aged parents, or don't have the same degree of responsibility to do so. And it's bad for the individual because you don't have to save or you have less reason to save for your old age. There's a certain risk that comes from the desire to be riskless. That is loss of virtue, loss of virtue as it's best understood in a liberal democracy and that's the virtue of self-reliance and responsibility.

HRP: Another provocative critic of modern America is Allan Bloom. What is your relation to Bloom's thought, and your view of *The Closing of the American Mind*, for instance?

Mansfield: Well he was a very close friend. I miss him very much. His book I read in manuscript, and I have the honor of having seen and told him that it would make him famous. It didn't realize it would be quite the success it was, but it did seem to me to be a marvelous statement which could not be ignored. And I still think it is. That is one of the books of our time. Anyone who hasn't read it should do so right now—or anyone who has bought it but hasn't read it. [*laughter*] What it does intellectually or philosophically is to show how Nietzsche became an American citizen. That I think is the part which has not attracted so much attention. That's a very important story. It is perhaps the essential story of the intellectual and even political history of our time. It's the third part of the book. The first part, where he talks about students, gets everyone's attention. It has this marvelous perceptiveness, insight into the problems of young people living now. That's what sold the book. I think this other investigation is even more valuable.

HRP: Do you agree with Bloom's pessimistic assessment of the intellectual caliber of young Americans?

Mansfield: No, it's more the moral caliber. They're too nice. And our virtue is being nice. That can be a kind of intellectual vice maybe. That's his chief objection to it. We're too nice and this means we're too open. Our receptivity is purely superficial because it doesn't challenge anything in us that we believe. So this niceness comes out of lack of belief, and learning does not occur because one merely substitutes for lack of belief a superficial acquaintance with other cultures or Others with a capital "O."

HRP: What you're saying seems to tie in with a claim Francis Fukuyama makes in *The New Republic*: "For many years now it has not been possible to speak too explicitly in polite society about the broad social character of various ethnic, religious, and racial groups or to suggest that certain cultures are superior to others in promoting certain economic, social, or moral values. To the extent that 'civics' is still taught in our public school system, the core teaching has been reduced to the view that other cultures are not 'worse,' just 'different.'" (April 1993, p. 91) Does this offend you?

Mansfield: Yes, yes it does offend me. It dismays me. People are being too easily and officially offended these days for me to want to use that word. But yes, that's just what I was thinking about. To appreciate another culture one should really try to see where it disagrees with ours, and why it does so. For example, why did the Hindus burn widows on the funeral pyre? It's not enough to simply reject that out of hand as an oddity. Why did they do that? What was the reasoning behind that? What about the caste system? In other words, what are the arguments on its behalf? One mustn't simply look at the cuisine of different cultures, so to speak, and sample it. These things which shock us, what does that tell us about ourselves?

HRP: Even though you suggested earlier that political philosophers who are liberal suburbanites may overestimate the reach of their abstraction, are you implying here that we can make some types of moral assessments of practices in other cultures that transcend the cultural division?

Mansfield: Yes, I think one can, sure. That's what political philosophy attempts to do. Political philosophy is about the best regime, and so it compares different regimes, judges the different claims that they make. Regimes always speak for themselves, claiming certain advantages, especially advantages over other regimes; they contrast themselves with other regimes. Liberal democracy usually contrasts itself with anti-democratic regimes. It gives itself certain virtues, and a political philosopher tries to judge whether it really has those virtues and if there are other virtues which are missing. So liberal democracy always looks more explicitly than implicitly at the picture of the best regime. It's essentially utopian, transcultural. But every political regime makes a transcultural claim. It may not be aware of all the cultures that exist in the world but it claims to be better than they.

HRP: Do you feel a pressure not to make those kinds of transcultural claims?

Mansfield: Sure, especially when it comes to something difficult and embarrassing to us. Our principle is "All men are created equal." It's hard to make judgments of different groups of Americans which implies that they're not equal, in other words, to make ethnic characterizations. A characterization is always saying that a certain group has a certain character, which means that it has more of this and less of that, which means that it is unequal in some respect.

HRP: That seems a key division between conservatives and liberals in contemporary America. Liberals to some extent would try to discourage an explanation of the differential success of different ethnic and cultural groups in the U.S. that involves a characterization of how their cultural differences might lead to different outcomes.

Mansfield: Or especially different virtues.

HRP: Or conservatives would be more willing, as Fukuyama is pointing to, to make assessments that some cultures hinder themselves in the American sphere and some do not.

Mansfield: That's another example of liberalism not living up to its own principle. This used to be as much a liberal habit as a conservative habit. It's not only that one becomes a conservative by not being a cultural relativist. Liberals used to have no qualms about denouncing illiberal regimes and illiberal practices by people within a regime. Now they've lost their own liberalism in multiculturalism or in relativism and they need to be reminded of what they ought, as liberals, to believe. Why is it necessary for someone who opposes grade inflation to be a conservative? There used to be a perfect consensus between liberals and conservatives that universities could not last without maintaining their standards. It's only since the late '60s that this has come about.

HRP: Is that a fair characterization of those who criticize you on this issue? Were people characterizing your opposition to grade inflation in general or your specific racial explanation?

Mansfield: Both, I think. There's a sign of movement among liberals and the Harvard administration on this issue. I am hopeful that change is in the wind on this one. Dean Lawrence Buehl's letter was a first. For some years now they've been sending around statistics on how each professor grades his students compared to how other professors grade those same students. This is the first time that an editorial came with that information, asking you whether it might not be wise to change your behavior. So if liberals want to join the anti-grade inflation crusade they are certainly welcome.

HRP: Do you think that enough evidence is available to an individual professor to make claims about the possible causes of grade inflation without the administration releasing information about the average grades received by different racial groups at Harvard?

Mansfield: No, and it would certainly be better to have some statistics. Lacking them, one has to speak on the basis of personal observation and what one sees in others. It's very common for white professors to over-grade blacks.

HRP: Do you think that the primary reasons for grade inflation were not the policies of draft boards in the Vietnam War but the increase in teaching by teaching fellows in the 1960s and 1970s, that is, graders who are younger and better connected to students?

Mansfield: The first I agree with and the second I think no. At a forum on grade inflation I quoted this old saw on aged professors: "The harder the arteries the softer the heart." When I began teaching, a young teacher was in a mood to be harsh so as to distinguish himself from the students by making it clear that one was enforcing high standards and being young meant being exacting. This, I think, is the same thing that Bloom was referring to when he spoke of the young nowadays wanting to be nice. Youth, I think, is much more intolerant than tolerant and so you need a special explanation for the niceness of young graders.

HRP: In the 1960s and '70s the universities opened their doors not just to blacks but to many other groups as well, including, for instance, students from rural and impoverished areas. Do you think that it is possible that grade inflation stemmed not from racial double standards but from a desire to make a university education available to many groups of people to whom it had not previously been available? In that light do you think that a degree of grade inflation, which allowed those groups to remain in the university and receive an education, was a bad thing for our society?

Mansfield: Well, I think that a more democratic movement in education had begun well before the 1960s. In fact, that was the whole idea of the state universities that were founded after the Morrill Act in the nineteenth century. I don't think that one encourages such groups by giving the less capable among them good grades. That's what's new. I would say that the draft deferment was a big part of the issue and still a bigger part, the most comprehensive of all, is the view that to grade someone is to impose an external standard, to exert power over somebody. This can be dressed up with the kind of reasons you gave that this person has valuable equipment and notions that we need to be aware of, and have in our university community, even though he's not so good at math.

HRP: Why wouldn't it be the case that in, let's say, admissions, not grades, that a university would feel that there is value in having a diversity of different groups and classes and backgrounds represented in the student body regardless of whether that desire for diversity might lead to the admission of some students who have demonstrated less merit, narrowly considered in terms of various criteria, than others?

Mansfield: Well, the merit narrowly considered is really our merit, the merit of scholarship. It's perfectly true that at Harvard we don't choose simply to admit the best future scholars and we wouldn't want to have a student body consisting only of future professors. Therefore, I think they take only a few of the top SAT scorers, and then after a while they stop and look at what else they've got, and that "what else" can be other kinds of merit like athletic ability or playing a musical instrument or demonstrated leadership. All of those I agree with as necessary and desirable qualifications of merit, narrowly considered, but I think it's very wrong to introduce race and race simply as such a qualification. It would be much better to find, among black students, merits or virtues which we would be lacking without them, but which aren't simply the possession of dark-colored skin.

HRP: You're suggesting that the university might chose to admit a certain number of individuals, regardless of their race, who had overcome particular obstacles that had been placed in their way?

Mansfield: Yes, that would be a good judgment to use, and therefore one would be better disposed towards the black from Harlem than the black from Scarsdale given equal or nearly equal abilities. The assumption behind your question is really quite different from the original justification behind affirmative action. The original justification was that in recruiting, that universities had followed consciously or unconsciously racist practices or had not been sufficiently encouraging or accessible to minority applicants. The original justification for affirmative action had a connection to the history of discrimination against black slaves in America. The diversity argument makes no reference to that wrong and of course applies to a majority, if you include women, of Americans at the expense of a minority of white males.

HRP: How do you feel about that original argument and about the argument that affirmative action was a limited program designed to redress past wrongs and put everybody on equal footing? Are you more supportive of that?

Mansfield: Yes, if that had ever been seriously intended or were now carried out. I think affirmative action deserves to be on its last legs. It has been a big failure. It was altogether unnecessary in the first place. We could have admitted the same or a perfectly reasonable number of blacks without abandoning the principle of merit and without introducing these harmful new criteria of affirmative action together with a huge bureaucracy that enforces it and corrupts everything at this university. It was totally unnecessary and it has been a failure. What we should do now is to begin to eliminate it first by confining it to blacks who are the really wronged portion of our population, and second by setting a time after which we declare that enough has been done to hurt their pride and their dignity and that it is now time to treat them like other Americans.

HRP: Do you perceive that there is more racial tension on campus than there used to be? Do you think that your comments in some way may have contributed to that?

Mansfield: No, I don't think that they contributed to that. They may have exposed it to some extent. I think a certain exposure is healthy. There are too many things being thought on both sides, which need to be said aloud and discussed openly. It's much less of a community than it appears. This is what I hear and what I see.

HRP: Could you discuss the difference in the teaching of philosophy between the government department and the philosophy department?

Mansfield: Here you have as colleagues political scientists who treat you as utopian, over-theoretical, abstract, incomprehensible. In philosophy you have colleagues who regard you, on the contrary, as too much concerned with fact, with contingency, with the illogical and the non-mathematical. If you want to study political philosophy you have to ask yourself whether you want to be with people who are interested in politics or people who are interested in mathematical logic. This philosophy department is mainly analytic and does very little in the history of philosophy. I can imagine myself having much closer relationships with a philosophy department that paid much closer attention to the history of philosophy. The analytic philosophers think that real progress has occurred in philosophy. They mean by that that certain questions have been resolved and it's no longer necessary to go back. Plato's ideas, for example, have been refuted so one doesn't have to read Plato seriously as someone who might have the truth. One has to be aware of Plato; so you take him in your first year or graduate school and learn a little about "the theory of the ideas," but one doesn't take that as a serious claim to truth. I do. I regard the professors of philosophy as having wrongly settled questions that are still open and having greatly and dogmatically narrowed the field of possible answers. I'm interested in the history of philosophy and of political philosophy not for antiquarian reasons but because I think that's where the truth lies, where the best statement of relevant possibilities can be found. That's what I learned—that's one of the main things I learned—from Strauss.

HRP: Why, from your point of view, do Anglo-American philosophers [such as those at Harvard] spend so little time considering European or "Continental" philosophy written after some mysterious dividing in the late nineteenth century?

Mansfield: I would say that the philosophy department has not come to terms with Nietzsche who was, I think, the philosopher of our time because he has revealed for us the problem of nihilism. I think that is the question that we face and I think that most of the analytic philosophers evade it. They don't take Nietzsche's searing criticism of Western liberalism and of modernity as a whole with sufficient seriousness. So they continue their liberalism, utilitarianism, positivism—logical or not—their linguistic game, their mathematical models, without a careful, unblinking look at our situation. Our situation is that, as Nietzsche put it, God is dead, by which he means not a merely personal God but any transcendent principle or ideal, because it has been killed by our historical consciousness. So, to overlook Nietzsche means to overlook the importance of history for contemporary philosophy and the power of historicism. Nietzsche's main representative in the twentieth century is Heidegger, so to come to terms with Nietzsche one has to go through Heidegger. This would be a personal recommendation to the Harvard professors of philosophy.

HRP: At Harvard, and perhaps at other prominent American universities, there seems to be a distinctive way philosophy is done in the philosophy department, and a distinctive way it's done in the government department. And there seems to be a third and equally different way in which philosophy is treated in the "literary theory" community. Why is the "lit crit" the subject of so much derision from the other academic communities that are concerned with philosophy? Camille Paglia is a good example of someone who heaps unbridled derision on those people, on their standards, on their historical knowledge. . . .

Mansfield: I think she's perfectly right. They do deserve all the insults she supplies. And I think their philosophy and their politics are equally and perfectly superficial.

HRP: Now, when you say "they." What community do you have in mind?

Mansfield: The community of deconstructionist literary scholars.

HRP: And at Harvard whom might that include?

Mansfield: I don't want to name names. Everybody knows that—I don't need to. Paglia, you ask about ... I think she is a serious intellectual commentator. She is sort of an autodidact in a way even though she was a student of Harold Bloom at Yale. And whether she's a passing fad or not, we'll have to see. But I think that the points she makes are serious and that her work is serious. She's a force to be reckoned with and a marvelous woman besides.

HRP: Could you expand on your view that literary criticism is pursued in a superficial way at Harvard?

Mansfield: Well, those people read each other, they don't read the fundamental philosophical texts, which in this case would be Heidegger, not just Derrida and Foucault, but the books of Heidegger which Derrida and Foucault read. So Heidegger and Nietzsche. And so it would require a serious coming to terms with the recent history of philosophy. And second their politics are superficial. They're politicized but they're not political. Their politics is a very small part of the current fashion—which is a fundamental trend in democracy—of the current fashion of egalitarianism. They simply assume, without argument, without examination of all the alternatives, that their view of human equality is the correct one, that no argument could be conceived in favor of traditional arrangements, or of alternative arrangements, but that everything which is the most advanced, is the most correct. So their politicization is as much an impoverishment of politics as of philosophy.

HRP: Why do you think that racial issues have so captivated current campus debate, instead of gender issues, at this point?

Mansfield: I think they are both equally controversial in principle. But, I think, from the very beginning, men have not argued with the feminist revolution. There are only or two books against it that I know of written by a man—some women have opposed it—but almost no man—there's no Bull Connor as a male antagonist to the feminist revolution.

HRP: What is the feminist revolution and what's wrong with it?

Mansfield: The principle of it is that men and women are equal in the sense of exchangeable. Anything a man can do a woman can do, and anything a woman can do a man can do. This is an extremely radical principle which has never been tried by any human society. Most of the feminists are moderates. A moderate feminist is one who believes that it's possible for a woman to have a family and a career, and a radical feminist denies that and is more or less openly opposed to the family. This revolution I do not think can succeed, because it denies natural differences that cannot be repressed. So it will lead to, and has already produced, a good deal of frustration in both sexes. Women will never succeed in being men, in being as successful in occupations which require aggressiveness as men are. And so, realizing this, or half realizing this, they are trying to change the nature of those occupations to fix it so that aggressiveness counts for less.

HRP: Surely, when you refer to occupation that require aggressiveness, you are not limiting yourself to the infantry?

Mansfield: No.

HRP: Could you expand on that? Are you including bond trading, are you including being a political philosopher?

Mansfield: Sure, yes. Anything that requires more get-up-and-go, less regard for others, more initiative, more ruthlessness. I use qualities deliberately which are good and bad, but all of which I think men have more than women. Men, in general have more than women—in general, because there are certainly examples of aggressive women and of—they used to be called effeminate men. And this is not to say, as the feminists say, that the aggressive occupations—that is, the occupations that require one to leave the home—are better. I'm not saying that—they say that. They say that the things that men have been doing are better and more honorable and deserve more credit than the things that women have been doing.

HRP: What about a moderate form of feminism that assumes that some occupations legitimately reward those who are more aggressive more than those who are less aggressive. That's—

Mansfield: They do it legitimately and illegitimately—either way they do it.

HRP: OK. Well let's say that's acknowledged by a moderate feminist and that a moderate feminist might say, "All I'm asking for is that we have a society that truly allows individuals to compete with other individuals to show what level of aggression they have, free from the expectation that because they are from a particular gender they won't be as successful." A moderate feminist might say, "Choose the criteria for success. I don't mind what they are as long as they are fairly applied. Don't subject me to the expectation that because I am a woman I can't be a bond trader. Give me the equal chance to enter into that realm of competition."

Mansfield: Well, that's already stacking it in favor of aggression, because it's that very competitiveness which women have less of than men. So no matter what the standards are, and this is why I think this applies very much more generally than simply to infantry, no matter what the standards are, if they are applied in a situation which contains competition, I think women are always at a disadvantage. And so they will always feel frustrated and cheated when they see someone of less intellect and character than they succeeds better. Men are more used to that and more tolerant of it.

HRP: Do you think that these differences to which you are referring are primarily socialized or are primarily the product of some difference in biology?

Mansfield: Primarily natural, but also partly socialized. The socialization can work to confirm the natural differences or to try to eradicate them. At present we are doing the latter and, I think, with some success but with the prospect of frustration and failure. I should also mention the consequences for the family of feminism, which are dire. The family and quite a few other things too, but especially the family, has long survived from the willingness of women to contribute more without being too concerned with the credit they get. And that is no longer, or much less the case, and I think it's hurting our families very much. A woman's responsibility used to be to do the things that the "responsible" people didn't do. That is, the everyday things. The things that are the real difference between human happiness and not—whether the house is in decent shape and the beds are made and dinner is there and the children are brought up.

HRP: Do you think that the real problem with the American family today is that many women in two-parent families are working, or the fact that many, many families today simply have no husband or father present?

Mansfield: Well, both. Irresponsibility is naturally greater in the male than in the female—that goes with aggressiveness and a certain desire to escape entangling attachments. But feminists fail to realize that a liberated woman also liberates a man. When the woman goes to work then the man no longer has to work for her to support her. When a woman has a right to abort on her own, without any say from the father, then it is hard to say that the father still has responsibility when she doesn't abort. Every child that's born in America today is so as this result of the sole discretion by a woman which, one could say, superseded the responsibility of the father who engendered it.

HRP: But in the decision whether or not to abort, one might argue that women deserve to decide that question because they will have to suffer unique personal hardships, physical hardships for a certain length of time, based on the possible outcome of that decision.

Mansfield: That's right, of course. That's too bad. For this, they get the compensating pleasure of a closer bond with their children. "Hardship" is too strong a word—"discomfort" in modern circumstances is, I think, the most one could say, or "inconvenience."

HRP: A libertarian might find the prospect of nine months of personal hardship so outrageous, so unfair that that would overcome the claim to—

Mansfield: Not if she were a woman. Women like to have babies. That's why they do, for the most part. And so do men, but not quite as much.

HRP: You used "she" for the first time in this interview. You don't subscribe to the trend of using gender-neutral language.

Mansfield: Right, because it seems to me to rest on the premise, which I deny, that men and women are exchangeable.

HRP: But why not, then, alternate the use of male and female pronouns so that the straw person to whom one is referring varies, so that the straw person could be conceived of as male or female? But to use only the male pronoun in the course of a discussion seems to possibly indicate that one thinks that only men could be the appropriate subject of the discussion.

Mansfield: No, it has never meant that. It has always been—in almost all cases—perfectly understandable when one is using "he" to refer to males and "he" the impersonal. And in those cases where it is unclear you can make it clear by using "he" and "she" as they used to be used and when you want to draw attention to the sexual difference. The ridiculous aspect of this new usage is that it means to deny the sexual difference and instead draws attention to it. And there's certain compulsiveness—here I am a libertarian—a certain imposition of somebody else's politics. If we were doing it again, and it weren't being proposed by feminists, with their crazy notion, I would be willing to entertain some sort of compromise.

HRP: Let's return to the abortion issue for the moment. Do you think that couples should, jointly, have a right to abort a pregnancy?

Mansfield: Yes, I do. I agree with President Clinton that abortion should be safe, legal, and rare. The problem is, if it is safe and legal, how is it going to be rare? So I would look for some way of reducing the number of abortions; a million and a half in this country a year is an extravagant number.

HRP: But if, let's say, an abortion, considered in the abstract, is not morally objectionable in the sense that it does not constitute the killing of a person, then why should the number that is performed matter at all?

Mansfield: It's, again, a terrible irresponsibility to treat a fetus as an inconvenience. It's not a person, but it's a potential person so it can't be just treated as a disease or an excrescence. It's a matter of life and death not of a viable human being but of a future human being. How is a mother supposed to look on a child as someone she could have chosen to kill? That seems to me to open up a freedom, which it would be better for us not to have. But, since we do have it and since there are cases of real hardship—even real danger—I wouldn't outlaw it altogether but I would put many burdens [on it]. One which my wife has proposed is a steeply progressive tax on abortions so that the more money you have, the more tax you would have to pay to get an abortion. One of the worst things about abortions is that so many of them are done by people who are perfectly capable of raising a child but find it inconvenient.

HRP: But if a man has a veto over the abortion of a woman whom he has impregnated, unless there exists mechanisms to force that man to provide economic assistance to the child and the child's mother, he basically has the ability to force a woman into economic hardship.

Mansfield: Or into the pleasure of having a child. You underestimate how much fun it is to have children. It's a lot of work too—I wouldn't call it hardship, I would just call it work. But it's the kind of work which is fun. I wouldn't have missed it for anything in my life. I've had a happy life in all stages, but the happiest is the time when my children were young.

HRP: If technology became available, would you put your notion of the pleasure of having children to the test and have one yourself?

Mansfield: Yeah, sure. But, I mean, that's totally . . . put it this way, I am ready for grandchildren.

HRP: Do you think a family leave bill is an effort to help families?

Mansfield: I think that's bad. No, I think it hurts families by producing greater independence of husband and wife from each other. And I'm against day care too—or government supported day care. I think it's better to have parents at home with their children, and [for them to have] a somewhat less affluent life.

HRP: But do you think that for the majority of Americans, the decision of whether a woman is going to work or not is really a choice between whether or not to purchase a second car, between affluence and membership to the middle class, or do you think it's a decision between poverty and—

Mansfield: No, I don't think poverty, no.

HRP: You don't think that that's the case?

Mansfield: Right, I think that's much overstated. But I can see why a woman might want to take a part time job [to] bring up the finances. That doesn't require, in most cases, I think, a full-time job or a full-time career, and that's different from the justification that most feminists would use. I have to say that there is certainly a problem here for modern women; there's not enough for them to do in the home, especially after the children grow to a certain age. It's boring. They certainly need something else than the work of a housewife, so I don't mean to sentence them to a life of tending the kitchen. But they should take advantage of leisure, which a lot of men would envy if only they would reflect, to improve their minds.

HRP: On a personal note, have you had to assure the female partners in your life that you do not in fact wish to sentence them to a life of household chores?

Mansfield: Yes, and my feminism is that I work around the house. It's more practical.

HRP: Where do you find the impetus to be a presence on campus, to be a crusader or to lead a fight which is often, at Harvard, not a popular one?

Mansfield: It comes from the horrible feeling that if I don't speak, no one will. It isn't really ambition, because I [don't] care about running things, or directing things, or administering. It's a strong sense that things are out of sorts and somebody needs at least to draw attention to a grave mistake we're making.

HRP: Do you feel that some of the positions you've staked out have possibly adversely affected your relationship with students who might want to take your classes? How might a black or female student view you as a professor?

Mansfield: Well, people do choose courses for the opinions of the professor more now than they used to, which is a very bad thing. I don't think I can use that as a reason for silence, and I just have to hope that there are sufficient numbers of fair-minded students who will see, I think, if they try it, that I do my best to run an honest course. And I don't think that that that's something that needs to be defined because everybody knows what that means. φ

W. V. Quine

Perhaps no philosopher has been so influential yet so unrecognized as Willard van Orman Quine. Though widely known, read, and deeply respected within the philosophical community, the name Quine is virtually unknown outside of the academy. Nevertheless, Quine's work provides the intellectual grounding for the "post-modern" revolution in English-speaking countries; he is the father of a fundamental change in the way people conceive the world.

Quine's early work focused heavily on logic, a subject about which he published two books in the early 1940s. His work, however, quickly began to incorporate the study of language. Quine was involved in a series of exchanges with Rudolf Carnap. Their debate centered around Carnap's sharp distinction between a language that one spoke and the statements that one made in this language. This view relied on a hallowed distinction in philosophy (at that time): the distinction between analytic truths (statements true in virtue of the meanings of their words) and synthetic truths (matters of empirical fact). With the publication of his article "Two Dogmas of Empiricism" (in *From a Logical Point of View*) in the early 1950s, Quine launched a ferocious attack on the analytic-synthetic distinction. In the process he shook a fundamental belief widely held by philosophers and began a debate that is, to this day, unsettled. His work in this period has had a lasting and profound impact on the history of philosophy, especially on the logical positivists (the most notable of whom was Carnap), contending that their philosophical project was misconceived.

Had Quine's philosophical career ended here, he would deserve to be considered among the giants of the twentieth century. But he was far from done. In 1960 Quine published *Word & Object*. In this book he developed his famous doctrine of the indeterminacy of translation. Quine argued that there were many ways, each consistent with all potentially available evidence, of translating between any two languages. In attacking the analytic-synthetic distinction and arguing for the indeterminacy of translation, Quine was attacking a "dogma" deeply rooted in the Western philosophical tradition—that words have meanings. The connection between these arguments and word meaning is this: if words were to have determinate meanings, then one could speak of two words being synonymous if they had the same meaning. It would follow, then, that an analytic truth would be one that could be turned into a logical truth by replacing some of the words in the sentence by their synonyms. Similarly, if words have meanings, then only one translation between two languages would be acceptable—that which mapped each word in one language to a word in the other language that had the same meaning. Quine's work in the 1950s aimed at destabilizing meaning. This notion of meaning being unstable, which has its roots in Quine, is central to the contemporary postmodern project.

Further, Quine argued that our knowledge forms a "web of belief." For Quine, no piece of knowledge was sacred or beyond potential revision. His work in the 1950s partially anticipates and lays the groundwork for Thomas Kuhn's *Structure of Scientific Revolutions* (1962), a work at the very basis of the postmodern canon. The idea expressed therein—that scientific theories are simply descriptions of observed phenomena rather than deep descriptions of "reality"—is a clear extension of Quine's web of beliefs.

Quine's style of writing was elegant and rigorous. His argumentation was famously clear and well-phrased. His work helped set the standard for philosophical rigor and clarity that is still dominant today in departments of analytic philosophy. In his later years, Quine continued to struggle with ideas in language and logic and produced much philosophical writing, including the *Philosophy of Logic* (1970), in which he revisits issues of logic, truth, and meaning.

W. V. Quine passed away December 25, 2000, having left an indelible imprint on the world he inhabited. The influence he exerted both on the philosophical community and the contributions he made to ways of thinking in general are of lasting importance. φ

W. V. Quine
Perspectives on Logic, Science, and Philosophy

Interview by
Bradley Edmister
and Michael O'Shea
in 1994

HRP: What is the role of philosophy vis-à-vis science?

Quine: I think of philosophy as continuous with science, but philosophy differs by degree in various respects. Philosophy undertakes to analyze the general, basic concepts of science—the sort of concepts the practicing scientist will typically take for granted. These are such basic notions as truth, existence, and necessity. Also, philosophy investigates questions of evidence for science—that's epistemology. It seeks a better understanding of the tremendous transformation that takes place between the input that we receive through the irritation of our sensory surfaces, and our torrential output in the form of scientific theory. It tries to analyze theory, and see[s] how much of it is really dictated by the input ("by nature," we say, but that's only going to be in the input), and how much is only a matter of our accommodation and organization of it. These are considerations that aren't ordinarily taken up by any particular science.

In these studies, philosophy will sometimes elicit paradoxes, which the scientist, even if he is told about them, isn't likely to worry about. In normal scientific practice, he can simply dodge that end of his theory. But the philosopher is going to be concerned.

HRP: So the existence of paradoxes in philosophy of science doesn't affect the workings of scientific theory?

Quine: Right. This is brought up most dramatically in the familiar paradoxes of set theory—Russell's Paradox and the like. Even mathematicians, as a whole, didn't worry about them, because they weren't going to be dealing with self-membership in classes, or classes of all non-self-membered classes. They worked in mathematical domains where, when intuitively surveying the assumptions and axioms involved, they felt they were on solid ground. It's the sort of thing that falls quite naturally into the philosopher's domain.

HRP: That view seems to reduce the work of philosophy to simply tying up the loose ends of science. Is that accurate?

Quine: Yes, I think "tying up loose ends" is a good way of condensing philosophy's purpose.

HRP: How much science should a philosopher know in order to do his job competently?

Quine: It's important that he have a respectable grasp, at least at the undergraduate level, of a hard science. It's extremely important to have had the experience of really knowing something without a shadow of doubt, even if it takes [on a] complicated argument, and having what one feels is a firm basis of evidence. Ideal for this purpose is mathematics, especially mathematical logic.

I have always felt that a good course in modern logic ought to be required, not only of every candidate for a philosophy degree, but for every undergraduate in every field. It could even be valuable for students specializing in the literary domain, where one doesn't aspire to logic's sort of certainty and conviction. It's important for those students to see the difference.

HRP: What is the role of first-order logic in the scientific project, in physics, for example?

Quine: In relation to physics, I don't see much of a role. I think that as far as elementary logic is concerned, the common sense of the physicist today (and of centuries ago, perhaps, before modern logic began) is enough. But modern logic is important for a systematic understanding of theoretical relationships; and when it comes to more analytical studies, both in foundations of mathematics and in philosophical analysis of concepts generally, logic is vital.

The illumination that modern logic has brought to philosophy of mathematics is the most illuminating instance. Gödel's incompleteness proof contradicted what everybody, even mathematicians, had taken for granted, namely, that mathematical truth consists in demonstrability. [It was thought that] you may not find the proof, but the proof can be found, if the thing is true—and a proof purely mathematical in content and formulation. This is what Gödel showed to be an impossible situation.

HRP: How has the role of logic in philosophy changed from the 1920s and 1930s, when there was a lot of excitement about the foundational role of logic?

Quine: I don't think the foundational role of logic has changed. But there's been a lot of progress in specialized directions, with perhaps the greatest being in axiomatic set theory and higher categories of infinity, and then also a tremendous amount of progress in proof theory, of which Gödel's proof is a shining example.

HRP: You crowned your recent *Pursuit of Truth* (1987) with the motto, "Save the surface and you save all." How have your empiricism and behaviorism affected your view of what it means to give a philosophical explanation?

Quine: That epigraph was accompanied with another one from Plato—"save the phenomena." I find it particularly interesting that Plato appreciated this attitude, but it's essentially just the statement of empiricism, the statement that what we're trying to do is explain what we can observe. If we don't respect our observations, and stick to them rather than revising them to fit our theory, then we're not succeeding in our effort to achieve truth.

Behaviorism, as far as I'm concerned, is only an intersubjective empiricism. It's empirical in attitude, but one doesn't settle, in the manner of Husserl and the old epistemologists, for private, introspective data. When you take as your data your own perceptions, and pool these with those of your colleagues, and get the common denominator, then you have data which are pertinent to science from the standpoint of intersubjective behaviorism. I don't see that as going beyond what every modern scientist would subscribe to as a matter of course.

HRP: In the reduction of common-sense terms for introspective human states to publicly accessible, empiricist terms, is there a danger of losing something? Can empiricism do justice to our inner lives?

Quine: Here one must distinguish two factors: the dreaming-up of hypotheses and the amassing of evidence for them. All sorts of undisciplined thinking can be valuable as a first step in thinking up bright ideas, way-out, highly imaginative, which turn out to be just what's needed once you get down to finding logical connections through experiments.

I don't think that this process neglects the natural mentalistic input—it just means not settling for it. Daniel Dennett was very good on this topic in an essay defending introspection, which took pretty much this line, as I read it.

HRP: You wrote in *Pursuit of Truth* that "there is nothing in linguistic meaning beyond what is to be gleaned from overt behavior in observable circumstances." Does the indeterminacy of translation hinder the intersubjective communication of scientific concepts, a communication which seems to be important for the project of "naturalizing epistemology"?

Quine: No, I think not. The indeterminacy of translation doesn't get in the way of translation—it allows that there are good translations and bad. It's rather a question of the data that are available to see whether a translation is good or bad. It proposes external, behavioral criteria for the test.

Here's the situation: you have two translation manuals that are both as good as can be. This is according to the empirical test of using them in normal communication with a native, and finding that they lead to smooth dialogue and successful negotiation, which could mean getting directions somewhere, or the native's giving up some priceless relic for some glass beads, or whatever you're trying to bring about. Those are the tests.

If you have two manuals, arrived at independently, which both pass those tests to perfection, then you try meshing them. Suppose it turns out that if you use one of these manuals for a given text, it gives perfect, smooth translation, and if you use the other one it works just as well, but when you try alternating them on the same text it turns out to give incoherence. This illustrates what I mean by the indeterminacy of translation. My conjecture is that [this situation] is to be expected when we get into theoretical dialogue. However, it's not something that would show up in entering into scientific communication; both of these manuals are completely successful on the empirical score. In that case, the moral is: stick to the same manual.

But translation isn't always possible in science. Today's physicist talks about Neutrinos, for instance, and says "Neutrinos are particles which lack rest mass." That sentence certainly isn't translatable into the English of 1930, because there's no translation of "Neutrino," not even a long paraphrase, because "Neutrino" has never been defined. None of the particles, not even "electron," has ever been defined in the strict logical sense of definition. There aren't even contextual definitions comparable to Russell's definition of singular descriptions. No word or phrase, either by itself or in context, can take the place of the word "Neutrino" or the word "electron." This is no obstacle; people use the word with no problem, and the native above can even use the word, given a certain substructure of explanation. Explanation, but not translation.

HRP: Your view explains intersubjective communication on the basis of readily observable events. But what happens when we're testing "manuals" about theoretical concepts or philosophical ideas? Presumably, such manuals could conflict with each other, yet they don't necessarily allow for observable evidence of the success of translation. This is more acute given the potential existence of radically different conceptual schemes among those communicating. What do we do in this case?

Quine: The way I see it, two different translators could in theory come up with quite different conceptual schemes for the same people. I see this as a matter of richness rather than poverty. It helps bring out the point that conceptual schemes are almost completely a matter of human creativity—creativity to the purpose, however, of matching up with the neural input.

Theory is so overwhelmingly much stronger and broader than the neural input that, of course, you expect slack, and that's what makes me believe in the thesis of indeterminacy.

In the case we're imagining, we have two accounts of the natives' metaphysics, which are not much alike. It is then a chastening experience to find that they're equally faithful accounts. Now what there is to be communicated of an objective, scientific kind is being communicated all the better, through our appreciating the theoretical latitude.

HRP: Would it be fruitful for philosophers to become irritated about this state of affairs and seek metaphysical explanations for this metaphysical looseness?

Quine: I don't think so. The distinctive thing about science is that there are checkpoints of observation. Everything that is compatible with those checkpoints [is acceptable]. One is always trying, as Sir Karl Popper pointed out, to "break" one's theory, devising the least hopeful experiment possible to subject it to. That's what marks the difference between responsible science and fancy, and it remains undisturbed through all this.

HRP: Your philosophy played a pivotal role in the demolition of the logical positivism of the 1930s. Do you feel any nostalgia for the philosophical optimism of those days?

Quine: I can see the attractiveness of that idea, but I also see something hopeful that seems to be taking its place: the tendency in certain philosophical circles (Dennett is again a shining example of this) to rub out, or at least blur, the boundaries between philosophy and various sciences. Here, Simon Saunders and others are trying to rub out the boundaries between physics and philosophy, along with others like Abner Shimony. It's not only getting physics into the philosophical circle, but philosophy into the physical circle—collaboration. These people take serious, advanced seminars in physics. Roger Penrose, in *The Emperor's New Mind*, is hoping that someone will come up with a new force, a new particle, that will give us a more intuitive understanding of new finds in quantum mechanics, of scientific concepts anyway. That's of as much interest to philosophers as physicists, and the addition of philosophers trained in physics might improve the situation in physics itself.

HRP: So the paradigm is not philosophy grounding physics, but rather a mutual strengthening and smoothing between philosophy and physics.

Quine: Exactly. Furthermore, it's not just in physics. This effect is present in the work of Dennett, with his seminars over at Tufts with people from neurology, computer science, linguistics, and psychology participating. The boundaries between philosophy and all these fields are wavering and disappearing, and this bears promise of a great new era.

HRP: Are we, then, on the verge of a new optimism about the role of philosophy and science? Is there a feeling of possibility finally "getting things right"?

Quine: I don't know about getting things finally right—it's an interesting question whether there's an end point, but I have no firm opinion there. There is certainly progress, that seems very clear. What excites me in this collaboration is the prospect of progress, not necessarily getting to the end of the line.

HRP: What have you found to be the most exciting intellectual development of the last twenty years?

Quine: Near philosophy, and of close philosophical relevance, I think of the work of Hubel and Wiesel in neurology, and the utterly new picture that they've given of the neurology of vision. It seems that it's not a matter of the visual field being reflected isomorphically somewhere in the nervous system, but a matter of various dominant features coming in separately from one another, and not even being clearly synthesized until the moment of reflection. All of this goes on in hundredths of seconds. It gives us a new angle of approach.

Reaching back before 1974, I think of advances in psychology of vision made by Edwin H. Land, inventor of the Polaroid camera, and his theory of color vision. There's no guessing what they're going to come up with next.

HRP: You seem to have considerable respect for the work being done in cognitive science. How do you feel about the attitudes characteristic of cognitive science, for instance, the conjecture that machines can duplicate the intelligence of humans?

Quine: First, I find the Turing test for artificial intelligence unhopeful as a test, because human behavior depends so much on everything that's gone on through many years, reaching back to infancy, and even to the distant history of our corner of the world. Intelligence, it seems, is a matter of degree, and I'm hindered by the fact that I have no satisfactory criterion for what constitutes "thinking." When we just go by output, of course, computers are already doing a quite remarkable job of thinking.

But I doubt that a machine could ever pass the Turing test. That was itself an arbitrary criterion to separate thinking from computing, and I have no hope for the development of a sharp criterion.

HRP: Famously, several of your papers written in the 1950s denied that the analytic/synthetic distinction had any foundational value, at least in the sense that Carnap and others wished. Does the distinction have any methodological significance?

Quine: In *The Roots of Reference* I suggested a definition of analyticity which seemed to me to approximate the layman's intuitive conception—not that the layman uses [of] the term "analytic." The analytic is what the layman calls "just a matter of words." He dismisses someone's assertion as just a matter of words, as a question of how to use the words.

But we still want a criterion for analyticity, and one that has occurred to me is that a sentence is analytic (for a given native speaker) if he learns the truth of the sentence in the course of learning one of its words. The obvious example is "No bachelor is married." A native speaker clearly learns the truth of this sentence by learning how to use the word "bachelor." A foreign speaker might have learned the word rather by translation. This criterion covers not only all sentences like that, but surely also all truths of elementary logic. Somebody who affirms "p and q" but denies "p" is, we say, misusing "and." He hasn't learned to use "and." That's true for all the basic principles of elementary logic, and from the basic principles you get all of elementary logic.

Elementary logic, in the sense I intend it here, is complete. It covers truth—functions, quantification, and identity—not set theory. This fits nicely with what Frege, Carnap, and Kant all held. I don't think of the rest of mathematics as being analytic. Furthermore, this isn't a concept that I can see applying across the board. This is what makes it unfruitful as a tool of philosophical analysis. Nobody remembers how they learned the truth of each sentence, and on the face of it, it shouldn't matter.

So a new word, "momentum," comes in. By definition, it's mass times velocity. No questions there, an arbitrary definition. We simply dig up an obsolete Latin word for this technical purpose. But even so, relativity theory denies that momentum is simply mass times velocity. You have to get something in there about the square of the speed of light. So there's nothing about analyticity that compels particular uses of words. That's why I felt that Carnap's blanket application of the term in theoretical contexts generally was obscuring the issues and getting on the wrong track. This matter of truth by virtue of language does come in as a component, but not, I would argue, sentence by sentence.

Clearly, verbal convention is a factor in the truth of any sentence. If the syllables of the words in any sentence, however empirical it may be, were used for another purpose, the sentence might be false instead of true. So the degree to which language contributes to this or that sentence, this or that part of science, can be methodologically and scientifically significant.

HRP: Is the gradation of analyticity and syntheticity in ordinary language a philosophically interesting topic? What are some ways it might be talked about?

Quine: I wouldn't think of it as coming into issue with particular words. But sentence by sentence ... it seems reasonable that there would be gradations, maybe consisting in the magnitude of the network of definitions that are necessary to connect what we learn ostensibly with a sentence in question. That's a highly theoretical question, and perhaps that would capture the gradation.

HRP: You gave us a sense in which elementary logic is analytic, but were just now careful to exclude set theory from that sense, presumably because of the implications of Russell's Paradox. What is the status of set theory, and given its use in grounding the axioms of mathematics, where does that leave arithmetic?

Quine: Russell's Paradox made all the difference. Frege thought the whole of set theory was analytic, although even in the days before Russell's Paradox he noted somewhere that the axiom that people would be most dubious about in terms of its analyticity was the universal comprehension principle [all predicates determine classes]. The question applies to higher mathematics generally, from set theory on up.

I see mathematics as sharing empirical content in a way connected with holism. In general, if you're testing a scientific hypothesis, typically you're going to need a whole cluster of other hypotheses before you get down to the level of observables with implied consequences. Among the auxiliary hypotheses you'll have to bring in, there will be some purely mathematical principles, differential and integral calculus, and so on.

So you might say that in general a cluster of scientific truths and hypotheses has an empirical "critical mass" if it is enough to imply observable consequences. And often, to get critical mass you're going to need some purely mathematical sentences. If you regard essential participation in a set of hypotheses with critical masses as what it means to have empirical content, it means that [all] applicable mathematics has empirical content. But it's not empirical in the sense of John Stuart Mill; that is, arithmetic is not the product of generalization from counting and counting again. Sometimes it is, I expect, historically, but that's not the point.

Then I would apply this in particular to set theory. But this matter of having empirical content must be separated from the old positivistic exclusion principle of the meaninglessness of metaphysics. I think it's a mistake to require that a sentence must have empirical content in order to be meaningful. In fact, I think that there's no end to the important [non-empirical] beliefs and truths of history and sociology, and perhaps theoretical physics. You can add a whole bunch of them together and they won't be enough to imply any observations, and yet they're important. They seem plausible by virtue of symmetry, simplicity, fitting-in to the things that we have well established by tests. These are indispensable, moreover, in suggesting further hypotheses which one can test. Science would be paralyzed if we excluded the untestables.

HRP: Within a "critical mass" of hypotheses in mathematics, exactly how do the purely mathematical sentences relate to the empirical ones?

Quine: Here's something characteristic of mathematics, but perhaps not only of mathematics: That these sentences are needed as components of sets with critical mass, but that no set purely of mathematical components has critical mass. This is a sense in which mathematics can be viewed as auxiliary to science. But then history—something as unlike mathematics as can be—would also be auxiliary in this sense. Again, just a set of historical sentences about, say, ancient Rome, and nothing more, can't be tested without the help of a lot more earthy generalizations. The tolerance that I'm urging regarding sentences that don't, of themselves, have empirical consequences, becomes, curiously enough, not merely a defense of highly speculative metaphysics or of history, but of hard mathematics itself.

HRP: Your work is marked by a clear concern for style of expression. What are your stylistic aims in writing philosophy?

Quine: Well, I certainly haven't thought about style enough to have principles of consequence, but one thing that I tend to try to avoid is mutually conflicting etymological metaphors.

One of the persistent errors that strikes me funny, which I first saw in a newspaper, and now it keeps popping up in print, is "stirring up tensions." Another is "it was at the height of the Depression."

Another specific thing I dislike is the heterogeneity of languages in new coinages. I like homogeneity of the components of a new word. For example, a mathematician's "hypernatural numbers." No! "Supernatural numbers." Hyper is Greek and natural is Latin. There's so much of that. I would hope that a scientist who needs a new technical word for something would consult a literate colleague, someone who knows Latin and Greek and could help him get it right.

In more general terms, I strive for clarity and brevity. It happens so often that by going over something and making it shorter I improve it.

HRP: Where did you pick up your rhetorical principles and skills?

Quine: When I look back to my first book, *A System of Logic* (1934), and articles from those years, I find that it's a more stilted style—I wasn't as sure of myself. My style's improved a lot since then. It's been mostly a matter of practice. I don't know of any source for my distaste for heterogeneities and so on.

HRP: At its best, it seems that American analytic philosophy tends toward a radically clear, taut style that one sees particularly in both your work and Nelson Goodman's. It reflects a very different spirit from the German philosophical prose of someone like Heidegger. Do you think that the tradition and the values of those who work in it dictate a particular style?

Quine: That's a very interesting point, and I believe perhaps it does. There are certainly affinities between [my writing] and Goodman's. But when I think of how clear and succinct Carnap's German was. . . .

HRP: Perhaps it's not national, but rather a divide between the analytic and Continental traditions.

Quine: Yes, I think that's it. It's the same sort of taste that makes for mathematical and logical elegance. It's linked to the desire for clarity and brevity. But my interest in overtones in etymological metaphors would be an independent factor. It comes from an interest in natural language as such that I've had from way back; it just happened. I got into etymologies when I was still in high school—I remember taking books out of the library about the origins of words. I still have the same urge; I'll want to know what the origin of a word is and have to look it up.

HRP: What modern philosophers do you follow with the most interest? Who do you think is on the right track?

Quine: I suppose that would have to include the work of my former student, Donald Davidson. I don't agree with him on everything, but we're after nearly the same thing, and along the same lines. We have very profitable discussions.

HRP: That's interesting—in a controversial reading of Davidson's philosophy, Richard Rorty has taken Davidson as an exemplar of his own type of ironist, relativist anti-representationalism. What do you think of Rorty's stance?

Quine: I was surprised by reading Rorty's big book [*Philosophy and the Mirror of Nature*], the one that made such a stir. He said very favorable things about my philosophical views, which surprised me because I didn't like his position. It strikes me as defeatist, and it shows a bit of the anti-scientific bias that is more extreme in people like Derrida and Heidegger.

HRP: Those "Continental" thinkers are often distinguished from analytic philosophers by saying that they do not take scientific inquiry as an intellectual model. Your own project of "naturalizing epistemology," on the other hand, reflects the conviction that scientific theory provides the paradigm for what philosophical accounts should be like. Do you think it's possible to do viable philosophical work that is organized around other paradigms, like poetry or belles lettres?

Quine: It seems to me that the place where that sort of thinking has a function, and is still within the domain of philosophy, is in philosophy of poetry and the graphic arts. Whether we choose to call it philosophy or not, there is a place for the strictly artistic use of language in conjuring up thoughts and visions, which help you get the point of an art work that you had missed before. I don't think that this function could ever be managed by strict scientific prose. But on the other hand, I don't see a place for it in scientific philosophy.

HRP: If a young philosophy student came to you for advice, and asked where the most pressing work in philosophy currently lay, where would you advise the student to turn?

Quine: One big project that has struck me as promising would be to take some limited part of hard science, like Newtonian mechanics, and try to trace out explicitly the logical connections of implication from its basic principles to the observational checkpoints. In other words, an explicit amassing of evidence. It would have the advantage not only of illuminating the epistemology of the science but also might even be a contribution to the science, by suggesting shortcuts and simplifications, or by showing how some bit of theory just didn't get used or serve its purpose. That method, if it succeeded with a sample chunk of science, might spread to other cases, and, if it succeeded, might help make philosophy a handmaiden to science, along with mathematics. φ

Alan Dershowitz

Alan Dershowitz is a nationally renowned lawyer, author, and journalist. He has been praised and criticized for taking the defense in notorious cases, from Claus von Bulow to O. J. Simpson, as well as taking positions on issues from the nature of Judaism to the Clinton impeachment hearings. By his admirers in the press, he is called the "winningest," "smartest," and "most peripatetic" of American civil rights lawyers, and he has appeared on major television shows from *Nightline* to *Crossfire*. Often obfuscated by his high-profile cases and controversial positions is Dershowitz's accomplished and serious work in the philosophy of law.

After graduating first in his class from Yale Law School, Dershowitz became, at twenty-eight, the youngest full professor in Harvard Law School's history, where he still teaches as the Felix Frankfurter Professor of Law. His best-known book is perhaps *Chutzpah*, published in 1991, which is in its twelfth printing. *Reversal of Fortune: Inside the Van Bulow Case*, another of Dershowitz's books, published in 1986, was turned into an Academy Award–winning motion picture by his son Elon. He has also written *Contrary to Popular Opinion*, which examined the U.S. constitutional and political process, and *The Abuse Excuse*, a collection of essays examining the relationship between individual responsibility and the law. Most recently, Dershowitz has published *The Genesis of Justice*, which examines biblical law in a search for "perfect justice," which Dershowitz acknowledges is rarely found on earth. His next project, *Shouting Fire*, is a collection of essays on civil liberties issues that, Dershowitz tells us, will discuss topics from the right to choice to the separation between church and state as well as the long-lasting legacy of the Holocaust.

Two themes that run throughout Dershowitz's work both as a lawyer and an author is his deep concern for the protection of the rights of minorities and his unremitting search for more perfect justice. His numerous successful cases, including Claus von Bulow (conviction reversed and acquitted), the Jewish Defense League murder case (reversed, all defendants acquitted), Michael Milken (sentence reduced from ten to two years), the Chicago Seven (convictions and contempts reversed), and John Lennon (deportation order reversed), have often had their defendants villainized and marginalized before Dershowitz takes the case. For this reason, Dershowitz is often seen as the Saint Jude of lawyers, the patron of lost causes. Philosophically, Dershowitz shies away from subscribing to one ideology in his works, instead resorting to intense searching for the truth in particular situations. Dershowitz is a rare thinker who is able not only to speak, write, and teach his ideas but also to go out and help make the world into what he sees as a better place. φ

Alan Dershowitz
On the Philosophy of Law

Interview by
Gil Lahav
in 1994

HRP: There has been some controversy at Harvard Law School about the proposed ban on hate speech. What are your views on speech codes?

Dershowitz: What I am in favor of is a specific provision that makes it clear that nothing can be banned unless it's specified by rule. And the only thing that I personally am prepared to see prohibited is harassment that borders on the physical. That is, an employer shouting at an employee in a racist, sexist, or otherwise degrading manner, because of [his or her relative superiority in a] hierarchical situation. But I am unequivocally opposed to any ban on any speech that is content-laden, classroom speech, or speech involving any political issues. I am as close to an absolutist on free speech as anyone in the Harvard University community. If we were to have any restrictions at all, I would prefer to see them in a code than to leave them to the discretion of some administrator. It is the arbitrary discretion of an individual that I am afraid of.

HRP: What do you think should be the philosophical mission of the Supreme Court?

Dershowitz: In the most general terms, the Supreme Court ought to do several things. It ought to clear the channels of democracy, [by ensuring] that voting is fair, that the democratic process operates fairly, that free speech is open and complete, that legislatures are properly apportioned. That's its primary mission: to see that democracy operates so that the legislatures can make [society's] decisions fairly. Beyond that, I think its other important role is to vindicate the constitutional rights of minorities who don't have the political power to have their rights prevail in the popular branches of the executive and the legislature.

HRP: In what ways is that mission compatible or incompatible with its political function?

Dershowitz: It's incompatible to the extent that the Supreme Court has become very politicized lately. It could be compatible. There is a proper role the Supreme Court could play, in which it is much more neutral on substantive issues but sees as its mission the vindication of minority rights that could not be vindicated by the popular branches.

HRP: How do you define "minority?"

Dershowitz: Well, it's not easy to define it. It's a continuum. The Supreme Court should have more power to vindicate the rights of those minorities who are weakest. Well-organized minorities deserve less protection than less-well-organized minorities, like atheists, criminal defendants, communists, or fascists. People who have no political constituency in this country can't use political processes. I don't define minorities in the way they're defined in civil rights statutes.

HRP: So what are your views on affirmative action as a way to protect minority rights?

Dershowitz: My views on affirmative action are very complex. I don't personally believe in race-specific or gender-specific affirmative action. I do believe in affirmative action based on how far a person has come from his or her personal origins. Universities ought to take into account where a person has come from, rather than only a static view of where that person is. But race [or gender] alone should be given little weight. I think race-specific affirmative action tends, in the end, to favor wealthy minorities over poor minorities, and more advantaged women over less advantaged women.

HRP: In *Doing and Deserving*, Joel Feinberg argues that legal responsibility, unlike moral responsibility, can be quite arbitrary. According to him this is the case because, with legal responsibility, the line must be drawn somewhere. Does that mean that there can be no right place to draw the line?

Dershowitz: I disagree with that formulation. In law you don't have to have a strict line; you could have a continuum too. We should not have a continuum when it comes to protected speech or areas where it's very important that we have clear lines, but it's in the nature of the legal system that we sometimes draw lines and sometimes have a continuum, and knowing when a line is appropriate [as opposed to] a continuum is a very important legal-philosophical consideration.

HRP: What makes one line more appropriate or better than another line?

Dershowitz: If we have to draw lines, we should draw them by the democratic process, because they're arbitrary and arbitrary decisions ought to be made in majoritarian ways, [and] not by judges. And for the most part, public decisions in the United States are made in this way. When we decide that eighteen year olds should vote, that's a legislative judgment—there's nothing right or wrong about it. We need a line. We don't want to inquire [about] everyone's capability of voting. We instead want to delineate a clear, but arbitrary line.

HRP: How removed should judges and Supreme Court Justices be from the world that they impact with their decisions?

Dershowitz: Judges should be familiar with how the world operates because they're being asked to make decisions that will have real effects, and these decisions must be based on [some] conception of how the world operates. For example, the current Supreme Court suffers from not having really experienced, excellent lawyers, and that shows in the quality—or lack thereof—of some of its decisions, particularly in the criminal justice system, which I know best. We see a series of naive decisions that don't reflect the reality of the criminal justice system.

HRP: What are your views on the movement to increase the number of court proceedings that are televised?

Dershowitz: It's not cost free, but I think it's worth the cost. My idea is to have a publicly owned station, much like C-span, that would cover the judiciary. It wouldn't try to focus only on the sexiest and most provocative cases, but [rather] on the most important ones, even if they're boring. It wouldn't have as one of its goals to bring viewers to the screen, but to make the judiciary more accessible to those interested in its process or decisions. It should be as open, in a democracy, as any other institution of government.

HRP: But don't you think that televising important or very emotional trials can create the danger of mob justice?

Dershowitz: Well, the alternative to mob justice is elite justice, and what we have to do is strike a balance. Mob justice is a phrase that was also used to criticize democracy. What's so delicate about the balance that our constitution strikes is that, on the one hand, it calls for a republican form of government with many attributes of a democracy and, on the other hand, it leaves some of the most important decisions to an elite, namely, the judiciary. Keeping that balance right is very difficult.

HRP: In the first lecture of your course "Thinking about Thinking" you seemed to deny that there could be any truth in the world of legal discourse. You claimed that lawyers simply select as premises the level of analysis that suits the needs of their client's case, and then argue the case from those premises. If that is correct, then does justice amount simply to the level of analysis that most impresses a judge or a jury?

Dershowitz: I think it is possible to have truth. I just think that it's something that few people care about deeply in our legal system. Our legal system is eminently manipulatable and good lawyers know how to manipulate it. There have been times in our history when the search for truth was genuine. Today our legal system has become so politicized that I see more manipulation than I do [any] search for truth. Justice is a process—a fair process. Since I don't believe in natural law, and I don't believe in legal positivism, I need to look at law as a fair process, which doesn't necessarily guarantee fair outcomes.

HRP: What would a fair process entail?

Dershowitz: A fair process entails fairly selected judges and jurors, clearly articulated rules, rules that don't differentially impact based on race, sex, poverty, or other such factors. Substantively clear rules that contain basic elements of justice. But it's very hard to define justice, or even fairness, in a paragraph. In some sense we know it when we see it. It's much easier to see its opposite than to see justice. I never expect to see absolute justice. I have seen absolute corruption, but I have never seen absolute justice.

HRP: Given the fair process as you've just conceived of it, what aspect of America's legal system needs the most improvement right now?

Dershowitz: Judges and the judiciary. We have too many cynical judges who don't believe in justice, cheat and lie, are intellectually dishonest in every way, and yet who are elected and re-elected, or appointed and promoted. And that combination is an indication of disaster.

HRP: What do you think accounts for the selection of inappropriate judges?

Dershowitz: The politicization of the process. The fact that the judiciary is seen as a plum. The fact that people aren't trained to be judges. In many parts of the country being a federal judge means being a mediocre lawyer who has a senator for a friend, and being a state judge means being a mediocre lawyer who has a governor for a friend. The process by which we pick our judges is an abomination. It's one of the worst processes of any civilized country in the world.

HRP: Do you think judges should be elected?

Dershowitz: No. That's the only worse system than political appointment, because then we essentially have one branch of government pretending to be divided into three. It's important that we have an elite branch of government that is picked for stability and selected without day-to-day accountability to the popular will. But I think they ought to be picked more professionally—more in terms of peer review and less in terms of politics.

HRP: If the United States had to improve its legal system by emulating that of another country's, which country would you recommend?

Dershowitz: I don't think any country can emulate any other country's legal system because every legal system has to evolve from the culture of the country. There is no country in the world that is as multilinguistic, multireligious, multiracial, as ours. So we have to have our own legal traditions. Any time that we've tried to borrow too heavily from other traditions we've failed. When other countries have tried to borrow from us they've failed. We have to improve our legal system on our own terms. There are elements we can borrow, but not the system. One of the reasons I generally refuse to consult other countries on how to write their constitutions is that I think too many countries borrow from other countries without thinking through what's right for them.

HRP: From your observations, which other countries have exemplary or fair justice systems?

Dershowitz: None. I don't think any country has a perfectly fair justice system. Every country that I've been to and examined has major flaws in its legal system. Some are better than others, and some systems are better than other systems in certain ways but not in other ways. For example, the military system is very efficient, but when any element of politics comes into play, it's terrible. The English system is very good, but it is [too sheltered from the press], and so its abuses cannot be as effectively monitored. The Israeli system is quite good, except when it comes to protecting the rights of Palestinians. So every system has its particular flaws.

HRP: Some opponents of the death penalty base their opposition on the skeptical claim that there is always doubt as to a defendant's guilt. What do you think of this view?

Dershowitz: They're wrong. Sometimes there is no doubt. There is no doubt that Adolf Eichmann killed many Jews. Sometimes there is undeniable evidence, like with a video tape.

HRP: But those opponents might counter that even video tapes can be doctored, and so there is always room for doubt.

Dershowitz: That's true. But not every video tape is doctored. I still believe in the existence of simple facts, like whether the guy pulled the trigger which caused the bullet to pierce the victim's lung. I'm not an epistemological skeptic. If I'm sitting in a chair, I don't doubt that it's a chair.

HRP: In more general terms, what are your views on the death penalty?

Dershowitz: I'm also opposed to the death penalty, but for another reason. In America, as in all other countries, the death penalty is applied inconsistently and unfairly. If you're a black man who kills a white man, you're much more likely to get the death penalty than if you're a white man who kills a black man. If one day the death penalty could be applied fairly and correctly, I might have to reconsider my position, but I don't think that day will come.

HRP: How would you classify your views on how the institution of punishment is to be justified? Do you subscribe to a retributivist or a utilitarian theory of punishment, or do you believe in some kind of Rawlsian composite theory?

Dershowitz: I don't subscribe to any prepackaged views. I think about each issue individually and form an eclectic opinion which borrows a little from whatever perspective or analysis seems appropriate to the issue. Above all, I ask myself what kind of society I want to live in and what kind of society I want my kids and grandkids to live in, and then I look for the principles whose application would bring about such a society.[1] φ

---

1. For an elaboration of this "experiential approach" to rights see Dershowitz's *Shouting Fire* (Little, Brown, 2002).

Richard Rorty

If the philosopher ought to play the role of gadfly, uncovering assumptions, asking unwelcome questions, mocking self-seriousness, then Richard Rorty is a contemporary philosopher with few equals. For more than twenty years, Rorty has been working out an original and iconoclastic vision of philosophy, of its history, and of its more recent troubles. He has also entered regularly and forcefully into dialogues and debates with people other than Anglo-American philosophy profes- sors. At a time when contemporary philosophy is unknown to almost everyone but contemporary philosophers, Rorty has made his views, political as well as philosophical, known to a larger audience. Rorty stands in a rather strange position to his contemporaries in philosophy: almost everyone knows and discusses his work, but scarcely anyone adheres to his philosophies whole- heartedly. It is a position, no doubt, that befits the gadfly.

Rorty's early career gives little hint of the philosopher he would become, though it explains his quick facility with both philosophy's history and with the questions bandied about in American philosophy departments in the last fifty years. Rorty took his degrees at Chicago and Yale, where he learned the history of philosophy thoroughly, and soon secured a faculty position at Princeton, then as now a locus for the most recent debates in analytic philosophy. His early papers were innovative contributions to the philosophy of mind.

In 1979, Rorty published the work that remains his deepest and most influential contribu- tion to philosophy: *Philosophy and the Mirror of Nature*. The book is a kind of symphony of anti-Cartesianism, culminating in the view that philosophy has, since Descartes's *Meditations*, been dominated by a metaphor of the mind as a mirror that reflects nature with greater or less accu- racy. This is, according to Rorty, a metaphor that has misled philosophy and would best be done away with, so that philosophy can see itself as what it really is: an ongoing conversation among human beings. Even more original than the conclusions of the book is its method: Rorty portrays the problems that philosophy has gotten itself into as the results of shop-worn images rather than of outdated logic, and he attempts to unravel those problems by persuading us to give up those images. It is a method that has been called sometimes in admiration, sometimes as rebuke, "lit- erary." Rorty would lay no claim to the originality of the method, which draws deeply from the later Wittgenstein, who, along with Heidegger and Dewey, is the inspiration and guide for this im- portant book.

Of that trio of philosophers, it is Dewey who has become central to Rorty's thought in the two decades since *Philosophy and the Mirror of Nature*. For the last twenty years, Rorty has become perhaps the leading voice among American philosophers for expounding and advancing pragmatism, which might be summarized as the view that a distinction that makes no difference in practice is a distinction not worth making. That is an unduly negative summary, for Rorty has drawn quite positive conclusions from pragmatism, conclusions arguably more helpful and hopeful than anything arising out of competing philosophies in this century. Pragmatism is as much a method as it is a theory, a method that favors the occasional over the systematic, and which freely crosses boundaries, intellectual and professional. It is a method that Rorty has carried out impressively. His writing since *Philosophy and the Mirror of Nature* has consisted largely of essays, writings that couple the clear and concise vernacular of the best American philosophy with a broadly historical view more frequently found in European philosophy. The pragmatists guiding concern—social and political affairs—has become Rorty's focus in his most recent works, *Achieving Our Country* (1998) and *Philosophy and Social Hope* (1999). Professionally, Rorty's lovers' quarrel with recent American philosophy (and it has always been a lovers' quarrel, for Rorty has drawn as much on Quine and his successors as he has on Heidegger and his) has ended in a kind of divorce: Rorty left Princeton for a non-departmental position at the University of Virginia, and now teaches in the Comparative Literature department at Stanford.

The idea that has occupied much of Rorty's attention and has generated the bulk of debate and disagreement about his views is this: there is no difference between our criteria for determining whether or not we are justified in believing a proposition and our criteria for determining whether or not that proposition is "true." Rorty argues that "true" is simply a "compliment" to views that we think well-justified, as that the notion of truth as the representation of the world "as it really is" is no more than dogma. This idea has a world-historical edge to it. Rorty claims that, just as Enlightenment thinkers managed to give up God as the basis of morality and to realize that it was only human beings who were to decide how they should act toward each other, so should we now give up the notion of truth as "answerability to the world," and realize that we, as human beings, are answerable to no one but ourselves. So to Rorty what matters, and all that matters, is whether or not a belief can be defended to one's fellows. To him, there is no court of appeal beyond humanity itself, particularly not "Nature." In Rorty's view, doing away with the dogma of truth as answerability will compel us to recognize ourselves as what we are: human beings trying to cope the best we can in this world, trying to achieve solace and solidarity with one another. φ

Richard Rorty
Toward a Post-metaphysical Culture

Interview by
Michael O'Shea
in 1994

HRP: What is a "poeticized" culture?

Rorty: A poeticized, or post-metaphysical culture is one in which the imperative common to religion and metaphysics—to find an ahistorical, transcultural matrix for one's thinking, something into which everything can fit, independent of one's time and place—has dried up and blown away. It would be a culture in which people thought of human beings as creating their own life-world, rather than as being responsible to God or "the nature of reality."

HRP: Do you see us tending toward that kind of culture?

Rorty: I think that since the time of the Romantics, there have been tendencies in European and American culture that have gone in that direction. There are Emerson and Whitman in America, and other lingering Romantic influences in Europe.

How long this can last, I don't know. It seems to be the product of a wealthy, leisured elite which has time to worry about this kind of thing, time to imagine alternative futures. The world may not permit the existence of this kind of elite much longer.

HRP: Could the ironic, poetic worldview characteristic of this elite ever become the property of the masses?

Rorty: Yes. I think that the success of secularization in the industrialized democracies suggests that. The sixteenth- and seventeenth-century notion that man would never be able to let go of religion has turned out to be wrong. The promise of the Enlightenment came true: that you could have a society which had a sense of community, without any religious agreement, and indeed without much attention to God at all. If you can secularize a society, you can probably demetaphysicize it also.

HRP: Given their training in metaphysics and similar fields of thought, what purpose could our current professors of philosophy serve in such a culture?

Rorty: I think that the main purpose they've served in the past has been to help us overcome old common sense, old common ways of speaking, past vocabularies; modifying these in order to take account of new developments like Enlightenment, secularism, democratic governments, Newton, Copernicus, Darwin, Freud.

One thing you can count on philosophy professors doing is what William James called "weaving the old and the new together," in order to assimilate weird things like Freudian psychology into moral common sense. Thomas Nagel wrote a good article in the *New York Review of Books* on how Freud's thought has become a part of our moral common sense. I think that illustrates the process nicely. Philosophers have helped with that process.

HRP: So philosophers are professional renderers of coherent worldviews?

Rorty: Yes, and the reason they'll probably always be around is that there will always be something exciting happening [in culture] that needs to be tamed and modified, woven together with the past.

HRP: Do you see the de-transcendentalization of culture as an inducement to political involvement? Jürgen Habermas and others have seen it as the opposite.

Rorty: I do see it as an inducement to involvement, and I think that Dewey did too. Dewey is saying: suppose you're a pragmatist about truth, i.e., you think that truth is what works. The obvious question, then, is: whom does it work for? This is the question that Foucault raises. You then ask political questions about whom you want it to work for, whom you want to run things, whom you want to do good to; these come prior to philosophical questions. Then you can let democratic politics set the goals of philosophy, rather than philosophy setting the goals of politics.

Habermas, however, seems to think that if you don't have philosophy out there as point man, telling society and politics where to go, then you're somehow stuck.

HRP: Do you have doubts about the same things that people like Habermas do, namely, that the sort of large-scale discourse about values that is needed in a democratic state can go on without an extralinguistic norm of rationality, a "master narrative"?

Rorty: Not really. I don't see why Habermas thinks it can't go on. He has this view that every assertion is a claim to universal validity, and that if you give up thinking of assertions in that way, you won't be able to take yourself seriously, or take communication seriously, or take democracy seriously. I just don't see the reasoning there. It's something like what [Hilary] Putnam thinks, when he claims that we need a "substantive" notion of truth. I never got that one either.

HRP: Perhaps such notions are meant to capture the idea of a certain responsibility that attaches to our utterances.

Rorty: Yes, but that seems an unnecessary detour in the attribution of responsibility. I think we ought to be able to be responsible to our interlocutors without being responsible to reason or the world or the demand of universality or anything else.

HRP: Is there a way to change current patterns of education and acculturation in order to bring this sense of responsibility about?

Rorty: I don't know. But I think that a lot of that change has already been accomplished by the emergence of literature as an alternative to science. Philosophy, at the moment, is sort of occupying a halfway position between the sciences and literature. But just for that reason, it's tending to fall between two stools and to be ignored by intellectuals. Philosophy in the English-speaking world is simply not a big deal to most intellectuals, and the reason is that the weight of non-scientific culture has gone over to literature. The analytic philosophers are viewed by most intellectuals as being nostalgic for the days when science was the name of the game.

HRP: What, then, do you find problematic about contemporary attitudes toward physical science?

Rorty: There's still a tendency to want somebody to occupy the social role formerly held by the priests. The physicist tends to be nominated for that role, as someone in touch with the nature of reality, with, as Bernard Williams puts it, reality apart from human needs and interests. This tendency to need a priest-figure is unfortunate; it seems to me a form of self-abasement. But I'm not sure how serious science-worship is anymore. You do still find a little of it in contemporary debates; in [John] Searle's debate with Jacques Derrida [about the philosophy of J. L. Austin; a debate reiterated in Derrida's book *Limited Inc* —ed.], for instance.

HRP: Is the situation changing in philosophy?

Rorty: Not that I can notice, at least in the English-speaking countries. It's going to be very difficult for analytic philosophy, given its professional self-image, ever to outgrow its association with the so-called hard sciences. That association really doesn't exist in non-Anglophone philosophy, and that's why I think it's going to be hard for the two [traditions] ever to merge.

HRP: Hilary Putnam, analyzing parts of your critique of reason in his *Renewing Philosophy*, declares that "relativism à la Rorty is rhetoric." Are you comfortable with this evaluation of your work? What role do you intend your work to play?

Rorty: Primarily persuasion. I don't much care whether it's called rhetoric or logic. I think of my work as trying to move people away from the notion of being in touch with something big and powerful and non-human. The reason I prefer Donald Davidson's work to Putnam's is that Davidson's views on philosophy of language and mind go further in that direction than Putnam's.

HRP: Is yours the kind of work that creates a foundation that someone else could build upon? Could it found a school?

Rorty: I would hope not. Founding a school is relatively easy. You can set up a problematic within which a generation can happily pursue professional activity, but you can never quite tell whether you've actually done something useful, or simply encouraged scholasticism.

One of the things I rather like about people like Derrida is that they have no real disciples. Derrida has a lot of American imitators (none of whom, I think, is any good), but he really is inimitable. There's no such thing as a "Derridian problematic." He doesn't give anybody any work to do—nor does Harold Bloom. And I admire that.

HRP: It might be argued that while your work has helped to dismantle a number of traditional philosophical dualisms, the ironist worldview you espouse seems itself to culminate in a strict dualism of the public and the private. You say that we should read some authors (Nietzsche, Derrida) in order to enrich our private, poetic existences, but others (Rawls, Mill) should be read in order to make ourselves better citizens of a liberal democracy. Is this distinction tenable? If our private beliefs are prevented from informing the social sphere, then what substance do they have?

Rorty: I don't think private beliefs can be fenced off [from the public sphere]; they leak through, so to speak, and influence the way one behaves toward other people. What I had in mind in making the distinction was this: the language of citizenship, of public responsibility, of participation in the affairs of the state, is not going to be an original, self-created language.

But some people, the ones we think of as poets or makers, want to create a new language—because they want to invent a new self. And there's a tendency to try to see that poetic effort as synthesizable with the activity of taking part in public discourse. I don't think the two are synthesizable; but that doesn't mean that the one doesn't eventually interact with the other.

When people develop private vocabularies and private self-images, people like Nietzsche, Kierkegaard, and Derrida, it's very unclear what relevance, if any, this will ever have for public discourse. But over the centuries, it sometimes turns out to have had a certain impact.

HRP: If a reader of Heidegger, for example, is struck not only by the idiosyncratic, "world-disclosing" accomplishment of his writings, but is also attracted by his vision of responsiveness to Being as the fundamental aim of man, how will this attraction show up in public behavior?

Rorty: I don't know, but I think it pays to bear in mind that during the 1950s and '60s, Heidegger managed to grab hold of the imaginations of all the interesting people in Europe. When Habermas, Foucault, and Derrida were in school, Heidegger was "their" philosopher. What they each made of him was, God knows, very different, but it's clear that we won't be able to write the intellectual history of this century without reading Heidegger. Just as there were sixteen different ways of reacting to Hegel in his day, there are now sixteen different ways of reacting to Heidegger, and I think it's pointless to ask what was the "true" message of either Hegel or Heidegger—they are just people to bounce one's thoughts off of.

HRP: But you have written in *Contingency, Irony, and Solidarity* that "as a philosopher of our public life," Heidegger is "at best vapid, and at worst sadistic." Is the sense of using Heidegger that you were discussing there a different sense than the one we're talking about here?

Rorty: I think that attempts to get a political message out of Heidegger, Derrida, or Nietzsche are ill-fated. We've seen what these attempts look like, and they don't succeed very well. Hitler tried to get a message out of Nietzsche, and Nietzsche would have been appalled by it. People who attempt to get a political message out of Derrida produce something perfectly banal. I suspect it isn't worth bothering.

But that's not to say that these figures will always be publicly useless. Having a great imagination and altering the tradition in insensible ways may make a difference in public affairs somewhere down the line. We just don't know how.

HRP: Given your view that our epoch is one of increasing secularization, what do you make of the existence in this country of a fundamentalist, religious Right that does have a noticeable effect on public policy? This seems to show that traditional religion, and other forms of non-ironic belief, are alive and well in the public sphere.

Rorty: I think it's what happens whenever you have a middle class that gets really scared and defensive. It starts to look around for ways of dividing society into sheep and goats, in order to scapegoat somebody. The American middle class has excellent reason to be scared about its economic future, and the economic future of the country. The more there is of this fear, the more you'll see cults, quasi-fascist movements, and things of that sort, all the stuff we classify as the "crazy Right."

HRP: What is there to stave that off, beside economic recovery?

Rorty: My hunch is that the normal cycle of boom and bust doesn't matter much, as long as the long-term average income of the middle class keeps going down, and the gap between rich and poor keeps growing. I don't think there's anything that's going to reverse that. I don't have any optimistic suggestions.

HRP: Are you then a pessimist about the future?

Rorty: I'm not confident enough about economics to say anything with certainty, but all the predictions about how the globalization of the labor market will effect the standard of living in the industrialized democracies seem to me fairly convincing. I think that as long as the standard of living of the middle class in the democracies is in danger, democratic government is in danger.

HRP: You once described yourself as a "postmodern bourgeois liberal." Given that self-designation, how do you see the contemporary academic Left, a Left alternately informed by the Frankfurt School thinkers and the French poststructuralists?

Rorty: That designation ["postmodern bourgeois liberal"] was supposed to be a joke. I thought it was a cute oxymoron—but no one else seemed to think it was funny.

I think there are really two Lefts. The Frankfurt School, for example, is an attempt to modulate Marxism down into plain, social democratic, reformist Left politics. And I think of myself as belonging to that Left—it's the same as the so-called Old Left in America, the anti-Stalinist, social democratic Left centered around Dissent. Irving Howe and people like that.

There's also what I regard as a pretty useless, Foucauldian Left, which doesn't want to be reformist, doesn't want to be social democratic. Fredric Jameson is a good example of that sort of Left. I can't see it as having any sort of utility in America; it seems merely to make the Left look ridiculous.

HRP: What do you think has been the effect of the contemporary, Foucauldian academic Left on American universities? Do you agree with the criticisms often leveled against Left-leaning academics these days?

Rorty: The Foucauldian Left is about 2 percent of the faculties at American universities, and it isn't very important, except that it gives the Right a terrific target. It's enabled the Right to generate an enormous amount of hostility against the universities, because it can point at these few people.

HRP: Where is the political center of gravity of the humanities faculty at a typical American university?

Rorty: It's still Left-liberal, social-democratic, and reformist. But the Foucauldians make a lot more noise.

HRP: In the fall of 1994, you wrote an editorial about the Virginia Senate election, in which you analyzed the candidacy of Oliver North as a symptom of a crisis of values among Virginians. Is the flight toward the sort of old-style, "manly" virtue that people find in Oliver North analogous to the kind of cultic flight that you see in the contemporary American middle class? Is it born of the same fears?

Rorty: Yes. The fundamentalist preacher and the military officer become figures of strength and purity more or less simultaneously. They're both seen as people with no time for moral weakness, or any other weakness, and therefore no time for the bad people—the liberals. They're strong guardians of virtue against the weak, confused, addled eggheads.

HRP: What resources does American pragmatism offer us today?

Rorty: Among the philosophy professors, in the form of Davidsonian philosophy of language and mind, it offers a way out from the boring realism-vs.-anti-realism issue, which I think has been done to death. Davidson gives us a way of getting out from under the dogmatism/skepticism oscillation that's plagued philosophy since Kant. I see Davidson as rewriting in terms of language the same things that James and Dewey did in terms of experience.

Actually, I've just finished reading John McDowell's book [*Mind and World*], and he thinks that Davidson will keep the oscillation going—because no one will ever accept Davidson's view that beliefs are mostly veridical. As a sociological point about the philosophy professors, this may be right. But I don't see why they won't accept it.

Outside of the philosophy profession, I think that pragmatism is just a continuation of the idealistic, onward-and-upward Emerson/Whitman tradition of viewing American democracy as the greatest thing ever invented, and the source of all good things.

HRP: The sort of "Emersonian theodicy" that Cornel West talks about in his history, *The American Evasion of Philosophy.*

Rorty: Yes. I think West gives a very good description there of the politico-spiritual dimension of pragmatism.

HRP: You have often spoken of Anglo-American philosophy professors' reluctance to accept a vision of philosophy that doesn't break down along fixed problematics. Do you have an idea about how to reform undergraduate and graduate education in order to change this?

Rorty: Not really, because I think the philosophy professors are in a bind in the English-speaking world. The undergraduates would really like to hear more about Nietzsche and the other Europeans, but the professors feel that this is bad for the poor kids, that it will tempt them toward irrationalism, literature, unscientific thought, and things like that. If [the professors] can't get over that block, I think they're going to paint themselves into a corner.

So philosophy departments in the English-speaking world are cutting themselves off from the rest of the university in a way that will eventually prove debilitating. And I wish they'd stop.

HRP: In *Consequences of Pragmatism*, you suggested that we might end up with two different disciplines being taught under the rubric "philosophy": Continental thought and literary criticism on one side, and science-oriented analytic philosophy on the other. Does that diagnosis still hold?

Rorty: Yes. I don't think the issue is so much the involvement of literary criticism, as it is historical orientation. Outside of the English-speaking world, training to be a philosophy professor is pretty much training in the history of philosophy. In Europe, you're a good philosophy professor just in so far as you have a good story to tell about [that history] which relates it to the present.

That kind of professional training is so different from the professional training you get in the English-speaking world, where you're supposed to keep up with the "preprint culture," and spend your time getting in touch with the hot new problems in the field, that it's hard to imagine the two ever coming together. What the [two groups of] kids are trained to do in graduate school doesn't have anything in common. And by the time they're done with graduate school, each group hasn't the slightest idea what the other is worrying about.

HRP: What part of your own philosophical education have you found most valuable?

Rorty: The historical part, mostly acquired at the University of Chicago, where history of philosophy was practically all there was. The department was dominated by a historian of philosophy, Richard McKeon, and he kept your nose to the grindstone. You couldn't get a master's degree there without being able to rattle off an awful lot of history. If I hadn't been forced to read all those authors, I never would have been able to read Hegel or Heidegger, and I would have regretted that.

On the other hand, if I hadn't gotten a background in what we now call analytic philosophy, I wouldn't have been able to appreciate Wilfrid Sellars and Donald Davidson, and I would have regretted that, too. φ

Henry Allison

The history of philosophy has allegedly not fared well in American philosophy departments in this past century, but this commonplace belief is belied by the immense influence that Kant's work continues to exercise on contemporary thinking. Many contemporary metaphysicians work in a framework forged by Kant, and would call themselves, in some sense, neo-Kantians. Kant's ethical and political writings are the backbone of the work that stands at the very center of discussions in political philosophy: John Rawls's *A Theory of Justice*. After Kant, the thinkers who deserve the most credit for this ongoing Kantian Renaissance are those scholars who have been able to couple sensitive historical understanding with acute analytical abilities: foremost among these philosophers is Henry Allison.

Allison spent most of his early years in New York and its environs: born in New York in 1937, he studied at Yale, Columbia, the Union Theological Seminary, and the New School for Social Research, where he took his Ph.D. in 1964. For more than two decades, Allison taught at the University of California, San Diego, which became, during his tenure there, a locus for the historically minded study of European philosophy in America. Since 1996, Allison has taught at Boston University, where the following interview was held.

There are two books that are almost always assigned in courses on *Kant's Critique of Pure Reason*: the *Critique* itself, and Allison's *Kant's Transcendental Idealism: An Interpretation and Defense*. More even than a careful and insightful summary of the project of the *Critique* (though it is that as well), Allison's book is precisely what its subtitle promises: Allison resurrects Kant's theoretical philosophy, which most of his contemporaries had treated as a piecemeal assemblage of philosophical positions, as the systematic philosophy that Kant intended it to be. More importantly, through Allison's work, the *Critique* becomes an entirely viable philosophical system, one that holds its own against its most recent and sophisticated critics. This is not to say that Allison has convinced all of his colleagues to accept Transcendental Idealism—since its publication in 1983, Allison's book has generated extensive debate. But the idea that a book on the *Critique of Pure Reason* could ever be the subject of such debate and that one could be convinced by Kant's theoretical philosophy in its entirety would have both seemed highly unlikely before Allison's book. *Kant's Transcendental Idealism* was followed by *Kant's Theory of Freedom*, which constitutes an extended explication and defense of that theory.

Published in 1990, *Kant's Theory of Freedom* deals with a problem that had occupied Allison, as he notes in our interview, since he was a sophomore at Yale. In 1996, Allison published *Idealism and Freedom: Essays in Kant's Theoretical and Practical Philosophy*, a work that defends and extends the thoughts put forth in his previous two works. Most recently, Allison's thinking has turned, as Kant's did, from the theoretical and the practical to the aesthetic. He recently published *Kant's Theory of Taste: A Reading of the Critique of Aesthetic Judgment*.

Allison's writings on Kant, however, are only one aspect of his work and thought. Allison's earliest philosophical interests lay in the work of Kierkegaard and Sartre, and he has continued to focus his intellect on many of the central figures in the history of philosophy, helping us to understand, in the process, why these figures are as central as they are. Allison's broad interests have brought him to study many thinkers who have not fared as well as Kant among Allison's contemporaries. His first book was *Lessing and the Enlightenment* (1966), and since then he has written dozens of articles on Lessing, Kierkegaard, Locke, Spinoza, and Berkeley, among others. The dissimilarity of these thinkers indicates the vast range of Allison's interests and his ability to incorporate the tangled and crossing routes that these thinkers have followed into a broad and sensitive vision of philosophy and its history. Allison is currently working on a major revision of *Kant's Transcendental Idealism* and a book on Hume. φ

Henry Allison
Personal and Professional

Interview by
Steven A. Gross
in 1995

HRP: Perhaps we might begin historically—that is, biographically. What led you to become a historian of philosophy and to focus on the specific figures you have?

Allison: I have to begin with what led me to study philosophy in the first place. I initially went to Yale with the idea of becoming a poet or writer of some sort. Two things—one positive, one negative—changed my mind and led me into philosophy. The positive was taking a freshman course with Brand Blanshard, who was a wonderful lecturer, a marvel of clarity and precision. That was my first real exposure to philosophy, and I certainly became hooked on it. The negative occurred during my second year, when I enrolled in a notorious course called "Daily Themes." The course required that one write a brief sketch or story of some sort five days a week; and after some very severe criticism by very distinguished faculty and a rather mediocre grade, I came to realize that I was not cut out to be a successful poet or novelist, so I shifted to philosophy. So that's how I got interested in philosophy.

Now, moving to the history of philosophy, that's more complicated. I think it was largely a collection of accidents—the nature of the orientation of some of the people I studied with and where I studied. Although I started with Blanshard, who was the last of the great rationalists, and who was wonderful because he would have fourteen arguments against this and that and was very systematic, I soon became interested in messy things like existentialism. So Kierkegaard and Sartre were the first philosophers I studied in any depth. And there was another professor at Yale—this time a bright young assistant professor, Louis Mackey—with whom I began to work, who went on to write a very important book about Kierkegaard.[1] I got interested in some of these things largely through him, but he also gave a history of philosophy seminar. So I had some interest in the history of philosophy and, I

---

1. Louis Mackey, *Kierkegaard: A Kind of Poet* (Philadelphia: University of Pennsylvania Press, 1971).

suppose already then, in Immanuel Kant. Of course, he came across as a very forbidding and challenging figure. But perhaps the first philosophical issue that I really got interested in—and Kant played a large role in this—was the problem of freedom, how freedom could be reconciled with causal determinism. Somehow back as a sophomore I thought this was a deep problem, and I also thought that Kant had something very important to say about it. And thirty some odd years later, in 1990, I finally published a book in which I tried to say what that was.[2] But basically, my initial interests were more or less what we would now call "Continental," and Yale was sort of a mixed department at that stage. I suppose that I initially had a kind of negative attitude towards analytical philosophy—mainly because I was ignorant of what was going on. But I certainly didn't have any sense of specializing in the history of philosophy. In fact, I was interested in the philosophy of religion and, I guess in a broad sense, German philosophy—mainly Kant and Hegel—because they seemed to me related to existentialism.

After graduating from Yale in 1959, I went to graduate school with the idea of concentrating on the philosophy of religion. I chose Columbia because it had a joint program in religion with Union Seminary. My thought was that just as a philosopher of physics should know some physics, a philosopher of religion should know some religion. So I learned a little bit about the Bible, studied some comparative religion and the like, and got an M.A., after which I shifted to the philosophy program at Columbia. By this time I developed some more historical interests. I became particularly interested in Greek philosophy—though I had some interest in that field from my undergraduate days, because I had studied Plato and Aristotle with Robert Brumbraugh. But I took a seminar on Aristotle with Randall, Kristeller, and Charles Kahn, and that was really very exciting. So at that stage I was torn between Greek and German philosophy. But I guess that what really clinched things for me was that while at Columbia I noticed and signed up for a seminar on the first *Critique* that was given at the New School by Aron Gurwitsch. I had heard of Gurwitsch (mainly as a phenomenologist). But I went down to the New School while still at Columbia, because no one was doing much Kant there, and signed up for the seminar—it was a full year seminar which got through the analytic—and this struck me as pretty good and important stuff. Although I didn't give up all my other interests for Kant, particularly not the philosophy of religion, I did decide to transfer to the New School and work with Gurwitsch. And, after studying Leibniz with him, I ended up writing a dissertation, not on Kant, but on Lessing and Lessing's

---

2. Henry Allison, *Kant's Theory of Freedom* (Cambridge: Cambridge University Press, 1990).

philosophy of religion and its relation to Leibniz. Thus, although I retained my interest in Kant, I also developed a broader interest in the history of modern philosophy. In fact, I worked not only on Leibniz but also on Spinoza, the empiricists, and German idealism. It was a real classical, European kind of philosophical education that I was lucky enough to get. And that is what finally pushed me in a strongly historical direction. It's not that I woke up one morning and said, "My God, I'm going to be an historian of philosophy"; it's rather that my training led me naturally in that direction.

HRP: Given this sort of education, would it have occurred to you—did it occur to you—to pose the question to yourself, "Do I want to be a historian of philosophy, a scholar in that sense, or ought I to be approaching the questions of philosophical interest to me in some other way?" Or would that way of posing the question just not have come up, given this sort of education?

Allison: Well, I think it's something like the latter. I don't believe that I ever felt that kind of sharp dichotomy, which I guess one would feel if one began with a more traditional, problems-oriented kind of education, where you're reading the latest publications in the *JP*[3] and then you might decide, "Well, maybe there's something historically interesting about the background of this topic." Thus, again, because of my training and experience, that kind of dichotomy or dilemma never arose for me.

HRP: This might provide a nice segue, then, to talking about the status of the history of philosophy in the English-speaking philosophy world in general. Many of the historians of philosophy in the contemporary English-speaking philosophy world did not receive this sort of philosophical education, but perhaps came from departments where there was more of a sense of a dichotomy. And this is still the case in many major departments, though perhaps to a lesser degree. The history of philosophy—the discipline, that is—has changed greatly over the course of your career, both in and of itself and in its relation, or relations, to the rest of philosophy. So, remaining in this historical mode, I'd be interested to hear what to your mind have been some of the most significant of these changes and to what you attribute them.

Allison: Well, I think you're right about that—I mean, you're certainly right about the training. In both cases you're right: you're right about the training that most Anglo-American historians of philosophy have received, that it was different from mine—although many in recent years have spent time studying in Germany—the Humboldts and things like that have made for quite a rich interchange; particularly, I think, for younger scholars like Fred

---

3. *Journal of Philosophy.*

Neuhouser, for whom it's typical to spend one or more years studying in Germany, which I actually never had the opportunity to do. I wish I had.

Now, I guess the other part of your question concerns the changes within the approach to the history of philosophy. Well, certainly it's gotten much more respectable. I think that a thoroughly dismissive attitude towards the history of philosophy is in most cases and in most departments, though not in all by any means, pretty much a thing of the past. And I think that's because there's been a gradual deeper realization of the interconnection between philosophical problems and concerns of the present day and past philosophy and, really, the inseparability of doing good philosophical work from some understanding of its history. Now, within the history of philosophy itself, I think there has been a very healthy development, in the sense that there's much more concern and greater respect for the scholarly dimensions of work in the history of philosophy. Now, in most cases, if one's planning to work on Kant, for example, one's expected to know some German—which I think is a good thing—and to know something about people like Wolff and Baumgarten. So this has become more part of the mainstream. Current work in the history of philosophy is much more historically informed, whereas if you think of what was going on back in the '60 s, things like Jonathan Bennett's books on Kant (one in the '60s, one in the '70s), a series of potshots, some very brilliant, insightful, others just completely missing the mark.[4] I don't think we see too much of that anymore.

HRP: I'd like to pick up on several aspects of your answer. First, perhaps I can play the role of devil's advocate and ask you to respond to the dismissive professor. There do remain those who view immersion in, or even fair familiarity with, the history of philosophy as at best unnecessary for, at worst a hindrance to, the doing of philosophy proper in some sense. Clearly, this isn't the line you'd take. What would you say, at a faculty meeting, for example, if you encountered such a person? This naturally has practical consequences for who gets hired, for graduate student requirements, and the like.

Allison: Well, I'm not sure that putting it in those practical terms is the best way, or the way I'd want, to address it. Obviously, implicit in such an attitude is a certain conception of what doing philosophy is, which I suppose is based on adopting a model taken over from the sciences. Now, if you're going to be a biologist, knowing something about the history of biology may be very nice, but it's not really essential to doing one's work as a practicing scientist. These are two quite distinct disciplines. I think there is a kind

---

4. Jonathan Bennett, *Kant's Analytic* (Cambridge: Cambridge University Press, 1966) and *Kant's Dialectic* (Cambridge: Cambridge University Press, 1974).

of, for want of a better expression, "scientistic" prejudice in at least many of those who take this kind of attitude. And so I guess I'd have to challenge their conception of what philosophy is really all about. If philosophy is thought of as resolving a set of discrete, well-defined, and manageable problems in their own terms—if that's what you think philosophy is—then I suppose there is no essential reason to study the history of philosophy, although there is still a general intellectual reason, which is still recognized as important, even necessary, among departments, to teach, at least undergraduates, something about the history of philosophy. I suppose that conception of philosophy came about historically—or one strand of it, certainly the main strand—through logical positivism and what came of that. So, this attitude towards philosophy itself evolved historically.

HRP: The attitude certainly has survived the demise of logical positivism and so I suppose someone might reply—as I continue in my role as devil's advocate—that the attitude could express a truth even if it's historically conditioned itself. Now, you say it's a claim you would challenge as expressing merely a prejudice: how would you challenge it?

Allison: I don't think I necessarily want to put it terms of truth or falsity. It's a sense of philosophy I don't share. And I would say that if that's all philosophy is, then I'm not deeply interested in it, and would not want to devote my career to it, which is not to say that there's not good, valuable, intellectual work being done by bright people on solving specific problems. My claim, I guess, is that the view that this is all there is to philosophy is a prejudice, which, as I was trying to suggest, probably does have its start in, though you're quite right, it has more life than good-old logical positivism. But so much of contemporary analytic philosophy is a direct off-shoot of logical positivism. Indeed, if I may be allowed some Hegelian jargon, a lot of it could be viewed as the abstract negation of logical positivism, which is still haunted by the shadows of what it had supposedly gotten rid of.

But you used the notion of truth. What truth do you have in mind?

HRP: That the majority—or perhaps all—of the central problems in philosophy are such that they needn't be approached historically. There might be practical benefits to approaching them historically. I suppose this view would have it: in exposing oneself to the past, one gets exposed to many different views and arguments. But it's not necessary to approach them historically. So, the negative way of putting this would be that there are no, or very few, central problems in philosophy that must intrinsically be approached historically. Again, I'm acting as devil's advocate in putting the question this way. Now, it might be one answer to such a person to say there's more to philosophy than just these central problems, but there might be a stronger position that held that even these problems, or some of them, can't but be approached historically. So, would you subscribe to something like this stronger claim, and if so, how would you argue for it?

Allison: To begin with, I would certainly subscribe to the weaker claim. But I think there are at least two versions of this idea that there's more to philosophy than these major problems. (Obviously, there are the less-than-major problems. But that's not the issue.) But what is also missing in this approach to philosophy, and therefore from the weaker view as you presented it, is, I think, the sense of the interrelation of these problems. And this is what leads one inevitably to some sort of synoptic or systematic view, which is what is generally rejected. As soon as you see the task of philosophy as involving essentially some kind of synoptic view, which is, of course, traditionally what philosophy has always been concerned with, then I think you're led almost immediately into the history of philosophy. It's one of the interesting things about twentieth-century–Anglo-American philosophy that there just are not many systematic philosophers around. (Although, interestingly enough, at this late date in the twentieth century, a number of the main analytical philosophers now seem interested in tackling the "big questions." But when they do it, it's often in a casual essayist style, as if they're almost embarrassed by it.) This attitude towards philosophy, then, or part of it anyway, ignores what I've always taken to be something that's certainly part of philosophy—perhaps even essential to it—namely, this synoptic vision, which involves the interrelation between the major problems. Because I think that if philosophy gets completely compartmentalized, ultimately it falls in danger of becoming a completely sterile exercise. And I think that a number of people have pointed out the analogy between some of the developments of analytical philosophy in the middle of this century and some of the things that were going on in the fourteenth century, when narrow scholasticism had lost sight of what was really at stake.

Now, the other view, I guess what you presented as the strong view—namely, that one can't understand these problems apart from history—yes, I suppose I would be committed to that view also. But I think that here you obviously have to distinguish between different senses of understanding. Clearly, there's a sense in which one can abstract from the history of a problem and deal with (I'm trying to think of some example)—well, just as an example, there's knowledge and the Gettier problem, to which people have made interesting and sophisticated responses. But yet what have we ended up with? An analysis of what we might mean by "knowledge," or what are the necessary and sufficient conditions for saying that X knows that Y, or something like that. But is that really all we'd like to know about knowledge? Why should that very problem be a problem? In order to understand why a problem is a problem, it seems to me, you're driven to some kind of historical perspective.

And then there's also the issue of continually reinventing the wheel. One of the things that I found that was fascinating to me when I was doing some work on Kant's critique of Eberhard, who was a Wolffian critic of Kant during his lifetime, was that all of those interesting issues about the analytic/synthetic distinction were brought up and criticisms of Kant's formulation were made that are in essence equivalent to a large number of contemporary classical, or well-known, criticisms. So I think simply having knowledge of what was going on—what Kant actually said, what the real responses to these criticisms were—itself enlightens the contemporary discussion of the analytic/synthetic distinction. So a lot of contemporary analytic philosophy I think does consist in a kind of reinventing the wheel, in the sense of offering solutions or criticisms that had been presented in the past. So in that sense, again, it's dangerous not to know the history of the discipline.

HRP: This leads back perhaps to a practical conundrum, which ties into something you were saying earlier about the changes in the history of philosophy as a discipline. Arguably, this tremendous increase in scholarly activity has led to two opposing tendencies. On the one hand, as you've been arguing, there's a greater awareness of the relevance of the history of philosophy to philosophy generally. On the other hand, there's the tremendous increase in scholarly expectations. What is required, to seriously pursue the history of philosophy, is arguably such that it leaves no time, given that we are finite beings, to gain the knowledge and to engage in the activities that could seriously bring to bear considerations from the history of philosophy on still standing contemporary issues. Who has time both to be a Leibniz scholar and also to contribute to the metaphysics of modality, for example?[5]

Allison: Well, that has nothing to do in particular with the history of philosophy. I think this is just part of the plight of the contemporary academic. Leaving aside the history of philosophy, who can keep up with the latest developments in ethical theory and modalities, or philosophy of language and aesthetics? Obviously, some people do a better job than others. Some people can just sit down and read an article once, and they get it; it's with them forever, and they can recall it twenty years later. I can't do that. But to say that the history of philosophy is relevant to or essential to philosophy doesn't mean that every good philosopher has to be a historical scholar. It

---

5. Margaret Wilson, "History of Philosophy in Philosophy Today; and the Case of the Sensible Qualities," in the *Philosophical Review* 101, 1 (January 1992): 204–06.

means that every good philosopher has to have a good general knowledge of the history of philosophy—certainly, it should be part of graduate education—and I suppose some fairly comprehensive knowledge of, let's say, one or two of the greats that are directly relevant to his or her work. Some actually do have fairly comprehensive knowledge. In this department,[6] just think of someone like Hintikka, who has an impressive grasp of Aristotle, Kant, Descartes. Or Sellars, who really is an impressive scholar. Or Rod Chisholm, who, I think (in spite of the fact that his philosophical work certainly was very much on the analytic side of things), has a very substantial philosophical grasp of the history of philosophy. So it's that sort of thing, I think, that's really desirable, because I think this is what enriches, what makes philosophy better.

HRP: Perhaps this would be a good time to turn more specifically to Kant and Kant's relevance to philosophy generally. Perhaps here's one way of putting a question along these lines: what in your view is true in Kant, and not just true, but true and relevant to contemporary philosophical concerns? I'll accept, of course, something recognizably neo-Kantian.

Allison: Well, the expression "true" or "true in a philosopher" I find a difficult one to deal with. Perhaps a weaker expression like "significant" or "still alive" or "vital and important" or something like that is more appropriate. Because once one gets outside of logic and some very specific claims, I find it hard to say that a philosophical position is true. It's powerful; it's compelling. Something like that.

About Kant, the first thing I'll say is that I think that, more than any other figure, he defined the agenda for subsequent philosophy. That is, the very problems in so many different domains—how are synthetic judgments possible?—or, just raising the kind of question: "How is X possible?" has become one of the basic ways in which we think of philosophical problems. Of course, many philosophers are strongly anti-Kantian; but that's part of what it means to set the agenda. And for a philosopher to do that in so many different areas of philosophy is certainly a mark of greatness; perhaps it's the mark of greatness.

HRP: So, there's Kant's legacy—certainly not to be pooh-poohed, but now say someone asks (I'll use a weaker word than "true"): what's viable in what Kant has to say on these matters? If you prefer, I'll ask something more specific. Let's take Transcendental Idealism. You present a very compelling reading of Kant on Transcendental Idealism, but is it a position that's still viable in either Kant's specific form or in some recognizably neo-Kantian form?

---

6. The Boston University Department of Philosophy.

Allison: Put it this way: I think idealism in some form is always going to be a viable philosophical move, as long as there's philosophy. I think ultimately what you have in philosophy are a fairly small number of generic philosophical moves, and idealism is certainly one of them. I also think that Kant's Transcendental Idealism is the most sophisticated, at least up to his time, and compelling form of idealism. So in that sense I think it still is a competitor in the philosophical arena. I don't make a stronger claim for it, and I never claimed to have proven that Kant's Transcendental Idealism is true. All I try to argue is that many of the objections to it are based on complete misunderstandings; it's a much more interesting and powerful philosophical position than it is generally taken to be. My work has been mostly in that direction. It's obviously one that I myself find attractive, so I guess I have to call myself an idealist of some sort.

HRP: Kant presumably thought that Transcendental Idealism was not merely attractive, not merely viable, but indeed true. And not merely a viable move that would be available perennially to philosophers, but one that he had established as being the proper move to make for a wide variety of questions. Perhaps, then, your take on the status of philosophical questions, as to their answerability, whether the questions are intrinsically perennial or not, differs from Kant's.

Allison: I think that's fair enough. Kant wrote the *Prolegomena to any Future Metaphysics,* which is to be counted as a science, but I think that he is more typical than unique here. A philosopher has to place some kind of faith in the finalness of his or her position, as a kind of driving force just to create philosophically. But of course in that sense, every philosopher is refuted by future developments, and this is going to happen to the philosophers who are with us now. So I guess a historian, looking back a couple of hundred years, can certainly have a deep and appreciative attitude towards Kant's significance and continued significance without having to be committed to the idea that his is the last word on any topic.

HRP: Perhaps *Glaube* is a psychological necessity, though I take it that Kant thought he had more than that. And if he didn't, presumably there's a criticism to be made of his arguments for his claims. I take it that the philosophical claims he makes are themselves to have synthetic a priori status.

Allison: Well, that's a different issue, because certainly many—not all—of the criticisms of Kant in the theoretical realm have come about as a result of appealing to scientific, mathematical, and logical developments after his time. So the question is to what extent is the philosopher to be blamed for not being omniscient. So one can say that, well, the actual argument of the transcendental aesthetic has to be revised somewhat in light of later developments, though I'm not sure that really counts as a criticism.

HRP: I didn't mean to be criticizing Kant, but I suppose my original question was: what, at the end of the day, ought one to think now about these Kantian moves, without blaming Kant for what has come afterward? And if there are legitimate criticisms to be made, for example, in light of developments in science, mathematics, and logic, in what way might a Kantian accommodate these criticisms while remaining recognizably Kantian, so as to preserve the viability of a Kantian position?

Allison: Yes, OK. That's obviously a very difficult question. In a sense to be a Kantian is to be a neo-Kantian, unless you're a slavish follower of the letter of the text. So you have to ask yourself, "What is essential in Kant's analysis?" and that's of course itself a controversial question. In answer to it, I think twentieth-century philosophers like Cassirer have done very interesting things in trying to present a Kantian picture that is wholly compatible with relativity theory, etc. And I think that sort of thing is possible and is part of the job. That's not the job that I've taken upon myself, because I don't have enough of the scientific training. I wish I had; I think that's a very important kind of thing to do.

But leaving the details of the science behind, what I take to be really fundamental in Kant's theoretical philosophy—true, if you will—is something like the sensibility/understanding distinction, and therefore that knowledge requires something to be given to the mind and some activity on the part of the mind to deal with it. And I think that analysis of the givenness condition is going to lead to something like Kantian forms of sensibility that are ultimately subjective in nature, and therefore to something like the doctrine of Transcendental Idealism. But from general considerations such as these one can move in at least two directions, and this marks the dividing line between two contemporary approaches to Kant. On the one hand, there are those (like myself), who tend to try to develop Kant's thought on the basis of a very general reflection on the a priori conditions of knowledge, which aren't closely tied to any particular body of scientific knowledge. On the other hand, there are those, and here I have Michael Friedman primarily in mind,[7] who view Kant's thought in the context of his eighteenth-century scientific, mathematical, and logical agenda. And I certainly don't disagree with that approach. That's just part of being a good historian. But if you limit yourself to that approach, and then ask questions like "What is 'true' in Kant?" then

---

7. Michael Friedman, *Kant and the Exact Sciences* (Cambridge, MA: Harvard University Press, 1992).

it becomes more difficult to save Kant. Then the greatness of Kant becomes or consists in the fact that he was the philosopher who best expressed, or definitively captured, the basic presuppositions of Newtonian mechanics and, given the logical tools he had to work with, provided the best possible explanation of the nature and possibility of geometrical knowledge. So although I appreciate all that, I also want to ask whether some philosophical sense may be made of Kant's views on a more general, transcendental level that is not so closely tied to the science of his time.

HRP: Perhaps I might mention another feature of Kant's philosophizing that recurs in your writing and that I think is certainly of great moment in contemporary philosophy—that is, if you will, the non-naturalizability of the normative. This is a theme that, for example, came up recently in a talk you gave at Harvard on Patricia Kitcher's book[8] in which there's an attempt to naturalize Kant on the mind. Of course, Kant being the synoptic thinker he is, this is not unrelated to his idealism, but perhaps you'd like to say something on these issues. I ask you this because here's an issue where I find in your writings more explicit hints (if that's not an oxymoron) about Kant's direct relevance to sexy contemporary debates. So maybe I could draw you out a bit about how you'd apply Kant's insights here.

Allison: I think first of all, backtracking a bit, that this is a good example in that it illustrates my general view of the relevance of the history of philosophy. In a sense the debate between naturalism and anti-naturalism is as old as the hills, and I think one of the most interesting and philosophically fruitful segments of it is precisely the debate between Kant and Hume. So I think not just Kant, but the Kant-Hume debate is itself a kind of model or paradigm of, as well as an anticipation of, twentieth-century thought, because this clearly is an issue that's at the heart of contemporary philosophy. In fact, it's been at the heart of philosophy since Descartes and the origin of modern science. Throughout this period the issue has been, and remains, one of reconciling our conception of ourselves as autonomous agents who make normative claims with the scientific picture of the world. This is a deep metaphysical issue; but it has a history and wasn't always a problem, at least not in this particular form. Of course, its problematic status depends on something like the mechanistic, or quasi-mechanistic, view of nature. And to my mind Kant's greatness, or a large part of what interests me in his thought, lies in his attempt to preserve both the truth of the scientific picture of the world and the distinctive character of human agency and the rational norms that are inseparable from it, while at the same time rejecting the (still

---

8. Patricia Kitcher, *Kant's Transcendental Psychology* (Oxford: Oxford University Press, 1990).

fashionable) Humean project of absorbing both agency and normativity into the naturalistic picture. By contrast, the naturalistic response, which Patricia Kitcher certainly represents in a very forceful way, is to enrich your concept of nature or naturalism so as to encompass the normative. I think that a defining characteristic of the Kantian position, or at least of my own philosophical position which I take from Kant, is that a hard and fast line is to be drawn between the natural and the normative. And of course this is itself related to a whole bunch of other problems—putting it in the simplest form, it's the "is-ought" issue.

HRP: We've spoken both about the past and the past's bearing on the present. Maybe we can say a little about the future. First, let me ask what directions you would like to see Kant scholarship take in the future, or, if you prefer, what areas in Kant scholarship do you see as ripe for research?

Allison: Those are two very different questions. Because I think Kant scholarship—or Kant interpretation, to use a broader category than scholarship—has very often, and I think rightly, responded to developments in the field of philosophy at large. In a sense every generation rereads its Kant in relation to the problems of the day, and we can't know what these problems will be since we can't anticipate the future.

Nevertheless, within Kant scholarship I think there are a number of things that are ripe for being done. We can predict that there's going to be a lot more work on the *opus postumum*, and its relation to the classical critical philosophy. Of course, there are three options there. One, the most unattractive option, but the traditional view, is that this is a work of Kant's senility and therefore is to be rejected. And certainly the work that's been done on the *opus postumum* recently has been very much against that. Most of the *opus postumum*—which is simply a collection of notes and quite partial manuscripts and other notes associated with it, produced over a period of about five or six years—is now thought to be certainly not the product of senility, but of genuine philosophical importance. But among those who maintain its significance, there are still two quite different approaches. One is to see it as some kind of radically new departure that the elderly Kant made at least partly in virtue of his acquaintance with recent developments in German philosophy. In his last years he started to read Schelling and Fichte and so became a kind of incipient post-Kantian! Or at least that is what some people think. The other, I suppose, is to see the *opus postumum* in essential continuity with the classical critical position. And you find contemporary people working in both of those directions. But I think that there will probably be a lot of doctoral dissertations on the *opus postumum* in the next ten, fifteen years, because it is still largely unmapped territory.

Another interesting idea is in just the opposite direction; it's going backwards to the precritical Kant and seeing how the ideas of the *Critique of Pure Reason* relate to the very significant body of work that Kant wrote before the *Critique.* There's still an awful lot to be done in that area. And of course both the *opus postumum* and going back to the precritical texts, lectures and notes require an immense amount of scholarship. Since so much has been written about the transcendental deduction, and about the second analogy, and about the categorical imperative, well, I think that at least for a while these are going to be the kinds of areas in which some of the more interesting work is done.

The third is my own present area of interest, the *Critique of Judgment,* which is beginning to get a lot of well-deserved attention. So those are my big three main areas over, let's say, the next decade—I can't speak beyond that—that Kant research is probably going to concentrate on.

HRP: Before I turn in closing to ask you about your current project, maybe I can ask you a question which will tie in with some of what we were discussing earlier. As was said, there have been many changes in the history of philosophy as a discipline over the course of your career, and in Kant scholarship in particular. Now, you've mentioned what you think we will see in the future, but perhaps you could tell us what you would like to see in the future? In particular, have all of the changes you have witnessed been for the good—is there anything you miss from the bygone days which you'd like to see recovered in Kant scholarship or in the history of philosophy in general, whether they be particular works, say, or particular approaches, or particular attitudes toward scholarship or interpretation?

Allison: Well, I think most of the changes that I've liked could easily also be described as a return to earlier ways of doing the history of philosophy. Within the Kant world, just think of the classical people like Paton and Kemp Smith. They're very different, but in both of them there's a combination of philosophical questioning and historical fidelity and concern. So I don't think that there's anything all that novel in more recent developments in the history of philosophy, except by contrast to its immediate, very anti-historical predecessors.

HRP: So all is well in Kant scholarship and interpretation as it is now? There are no remaining or new areas of sickness? I'm not asking you to say anything nasty about anyone in particular.

Allison: Well, there are an awful lot of wrong-headed interpreters.

HRP: Fair enough. Well then maybe we should turn to what you're working on now. Maybe you could tell us something about your current projects.

You mentioned work on the third *Critique*. Perhaps you could tell us something about that, and if there are other projects, perhaps you could also tell us something about them.

Allison: What I'm actively engaged in now is the project on the third *Critique*. I guess I view it as the third great project of my career, and I hope it will result in a book. I felt from the beginning that there are three great ideas in Kant or, if you will, doctrines. One is the ideality of space and time, which I wrote about in *Kant's Transcendental Idealism*. The other is—we've already talked about it—this conception of freedom, and reconciling freedom and agency with the causal determinism of nature. And I wrote my *Kant's Theory of Freedom* on that, so I'm really running out of big projects. I just have one left, because I think the third great idea in Kant is a much messier one, this idea of the purposiveness of nature, which is manifested in the beautiful and in the teleological realm. So my current project is to try to work out a compelling interpretation of that idea, which is the central theme of the third *Critique*.

HRP: Has your deepening understanding of the third *Critique* led you to alter any of your views on the first two?

Allison: I have to think about that. Nothing comes to mind off-hand. But what I have found is that going back to the first two has certainly deepened my understanding of the third *Critique*. Specifically, I had done a lot of work on the transcendental dialectic after I had written my idealism book. I find that has become very fruitful for interpreting dimensions of the third *Critique*. There are parts that I had of course worked on for years, and that had been largely mysterious to me to say the least, that I'm beginning to get some insight into through my understanding of the first *Critique*. As long as that keeps on growing, I think I'm still alive philosophically.

HRP: Are there any other plans to work on other authors besides Kant? Earlier in your career you published on Lessing and Spinoza, for example.

Allison: Yes, although time has its limits. I would like to do more in Hume, and I certainly hope to return to Spinoza. I'm also becoming very much interested in some of Kant's immediate followers—not so much in Hegel, although I do have an interest in Hegel, but I'm thinking of the immediate period of the 1790s, which in Germany was a fascinating period, and so the kinds of criticisms of Kant that emerged during that period of time is a crucial period for research. Fred Beiser recently wrote a very interesting book dealing with that period.[9] And I'd like to be able to do some

---

9. Frederick C. Beiser, *The Fate of Reason: German Philosophy from Kant to Fichte* (Cambridge, MA: Harvard University Press, 1987).

more with it. I have a very good graduate student now who is writing a dissertation on Solomon Maimon and his critique of Kant, which in many ways anticipates a lot of the contemporary debate about the nature and status of transcendental arguments. It's another example of the usefulness of the past. φ

Michael Sandel

By championing Aristotle, cherishing Hegel, and criticizing Kant, Sandel has caused waves in philosophical
circles. While sympathetic to the liberal rights of the
individual, Sandel argues that the existence of society
precludes autonomous self-definition. His provocative
disquisitions—e.g., *Democracy's Discontent: America in
Search of a Public Philosophy*, *Liberalism and the
Limits of Justice*, and *Liberalism and Its Critics*—speak
of the necessity of a richly constituted individual self,
defined by his environment and his fellow man. For Sandel, man's nature is frustrated by our
splintered world where the successes of our global economy have meant the neglect of the
impoverished individual. He predicts inauspicious times ahead if the individual cannot grow
through the cultivation of his own community, through the growth of his fellow man.

Sandel questions the political paradigm of moral neutrality. He considers the challenges of
human nature: the difficulty of realizing ourselves as individuals in the collective context of society. In seeking to preserve man's community, Sandel looks to preserve man himself. In doing so, he
further preserves philosophy, which would become impossible within disaggregated human life.

As a professor of political philosophy, history of political thought, and moral reasoning, Sandel
has developed a complex conception of politics. As the setting for collective deliberation and
mutual rights, politics lay the groundwork for social living. Recognizing the Aristotelian conception of government as a good-in-itself, Sandel considers politics as the tie that honors man's
social nature by linking one man to the aggregate. Sandel further considers whether this good
might be the precursor to an even greater good, whether through politics we could uncover moral
truth. Is government the vehicle for maintaining the social connections among men and, if so,
mustn't it be, as man himself is, moral in nature? Sandel probes the issues such as slavery and
abortion—historically often treated as political but, he suggests, ontologically moral in nature.

Graduating from Brandeis University summa cum laude and Phi Beta Kappa, Sandel subse-
quently received his doctorate from Oxford University (D. Phil, 1981) as a Rhodes Scholar.
Writing and lecturing worldwide, his work has been published in *The Atlantic Monthly*, the *New
York Times*, *The New Republic*, and *The New York Review of Books*. He serves as a member of the
Brandeis Board of Trustees, the Rhodes Scholarship Committee of Selection, the Board of Syndics
of Harvard University Press, the Council on Foreign Relations, the Shalom Hartman Institute of
Jewish Philosophy in Jerusalem, and the National Constitution Center Advisory Panel. In 1998, he

delivered the Tanner Lectures on Human Values at Oxford University. His undergraduate and law school classes perennially attract hundreds of Harvard students, compelled by Sandel's dramatic dynamic: substantive philosophic discourse, methodical reflection warmly delivered with quick wit and unfaltering rhetoric. φ

Michael Sandel
On Republicanism and Liberalism

Interview by
Leif Wenar and
Chong-Min Hong
in 1996

HRP: You're known as a critic of liberalism. What exactly is liberalism and what is wrong with it?

Sandel: I take myself to be a critic of a certain version of liberalism. It's the version of liberalism that finds its most influential expression or statement in Immanuel Kant, but also in contemporary philosophers such as John Rawls. It's the version of liberalism that says government should be neutral among competing conceptions of the good life, in order to respect persons as free and independent selves capable of choosing their own ends. It's that, Kantian, version of liberalism that I have been a critic of.

HRP: And what, in your view, is wrong with that?

Sandel: In *Liberalism and the Limits of Justice*, I emphasized one criticism of that version of liberalism, which is that it rests on a conception of the self that doesn't enable us to make sense of certain moral and political obligations that may not flow from choice. And so I argued that this version of liberalism doesn't take adequate account of the sense in which we may be partly constituted by certain purposes and ends, or attachments and commitments, that may give rise to obligations of solidarity or membership. Another criticism of this version of liberalism that doesn't rest so heavily on the conception of the self has to do with the possibility and the desirability of politics being neutral with respect to particular moral and religious conceptions. So I would say there are two broad lines of criticism: one having to do with the conception of the self on which this version of liberalism rests, the other having to do with the possibility and the desirability of neutrality with respect to particular moral and religious conceptions.

HRP: You, along with Charles Taylor, Michael Walzer, and Alasdair MacIntyre, have been identified with a school of thought called "communitarian." In your new book, *Democracy's Discontent*, however, you do not use that term even once.

Sandel: It's true that I don't use that term in *Democracy's Discontent*, nor, for that matter, I think, in *Liberalism and the Limits of Justice*.

HRP: Are you dissatisfied with the "communitarian" label?

Sandel: You must understand that this term "communitarianism" is a label: it was introduced by others to describe the debate that flowed from some of the criticisms of liberalism that I made and that others made.

The reason I'm uneasy with the communitarian label is that "communitarianism" suggests the idea that the values that prevail in any given community at any given time are just. And I reject that idea, just as I reject majoritarianism. I don't want to claim that the way to think about justice is to consider the opinions that the majority in any particular community may have at any given moment, and call that "justice." That seems to me a mistake. And, to the extent that "communitarianism" suggests majoritarianism, or a certain kind of moral relativism, it misdescribes the view that I would defend.

HRP: The view that you defend in your new book is more accurately described as "civic republicanism"?

Sandel: It's true that in describing a rival tradition to the liberal tradition in American political and constitutional history, I emphasize the civic republican tradition. The central idea of that tradition is that liberty depends on self-government, and that self-government requires citizens capable of deliberating about the common good, capable of sharing meaningfully in self-government, in self-rule.

What casts that tradition in tension with the version of liberalism that insists on neutrality is that the republican tradition emphasizes that politics should aim to form or cultivate certain qualities of character—certain habits and dispositions—among its citizens, to equip them to share in self-government.

So this formative project of the republican tradition emphasizes the element in politics of soulcraft or character formation, and this puts it at odds, or at least in tension, with those versions of liberalism that say government should not try to cultivate any particular virtues among its citizens, or any particular qualities of character. It should simply enforce a scheme of rights within which people can choose their own ends, for themselves.

HRP: Your view must construe the nature and purpose of rights differently than does liberalism.

Sandel: Yes. In the liberal conception that we've been discussing, the justification of rights has to do with the importance of respecting the capacity of persons to choose their ends for themselves. For example, the liberal interprets the right to free speech as a right to form one's own opinions and to express them. The republican argument for rights is different. The justification for rights in the republican conception is bound up with a certain end or goal, namely, the end of shaping citizens who will be capable of sharing in self-government. So the right to free speech in the republican tradition draws its justification from the importance of enabling citizens to engage in political deliberation about the proper ends of the political community. The role of rights, I should add, is of great importance in the republican tradition. It's not that the liberal tradition favors rights and the republican tradition opposes rights, but that the justifications are different.

HRP: As you say, the civic republican tradition of thought places a particularly strong emphasis on the idea of self-government, especially as a good to be promoted by the state. But what is it about self-government and political participation that is good? Or, more philosophically, what theory of the good underlies the tradition?

Sandel: This is an important question. There are two versions of the republican tradition, and each would offer a different answer.

One interpretation of the republican tradition, which might be called the weak or modest claim, would say that sharing in self-government is important regardless of what one's other, non-political ends are. Without cultivating in citizens the capacity to share in self-rule, it would not be possible to sustain a democratic form of life that enables people to pursue their ends, whatever those ends may be. That's the weak or modest claim. It conceives of government as an instrumental good.

There is also a stronger, more demanding version of the republican tradition that answers your question in a different way. And this is an answer that goes back to Aristotle, and in contemporary philosophy finds expression, say, in Hannah Arendt. The stronger version of the republican claim says that to share in self-government is an essential aspect of realizing our full human capacities for living a good life. And the argument of the strong republican view ties government to the human good as such, and says that unless we engage in political deliberation, certain important human faculties—the capacity for independent judgment, for sharing with others in deliberation about common purposes; the capacity for sympathy with other people's projects, but also a certain detachment from our own immediate interests—will lie fallow, and that one can't fully realize the good life except insofar as one lives a life that has some political activity or engagement.

So, there's the weak version of the republican tradition, which conceives of self-government as an instrumental good, and there are the stronger versions which conceive of self-government as an intrinsic good. In *Democracy's Discontent* I don't come down—at least I don't think I do—explicitly as between those two versions, although I think there is something to be said for the stronger version of the republican claim.

HRP: I suppose I'm wondering why you're hesitant to say more, if you are. Is there something that's keeping you from resurrecting the stronger claim, given its powerful past?

Sandel: For purposes of the book, *Democracy's Discontent*, it didn't seem to me that I had to try to come down on this issue. I didn't have to force myself to choose between the two versions of the republican tradition because one of the main aims of the book was to try to interpret our political condition by exploring the public philosophy or the conceptions of citizenship and freedom that underlie it. And for the purposes of that project, it seemed sufficient to show, or to try to show, that the republican strand of American public life has been crowded out by a certain version of the liberal strand, and that this shift in self-understanding can account for the sense of disempowerment and frustration that attends contemporary American politics.

So that part of the project didn't require—I don't think—that I choose between the two. Still, it's an important question to ask why self-government matters: does it matter only instrumentally, or also intrinsically?

The reason that I hesitate in answering the question is that one can imagine ways of life that don't seem explicitly political but do call for capacities of deliberation and judgment and the taking of responsibility for common projects as well as for individual ones, that cultivate many of the virtues that the republican tradition emphasizes. And it may sometimes be unclear whether those ways of life really count as political or not. For example, a great many people may not be particularly involved in electoral politics or in the activities of the national government, and in that sense their lives may not involve political activity or engagement. And yet they might be involved and engaged in civic activities, whether in neighborhoods, or schools, or congregations, or unions, or workplaces, or in social movements. They may be involved and engaged in civic activities in those kinds of settings that some might argue are not, strictly speaking, political, though it seems to me they would be political in the relevant respect. So if "political" can be conceived expansively to include civic engagement beyond electoral politics and beyond government, then it seems to me a case can be made for politics being an essential ingredient of the good life.

HRP: And what about a philosophical life, a life of pure contemplation (if, as Aristotle denies, such a life were possible for a human being)?

Sandel: Well, this has always been the most compelling challenge to the strong republican claim, to the claim that politics is necessary to the realization of the good life. It's a challenge that Aristotle struggled with in Book X of the *Nichomachean Ethics*, even after he affirmed and in some ways gave the classic definition to the republican claim.

But the question is whether the life of contemplation can be autonomous with respect to politics after all. There are two reasons to wonder about the autonomy of the contemplative. One of them is a practical challenge, which Plato acknowledges: that philosophers need to worry about whether the city in which they live will be conducive to their philosophical contemplation. And the worry about the civic or political conditions of contemplation even for Plato calls into question the autonomy of the contemplative. The philosophers, after all, were dragged down into the cave precisely for this reason, to assure the conditions for the possibility of their higher activity.

That's the practical challenge to the autonomy of the contemplative. But there's also a philosophical challenge, and this I think one finds glimmers of in Aristotle. Is the activity of thought—or is the pursuit of the truth—something that can be engaged in without contact with some city and its tumult, and its controversies, and its disputes? Doesn't there have to be some occasion for reflection, and isn't the occasion for reflection—maybe even a form of annoyance—ultimately political in character?

HRP: What other classic philosophical texts have you found most helpful to draw on in elaborating your republican theory?

Sandel: Well, as far as influences, we've spoken some about Aristotle, someone who stands at the beginning of this tradition of republican thought. But there are important respects, it seems to me, in which the republican tradition needs to be reconstituted if it's to be relevant to contemporary politics, to politics of the modern age. The reason the republican tradition can't be applied directly to contemporary politics is that the republican tradition has always emphasized that the civic project, the formation of citizenship, and the exercise of self-government must unfold in particular places, as Aristotle wrote of the polis. But in many respects, politics, and certainly economic activity in the modern world, increasingly spills across the boundaries of particular places—even across the boundaries of nations, never mind cities or city-states. Add to this the insight that comes from the Enlightenment about the universal claims of political morality. So given the global aspects of political and economic life today, and also given the universal aspiration of moral reflection since the Enlightenment, it's not reasonable to try simply to appropriate Aristotelian conceptions of politics and apply them to the modern world.

Hegel, responding to the Enlightenment at closer range, grasped an important feature of modern social life that persists; he emphasized the interplay between particularity and universality in moral and political philosophy. He emphasized the way in which even to respect universal humanity and universal moral norms required institutions of meaningful differentiation. Even universal allegiances required for their cultivation and for their realization the persistence of the particular.

That insight of Hegel's is one that seems to me terribly important in thinking about the republican tradition in contemporary circumstances. It's not enough to emphasize the smaller, or local, or more particular forms of identity and community in an age when economic arrangements are global in their character. And so it seems to me that any attempt to organize a political response to the global economy requires on the one hand more expansive forms of solidarity and community and identity than the nation-state can, by itself, provide and at the same time requires shoring up more particular forms of identity and community in neighborhoods, schools, unions, social movements, and the like. Both at once, it seems to me, are necessary. And this double feature of identity formation in the modern world is something that Hegel sheds light on.

So Hegel's critique of Kant would be among the influences, to go back to the question. It's a critique that doesn't forsake the aspirations of universal morality—that's its power. It isn't merely nostalgic. And I think any attempt to reconstitute a contemporary politics of meaningful self-government has to take account of that double-imperative: the truth in the aspiration to universal morality, along with the indispensability of more particular forms of identity.

HRP: Your emphasis on the idea of self-government goes beyond mere voting, or other features of an ostensible democracy. Thus you would probably agree that there is something wrong with a system of electoral politics, if it doesn't allow people to promote the ideal of government?

Sandel: Yes, and I would go even further. Of course, I would say that in a totalitarian state in which people vote but do so without actually making decisions for themselves, or in sham electoral politics, as in Iraq for example, where 98 percent of the people turned out and voted for Saddam Hussein—that kind of electoral political participation does not count as calling forth the virtues we're discussing.

But even more, I think it could even be said that the routine electoral politics that are carried out in American democracy very often fail to call forth the qualities of character and judgment and deliberation and responsibility that the republican tradition is concerned with. That's a feature of mass electoral democracies whose content is unfortunately governed to a very large extent by money, by large contributions, by thirty-second television advertisements.

To be involved or engaged in political activity in this sense is usually to be a passive spectator to a not-very-edifying spectacle. And it's hard to see how qualities of judgment, independence, deliberation, and responsibility are promoted by that kind of activity.

HRP: Your advocacy of empowering groups and participation in governance will make some worry about the content of the rules that are decided upon through such a process of participation—that some groups, when empowered, will enact laws that insult or exclude other groups. This is the question about majoritarianism. How would you distance your own views from majoritarianism and its dangers?

Sandel: Well, what's wrong with majoritarianism is simply the principle that whatever policy is favored by the majority of people in a given community ought to prevail. That seems to me wrong. Whether it ought to prevail depends on its merits, and we can't know that without attending to the moral arguments in its favor. Sometimes the best policies, the just policies, or the morally most desirable policies fail to win the majority. So the most obvious objection to majoritarianism, it seems to me, is that it has simply to do with numbers, not to do with the moral justification of the policy.

Now you may be also asking a different question—or there may be a different question in the background—which may be this: doesn't procedural liberalism provide a more secure guarantee against majoritarianism than the republican tradition?

HRP: Yes—

Sandel: To this I give the following answer: the republican tradition, to go back to an earlier part of our discussion, does not reject rights. What constrains majorities institutionally are rights, and the republican tradition doesn't reject the idea that certain rights should constrain what majorities do. The difference between the liberal and republican tradition is not whether there should be rights that constrain the majority, but how those rights should be identified and justified.

There may be a further objection to that—I think the heart of the worry that you refer to seems to be that rights that are justified according to some end or purpose are less sturdy or less secure than rights that draw their justification from the notion of respect for persons as persons capable of choosing their own ends.

HRP: Isn't that an important worry?

Sandel: Yes, but lying behind that worry is the idea that if the case for a right depends on an end or purpose, that will be controversial or it won't be determinate and therefore people may disagree about whether this end does or doesn't sanction that right; whereas respect for persons as persons capable of choosing their own ends regardless of what they choose seems more secure. But it seems to me that neither argument for rights always yields a determinate answer. Both give rise to controversies.

So while it's true—to go back to the free speech example—that if the point of having a right to free speech is to enable people to share in self-government, there could be a dispute about what counts as sharing in self-government, such that certain types of free speech won't be covered. There could be a dispute about that, and it could be decided too narrowly, that's true.

But what counts as respecting persons as persons capable of choosing their ends also admits controversy and contest that can lead—and has historically led—to narrow construal of rights. For example, in the Lochner era, the liberal justification of rights as respect for freely choosing selves led the Supreme Court to strike down industrial legislation providing for maximum hours, or minimum wages, or safe working conditions for workers. And the reason those laws were struck down was in the name of rights, namely, the right to freedom of contract.

Others argued that that was one way of construing rights—that the relevant right to choose one's ends was not that one should be free as an employer and as an employee to make a contract for labor on whatever conditions, however onerous and horrendous they might be. Others argued that there has to be a certain equality of bargaining position truly to respect the right to choose one's ends, or a labor contract, for oneself. But in any case, there was a dispute about what counted as respect for the right of people to choose their ends for themselves. So it seems to me that both justifications of rights admit of competing interpretations—some wider, some narrower.

And furthermore, it seems to me that it's not possible to adjudicate among the competing interpretations of respecting persons as persons in the liberal conception. It may not be possible to choose among those competing interpretations—say, the libertarian interpretation as against the egalitarian interpretation of rights—without affirming a more particular conception of the good life and the good society. To resolve competing interpretations of what counts as respecting liberal rights, one may be forced back, implicitly or explicitly, into competing accounts of the good.

Thus the liberal justification of rights—though it may seem on the surface more secure, less vulnerable to dispute, controversy, or competing interpretations—on reflection, is not. And this we can see from disputes that have occurred in our own constitutional and political experience within the assumptions of the liberal right to equal respect—debates that have gone on at least since the Lochner Court and the New Deal—for instance, the debates between defenders of the welfare state and libertarian critics of the welfare state.

All these debates, by and large, have taken as given the idea that everyone has certain rights, that those rights should constrain majority rule, and that the justification for those rights is to respect persons as persons capable of choosing their own ends for themselves. Everyone agrees on that, but the interlocutors disagree about how to interpret those rights. And can those interlocutors defend their interpretation of liberal rights without having recourse to some particular conception of the good society or the best way to live that stands outside the procedural view?

HRP: One aspect of liberalism that is attractive to many people is its account of legitimacy: that coercive political power should only be used on grounds that everyone can accept—or, as Rawls formulates it, that coercive political power should be used only on grounds that all can reasonably be expected to endorse as free and equal citizens.

Do your own thoughts about legitimacy try to appropriate, or to redirect, or perhaps to deny the force of the intuitions behind this account of legitimacy?

Sandel: Those intuitions have appeal in particular if we think about the wars of religion, for example, where what it meant to govern according to a particular conception of the good was to consign ourselves to a kind of perpetual civil war, or to the rule of the powerful who would prevail and impose their views on others.

But now, when we don't live on the brink of the wars of religion that provided an important background to that intuition, do we want to say that there can never be a cause that might arise from within a comprehensive moral or religious conception that could justify coercion? Coercion is, generally speaking, a bad thing because there's much to be said for respecting people's capacity to choose their own life plans for themselves. And there's often great harm associated with frustrating people's desire to live as they please. But it seems to me we need to weigh, in any given case, those harms against the competing moral interests at stake. And we can only do that, it seems to me, by attending to the moral argument or the religious argument about the goods at stake—to weigh that on the one hand against the harm (which is typically very substantial) of coercing people on the other.

To acknowledge that coercion often is harmful and carries great moral costs isn't to say, it seems to me, that no competing moral claim could possibly justify it. And one could say the same of social cooperation based on mutual respect. It's a very great good, social cooperation based on mutual respect, but there's no reason to think that it's so overriding a good that we can say in advance that it defeats all competing claims that might arise from within particular moral or religious traditions.

The only way we can know is to attend to the arguments lying behind the moral or religious claim and to weigh them against the good—the very significant good—of social cooperation based on mutual respect. But there may be some moral or religious ends that are worth affirming even if they fly in the face of social cooperation based on mutual respect. So it seems to me one has to attend to the good on both sides and to the harm on both sides.

HRP: You write that from the republican point of view "what makes a religious belief worthy of respect is its tendency to promote the habits and dispositions that make good citizens."[1] This seems to put aside the question of the truth of various religions in favor of a focus on their possible role in a republican regime. Yet isn't this analogous to the bracketing of controversial questions by liberals that you have objected to, for example, in the liberal treatment of the abortion issue?

Sandel: It seems to me that there are two main reasons for according special protection to religious practice. One of them is the republican reason that characteristically, though not in all cases, religious practices, at least in the United States, have often cultivated in citizens the virtues and qualities of character that contribute to self-government. The passage you cited refers to this reason.

But a second, different reason would have to depend on the idea that religious observance and identification can be intrinsically an important part of moral life. This second reason is a non-political reason, and it has nothing to do with the republican tradition. This goes back to our earlier discussion about the instrumental and the intrinsic, though there we were talking about self-government. But, talking about religious liberty, it seems to me there's an instrumental reason, which the civic tradition has emphasized, and there is also a separate, intrinsic reason for according special protection to religious liberty that has nothing to do with its political consequences.

These two main reasons for according special protection to religious liberty are to be distinguished from a third reason, which is the reason offered by the version of liberal political philosophy that has informed many court decisions in recent decades. This has to do with conceiving religious liberty as one among the ways of respecting persons as free to choose their own values and ends for themselves.

So by emphasizing the first two reasons, I try to suggest that the third reason, which assimilates religious liberty to liberty and to autonomy in

---

1. *Democracy's Discontent* (Cambridge, MA: Harvard University Press, 1996), p. 66.

general, ironically restricts the range of reasons for protecting religious liberty. Some of the court cases that draw their justification from the third kind of argument that assimilates religious liberty to liberty in general wind up according less protection to certain free exercise claims, because once claims of religious liberty are assimilated to autonomy rights in general, it makes it much more difficult to single out religious liberty as having special importance. You see this, for example, in the peyote case, where Scalia says that we can't allow each person's conscience to become a law unto himself and to require government to show a special justification every time it violates some person's beliefs. And this is what happens with the indiscriminate reading of the free exercise clause. Once religious liberty is cast as just one instance among others of respect for people's right to choose their own values and ends, then it's very difficult to accord it special protection because it becomes too broad a category.

HRP: Finally, on a more personal note, how has your thinking on the importance of community and participation affected how you engage in the various communities of which you are a member?

Sandel: Having lived for some time in Southern California, I think I probably acquired a keener appreciation of the importance of particular forms of community and identity than I might have had I lived in other more rooted places, though that was really only in my high school years that I lived in California.

I come originally from Minnesota, just outside Minneapolis, which is often thought to be notorious for its civic-mindedness. So in contrast to your question, I think it worked the other way around. φ

Cornel West

In the spring of 2000 Cornel West co-taught a course entitled "Pragmatism and Neo-Pragmatism" with Hilary Putnam at Harvard University. Throughout the semester, West would begin his analysis of each philosopher studied in the course by writing a few key words or pairs of words on the board before proceeding to disclose their significance. For John Dewey, for example, he wrote: anti-dualism interaction/transaction; transcendentalism/contextualism; elitism/democratic sentiments. When it came to the lecture on West's own philosophy, Putnam, with a playful grin, borrowed West's habit and wrote what West had acknowledged as the primary concerns in West's philosophical landscape: death/desire; dogmatism/dialogue; domination/democracy.

West's landscape is shaped by a variety of traditions, particularly Christianity and the works of Kierkegaard, Chekhov, Marx, Schopenhauer, Hume, Melville, and Emerson. Each of these thinkers has reaffirmed the importance of existential questions in West's intellectual and spiritual pursuits. West's deep family roots, his strong faith in Christianity, and his early exposure to Kierkegaard helped him grapple with profoundly troubling issues like the fragility of life and the ubiquity of injustice. West's concern with these troubling regions of life propels him to insist that philosophy be both informed by insights from religion, political and social activism, and the arts (e.g. Coltrane and Chekhov) and made accountable to the thorny issues raised in these fields.

While many of West's philosophical interests have found a certain resonance in the American philosophical tradition of pragmatism, he offers an existential and political critique of this tradition because he is dissatisfied with its indirect description of the human condition. In his belief that philosophy must grapple with existential dilemmas, understand the historicity of its own ideas, and combat the ills it encounters, West envisions a philosophical enterprise that differs substantially in tone from many of the dominant strands of philosophy today. He follows and propounds the vibrancy of a lived philosophy—a way of confronting philosophy that makes one aware of the merits and limits of reflection.

Cornel West is currently Alphonse Fletcher Jr. University Professor of Afro-American Studies and the Philosophy of Religion at Harvard University. He is active in discourses on social and political issues such as race and religion. He has written sixteen books, including *Beyond Eurocentrism and Multiculturalism* (1993), *The American Evasion of Philosophy, A Genealogy of Pragmatism* (1989), *Race Matters* (1993), *Keeping Faith* (1993), *Breaking Bread* (1991), and *Restoring Hope: Conversations on the Future of Black America* (1997). φ

Cornel West
Philosophical Faith in Action

Interview by
Katherine Dunlop
and Scott Shuchart
in 1997

HRP: We were hoping you could start out by telling us how you got into philosophy and, in particular, into pragmatism and the philosophy of religion. Could you describe the history of your education?

West: I think it goes all the way back to family and church. I've always been obsessed with the problem of evil and I wrestle with various forms of unjustified suffering, unmerited pain, and unnecessary social misery. Early on it was Kierkegaard. We lived in a segregated section of Sacramento, California, and we had a little bookmobile—we didn't have libraries around—and when I first read Kierkegaard, I said, "My God! He's on to something very crucial for me," which was, how do you actually engage in forms of philosophical reflection that are inseparable from lived experience and concrete situations?

I'll never forget when I first arrived at Harvard. I knew I wanted to major in philosophy, and I walked into Bob Nozick's office. He was my tutor. [I told him I had read] Kierkegaard and the *Story of Philosophy*, by Will Durant, a popularizing, kind of philistine conception of what the major figures were, but very important for a young person, sixteen or seventeen years old. And Brother Nozick said, "Not bad, but we're going to introduce you to some high-powered philosophers." I said, "Oh, now that's interesting."

I think from there I continued on, obsessed with this same problem of evil, but had a chance to read some very, very crucial figures and texts. One, of course, was Hume's Part X of *Dialogues Concerning Natural Religion*, [where] you got a nice wrestling with a kind of existential analysis of pain and suffering as well as a powerful critique of forms of empiricist foundationalism. And then it was Kant's famous essay of 1791, "On the Failure of All Philosophical Theodicies." And then Schelling's great *Treatise on Human Freedom*, which is probably, I think, one of the most powerful and profound wrestlings with the reality of evil and why German Idealist systems fail because they cannot deal with the reality of evil. And [finally] Schopenhauer.

113

Those four texts really always sat at the center of my own wrestling, in terms of the modern European philosophical tradition.

Now, [I was introduced to pragmatism] under Israel Scheffler and then of course my good friend [Richard] Rorty, at Princeton. Pragmatism struck me as a way of making certain kinds of contextualist and historicist moves that relate philosophy to culture, history, struggle, and so on. And it was there, actually, I discovered old Josiah Royce and so I became a kind of—never a card—carrying pragmatist, because I felt in some ways Royce was more profound than all of them. "Lecture Eight" on Schopenhauer, in the *Spirit of Modern Philosophy*, 1892, is to me still one of the great moments in American philosophy.

So I come at it in a very, very unique, idiosyncratic—some people might say "confused" way. When you come in through the Kierkegaardian-Schopenhauerian route, then you get a very different set of concerns. But you resonate deeply with the critiques of, not just foundationalism and not just forms of ahistoricism, but really trying to relate philosophy to lived experience and understand it fundamentally as a quest for wisdom, the kind of thing Dewey does in "The Quest for Certainty," the famous Gifford lectures of 1929. You really relate it to a quest for wisdom and that critique of the quest for certainty that you get.

HRP: You've identified Quine as a key figure in American pragmatism. In *The American Evasion of Philosophy*, you write: "The genius of W. V. Quine was to intervene in the most sophisticated discourses of symbolic logicians and logical positivists with pragmatic formulations and Emersonian, i.e., human-making, sensibilities." Some people might object that Quine's move to replace epistemology with behaviorist psychology, however, is not particularly humanizing at all. How would you square Emerson's view of radical self-reliance with a Quinian approach that sees individuals not as radically self-defining, but as a bundle of speech-dispositions?

West: It's a good question. I view Quine first and foremost as a naturalist, rather than a pragmatist, but there are pragmatic elements in his naturalism, in the same way that I would view Nelson Goodman's stress on human-making and world-making as a result of that human-making is, I think, continuous with the conception of Emerson's concerns about human beings and human creativity being at the center of things.

There's a certain ambiguity in understanding what we mean by "humanizing." Quine certainly, I think, understands science as human praxis enacted by human communities in that sense. And I think in that regard he demystifies certain older styles of positivism—but see, Quine remains a positivist in the end, I think. Part of that has to do with his deference toward physicists, his secular priesthood, as it were. And I do believe that the physicists have much to tell us, they have their own versions of world-making, to use Goodman's language, and they predict better than any of the other groups. So we do defer to them when it comes to predictive powers. But there's more to life than just predictive power, and that's where I would go at Quine.

Quine and I used to have these wonderful discussions when I was an undergrad. I would ask him, I would say, "Professor Quine, what meaning do you find in life?" He'd say, "Well, that's a very interesting question, Cornel. I have hobbies, I collect rocks. I go around the world and I have a fascinating rock collection, and I find great meaning in that—to see the variety of rock formations in the world," and so forth. I'd say, "That's interesting. What is it about rock collecting?"

"It reveals intellectual curiosity."

Aha! Interesting! "Is that intellectual curiosity linked in any way to issues of love, and death, and affection, and so forth?"

He'd say, "Sure, we all have these needs."

I'd say, "Ah, are you planning to write more about that?"

"No, no, I'm not really concerned about that, you know."

I was just trying to tease out the existential dimensions of his own life. He was quite open to it, but you don't see it reflected in the writings.

HRP: In *The American Evasion of Philosophy*, you point out that the very notion of a purely philosophical question, or a question only of philosophical interest, is a historical notion, one that really only comes about in the early modern period. Someone could read your emphasis on the practicality of pragmatism, its connection with lived life, as a move away from asking purely philosophical questions in that way. Would that be fair?

West: Well, so much hangs on what we mean by "purely philosophical." I mean, there certainly are questions that ought to be asked that do not have immediate instrumental use or do not have immediate practical bearing. Those questions ought to be asked, and, in some sense, they are "timeless." You see it in various cultural myths, narratives, stories, symbols, and so forth asking these fundamental questions. What does it mean to be human? What is the nature of death? Why is there something rather than nothing? What is the origin of evil? These in some sense are timeless questions—they're always couched within various historical forms, but they're questions that do not have this immediate practical bearing that I think ought to be asked.

Yet I also follow Rorty: I really do believe that the way in which philosophy in the modern period emerges as an autonomous discourse, self-contained, autotelic, and so forth, is a story that's worth telling. It's a very complex story—nobody's really got it right, but we know that something happens in which, for example, skepticism is viewed much more as an epistemic matter than as a way of life. It's interesting. Royce used to talk about the spirituality of genuine doubting, which is a way of talking about linking the philosophical to forms of, not spirituality in the ephemeral sense, but a way of beckoning us or luring us to various forms of awe and wonder and curiosity. You see, I'm all for that. A lot of people would associate that with the purely philosophical. If that's what you mean, all right. But on the other hand I want to historicize the purely philosophical, and then we're forced into a story-telling.

HRP: In *Keeping Faith*, you comment on the depth and intensity of your "commitment to what I call a prophetic vision and practice primarily based on a distinctly black tragic sense of life." There seem to be two parts of this commitment. There's the willingness to look at facts of death and despair, and to affirm moral agency in the face of those, and there's also a strand of Christian thought that is "so skeptical about our capacity to know the ultimate truths about our existence that leaps of faith are promoted." Now, certainly there's a place for philosophy in the first aspect. However, while leaps of faith provide a subject-matter for philosophy, and Kierkegaard's *Fear and Trembling* certainly comes to mind there, it seems that as practice the second strand could almost be seen as anti-philosophical.

West: Yeah, or at least holding the philosophical at bay in light of certain conceptions of the limits of philosophical inquiry. "Anti-" might be a bit too strong a claim, I think, because in some way "anti-philosophical" is parasitic on a certain conception of the philosophical which brings you right back in. When you're trying to hold it at bay because you're both using it and still concerned about the limits of it then that might put you in a very different discursive and existential space. And that's, I think, more what I have in mind. It's like, again, Kierkegaard—he doesn't really call for the crucifixion of reason, though at times he uses that language, but it's much more a use of all of the resources available, of rational reflection and acknowledging that it still has boundaries, borders, and limits, and so forth.

Now, it's also true, too, that one could say, well, aren't you making metaphysical claims about the nature of reality when you [speak of] the absurd, the capriciousness that sits at the center of it? Schelling talks about the veil of sadness spread out over all nature and the deep indestructible melancholy of all life, in the great treatise of 1809, and he's deeply disappointed! He had opted for the German Idealist project, the rationality of the world measurable by means of an analysis of human consciousness. And he ends up thinking, "God! It's darker than I thought! This preponderance of unreason, understanding nothing but regulated madness." See, he's on to something: if in fact there is a certain ineradicable, unsubsumable, non-rational element, then how do we talk about it?

It might be a question of trying to relate metaphilosophical critiques through certain dramatic conceptions of the life of the mind and dramatic conceptions of living one's life. And in that regard I really do believe (here I think I agree with Brother Stanley Cavell) that there ought to be much, much more dialogue between, not just literary critics, because there are so many schools of literary criticism out there, but certain conceptions of the dramatic that we find in plays and novels and so forth, and philosophical discourse that's concerned about lived experience.

You think about it, you know, Schelling died in 1854, wrote the text in 1809, never published a word after. That was it. Powerful. He wouldn't publish a word. That's a long time in exile, forty-five years. Schelling's coming back, too. We talked about Schopenhauer coming back. But he's not coming back as the old German Idealist, no, no, no. He's coming back as a metaphysician of evil, to use Heidegger's language. The metaphysics I think have to be curbed, curtailed, demystified rather than deconstructed, but [they're] certainly coming back. All the philosophers of darkness, I think, very much like the artists of darkness, are going to be so relevant for the twenty-first century. Paul Celan's poetry is going to be central in the next century, Kafka central, Hardy central, the Schellings and Schopenhauers. Not because their conclusions are convincing, but [by] the nature of their wrestling. There's a sense in which in analytic philosophy we overlook the tonality of the philosopher, and the Schellings and Schopenhauers and Kierkegaards will come back in part because of their tonality, that chimes well with the zeitgeist, as it did in Europe in the '30s and '40s after the war, with Sartre and others. It's going to come back in a very, very different form—I mean, I'm just pontificating at this point, but still—that's where I'm headed.

HRP: It seems like Schelling and Schopenhauer would have something to say about the nihilistic threat that we all face.

West: Absolutely, as human beings. Globalization of capital, uprooting of various communal structures, community-based structures of meaning, deracination and rootlessness of individuals, it's going to be global. It'd be very interesting to see Schopenhauer in Africa. We know his deep interest in Eastern philosophy—reading the Upanishads every night, Buddhism has such elective affinities with his philosophy—but Schopenhauer in Africa,

Schopenhauer in Latin America, not as the sole source of philosophical reflection but as a crucial voice. There's always going to be the more upbeat figures in the tradition, be it religious or be it secular. You have to have that balance, you need to have the balance.

Part of the greatness of Royce is that he's holding on to his Christian faith for dear life, very much like myself. But he knows that the truths that Schopenhauer and others are putting forward are inescapable, so what are you going to do? What are you going to do? Phronesis, practical wisdom, what does it require? How do you talk about courage, strength, endurance, struggle? Is it like the conclusion of an Aristotelian syllogism? Action? Well, no, it's more complex than that, but it has something to do with that. What kind of person are you?

HRP: Perhaps what a lot of people find very interesting in your work is the connection you're able to draw between philosophy on the one hand and action on the other. In particular, you had said earlier how some of these "timeless" questions with which philosophy has concerned itself have a lack of immediate, practical bearing. On the other hand, for instance in *Race Matters*, you identify the greatest threat facing black Americans as a "nihilistic" threat. You criticize liberal and conservative discussions of race as failing to confront this threat, and in particular you say that liberals ignore the importance of identity for black Americans. Also, the idea of a "love ethic" is central to your answer. These notions of identity and moral reasoning seem to be very philosophical, or at least notions about which philosophy has quite a bit to say.

West: No, that's true, it's true. Got in a lot of trouble using that term "nihilism," actually, because of course it has its own history, its own genealogy. I probably was linking it much more to a literary tradition, goes back to Turgenev's Bazarov in *Fathers and Sons*, than philosophical discourse, in a way, and then was trying to apply it in a very postmodern context, chocolate cities, in light of various ways in which it has been constructed, given the history of segregation, given the disinvestment, the level of unemployment, underemployment, and so forth. And yet I would still want to defend it, because I think you're right, I think there certainly are ways in which we can talk about that, where it overlaps with some of the philosophical concerns about meaninglessness and hopelessness.

Linked to lived experience, again. We're much closer to the philosophers of life and will than we are analytical philosophers. At that point it does become very much an existential question, a historical question, and a political question, at the same time. The existential question has to do with what resources we have available to create some new structures of meaning and value, so that people will feel as if life's worth living. The historical question is, what various contexts are in place and can be created? And that has to do with institutional and structural analysis: the economy, information, nation-states, the culture, and so on. And then the political question, forms of agency and insurgency, from below but also linked to progressives in the middle and upper strata. That's where the radical democratic project comes in, where you really have to have both vision and analysis, and try to make that vision and analysis more visible and accessible to people, by any means—media, texts, teaching—and then come up with institutional vehicles that can carry it for you. And maybe at some point contest with state power, even if it's just at the local level, and later regional and federal, at the end probably global level, given transnational corporate power and its disproportionate amount of wealth and influence around the world. All three of those have to be noted at the same time, and that in no way really comes through in that essay. I was simply describing the situation, not viewing it as the major [explanatory] causal factor.

You can't generate agency and insurgency when people feel themselves lacking worth, self-respect, and so forth, and that's been a deep problem, especially among people of African descent—who've been such a hated and haunted people. If you don't talk about a love ethic for a people who've been hated for so long, they'll never be able to conceive of themselves or ourselves as agents in the world who can make a difference in it. And of course that's been one of the fundamental roles and functions of the black church at its best—it created that black space that can hold at arm's length the white-supremacist bombardment to affirm one's sense of self, even if it was transcendentally invoked. "God loves me, folks on the other side of town don't, for the most part. [Laughs] And those folk who are close to me usually linked to that same God also love me, hence I can get a different vantage point to view myself than what the media's telling me, what the churches are telling me, what science is telling me," and so forth, and so on. This is true for oppressed groups across the board. Women have had the same problem, in terms of 2,000 years of patriarchy and so on. Where do you find those sources of self-affirmation, self-confidence, that view you as an agent-subject in the world? But what happens when those institutions themselves begin to unravel? That's part of what that essay is about: the family, churches, apprenticeship networks in music, apprenticeship networks in athletics—those are four crucial sources for black self-formation in white-supremacist America up until the '60s, when we finally break the back of American apartheid.

Fifty years ago, the only space where black people could find some sense of fairness was a boxing ring. Joe Lewis took on tremendous weight and gravity, because every other sphere of American life had a structure of unfairness; but at least that referee, he was going to be fair! If Joe knocks Max out, Max is down! It's not where, if you're white you've got twenty counts and if you're black you've got five. No, it's ten for everybody. If you hit him below the belt—you better not do that! "It's a black man, I can do whatever I want to a black man." No, we're in the ring now, this is fairness. Jackie Robinson, same thing. And so, of course, athletics will play a fundamental role, as will apprenticeships in music and entertainment play a fundamental role in terms of sustaining black self-confidence. How do you translate that into the other spheres? That has been the challenge of the last twenty-five years. And if the institutional buffers that once provided a source of self-confidence themselves waned, what happens? There are some young black Americans wrestling with that in a serious kind of way. Because the levels of self-loathing, self-hatred, self-doubt are running amok, with the result of self-destruction, destruction of others, and so on, and it has implications for the country as a whole. It has implications for the prospects for the American republic, the future of American democracy, which a lot of Americans don't realize, but it actually does. Race may bring down the curtain on the American experiment. That's another issue, but it's a crucial one.

It's striking to me that when you look at philosophical discourse, most American philosophers have been reluctant to say a lot about race. You think of the great American philosophers, what did they write about race? Royce wrote a book on race, *Race Questions*—the only one. But the great William James, who of course was probably more sensitive to issues of race ... his famous letter to a Springfield newspaper condemning lynching is the only literary example we have of a philosopher during the golden age who took a stand on race. John Dewey, of course, who was one of the founders of the NAACP, was quite active against racism, but he never writes about it. When you turn to a Whitman, *Leaves of Grass*, first edition, race everywhere. Mark Twain too, of course. Melville, Benito Cereno and Moby-Dick. The great figures in literature have had something to say. Faulkner, oh my God! You can't get too much deeper from the white side of town! Toni Morrison, black side of town. And we can go on and on. Philosophers—a Martian could come down and read great philosophical texts in America and not even know they had a race problem.

There are black philosophers like Lucius Outlaw, Howard McGary, and Charles Mills around now who are really forging a fascinating critique of a lot of the mainstream, and it's important. We don't know exactly where it's going to go, but it's very important, and begins to overlap with some of the very powerful feminist critiques that have been at work, the Sandra Hardings and others, also the homophobia and heterosexism that's also at work. It'll be very interesting, the next twenty or thirty years, how this spills out, what form it takes.

HRP: You mention the crisis of belonging that faces black Americans. This seems to be one of the problems that afflicts black intellectuals. Certainly the crisis as a whole goes beyond the academy. What changes do you think might be made in the academy to make it more hospitable to black intellectuals?

West: That's a good question. We've made some breakthroughs, of course. I wouldn't be here twenty-five years ago. The great Du Bois, who's probably the greatest black intellectual of the twentieth century, couldn't set foot in a Harvard faculty context, though he was the first black Ph.D. here. So we've made some breakthroughs, no doubt about it. I think that one of the challenges of the black intellectual is a philosophical one, which is the courage to be themselves. You have a Harvard, you respect the richness of its tradition, both keeping track of good and bad, you much more shape Harvard in your image than try to shape yourself in Harvard's. Which is to say, be yourself—in a self-critical way, not in a self-righteous way. I think that's true for a number of groups that have been excluded: the anti-Catholicism, the anti-Semitism, the anti-women practices that have been part and parcel of Harvard's history at its worst. But when they arrive, if it's simply a matter of wearing a mask and assimilating in a cheap sense, then you're going to be in deep trouble, in terms of intellectual creativity, in terms of existential sustenance. But in being yourself you recognize that Harvard will be a part of you.

I would be dishonest if I said that Harvard wasn't a part of me. My undergrad years here, I was so liberated, empowered, emancipated, I can never deny that. But liberated, emancipated, empowered into what? Not into just another typical Harvardian, but to a unique kind of hybrid figure of which Harvard is a part as well as a whole lot of other things: black church, black street, James Brown, George Clinton, all that, together. I think in the end people have much more respect for that kind of honesty and candor, so you end up not imitating or emulating, but just having the courage to be. And I think when black students see that, they say, this place can be as much mine as it was Harry Wolfson's in the '30s and '40s, though you must be willing to change. And of course you will change it. When there are figures who exemplify that kind of hybridity, then I think it opens the possibilities for black students coming through. Because, in the end, we're really talking about young people, who represent the future.

And of course it has implications for non-black students, white, brown, red, and yellow, and so forth. Because in the end the courage to be is a human thing, across the board: you can be upper-class, WASP, male, and still have no courage to be. You can think you ought to be black, black proletarian; nope, you're not black proletarian, you're upper-class, WASP, male, it's nothing to be ashamed of, if you have enough courage to be, to wrestle. If you just want to wear a mask and assimilate downward, same problem. And so in that sense it becomes a lesson not just for black intellectuals or black academics, but it becomes a human lesson that cuts across the board.

HRP: There's something you touched on a little bit, something about the individualistic component of a lot of the views we've been discussing. You point out in *Keeping Faith* that there's something in American philosophy of religion that takes individualism more seriously than Marxism in the context of, as you say, modern globalization, international capitalism. What is the state of, or the fate of, individualism? Is the early-pragmatist emphasis on it too much, is it something we need to realize in a different way?

West: One would want to keep in mind that, let's say with Emerson and James, you get the stress on individualism. Peirce and Dewey had rich notions of individuality which are very different than the kind of individualism you get out of Emerson and James. And yet, I'm deeply wedded to the notion of individuality of persons constituted by communities, even a notion of personality, which is not the same, but also one that connects individuals to lived experience, [such as] processes of socialization, acculturation, and so on, which makes them historical beings. But what happens these days is very sad.

You know who actually is quite profound on this is Robert Penn Warren, who is again a very overlooked major American writer, poet, and novelist, probably the greatest poet-novelist we've ever had. What Robert Penn Warren understood was that de-culturalization went hand-in-hand with a lack of history and a lack of connection to tradition, and the lack of historical consciousness, and the de-coupling of individuals from traditions makes it very difficult for people not just in getting rich and getting their footing and bearings and so forth, but leads them much more into very cheap forms of conformity.

HRP: Of course the interesting thing about Penn Warren is that he's a student of history.

West: Absolutely. You're thinking of the great novel [*All the King's Men*]. Indeed, and that's one of the great American novels, no doubt about it, a political novel. And poor Warren, you know ... He hasn't received that much attention. My good friend Harold Bloom calls Robert Penn Warren the most un-Emersonian of American writers. Of course that's a compliment for Penn Warren—for Bloom it's a critique, but he deeply appreciates Penn Warren's work. And in relation to your question: namely, that, ironically, without the sense of history and connection with tradition, all the rhetoric about individuality becomes more and more empty because the individual becomes simply a certain moment within the conformist project, usually for market purposes, fashion, fads, and so forth. At that point, even Emerson and James would thoroughly object, because their notion of individualism is all about nonconformity. It's all about cutting against the grain, as it were. *Self-Reliance* is about abandonment, and [for] James, individualism is always holding [it] at arm's length: "I hate bigness, I can't stand those prevailing paradigms, that Ph.D. octopus system reproducing these graduate students, giving them the stamp of professionalism, I can't stand that." And of course as a Christian for me that is fundamental; as a radical democrat, fundamental, because conformity is a certain form of authoritarianism, if it runs amok—power imposed, arbitrary power, unaccountable. It's not just a question of peer pressure and so on. It has deep implications for anti-democratic self-formations. We can't have democratic cultures without some source of democratic personalities, democratic individualities.

Again, I think it takes us back to issues of courage, strength, endurance, sacrifice, cutting against the grain. Once the sources of the courage begin to wane, you get cowardliness, cowardice, the real raw stuff of authoritarian politics, and so on. Cowardice goes hand-in-hand with hatred. Christians talk about love, about courage. Kierkegaard shows Christian life is living dangerously—ah, proto-Nietzschean, but he's got it under Christian auspices, right? Bernard Shaw says hatred is a coward's revenge to being intimidated, so that you can't deal with otherness, you can't deal with strangeness, in the courageous way that trying to relate, commune—it's almost Levinas-like. No, what you do is you're intimidated by it, you're fearful of it, and therefore you either want to dominate it or associate that difference with disgust and degradation, which becomes a rationalization for hierarchy imposed upon it, as forms of subjugation, you see. And so in a very interesting kind of way the issues of courage, love, cowardice, hate go hand-in-hand, and we've got a lot of cowardice spreading rapidly. It's always been there, no one could argue, but it's even more so, especially when you have alternatives that are hardly credible. People can't believe that there's really an alternative to the present, they figure they just have to fall in, lock, step, and barrel, because—no chances. There ought to be a few who will take a chance even when there's hardly a chance, because it's right, moral, and just, and so forth. That's a form of courage.

We know, philosophically speaking, that intellectual courage puts philosophy at its best. Socrates—if we believe what Plato and Xenophon said about him—has intellectual courage in a deep way. And for me, of course, Jesus is not so much intellectual courage, but it's courage as compassion, which I think in the end is much more profound than Socrates; Socrates never weeps the way Jesus weeps. Jesus weeps uncontrollably; we don't have Socrates crying and he laughs only once, which is interesting, gives me a hint that he missed out on something, a lot of things. What I also want to encourage is compassion, that may lead to weeping. And that takes us back to Chekhov, because you really do have Socrates, Jesus, intellectual curiosity, scientist, medical doctor, and deep Christian backdrop but agnostic in belief. Christian temper without the Christian consolation, see, that's good stuff! All that love and compassion, courage, but still Socratic, in terms of intellectual engagement, go wherever the conclusions take you and so forth, but you're still loving. Look into the abyss, whew! That's Chekhov. See, Chekhov's got all that Schopenhauer in him, but yet he's still able to use it in such a way that he ends up sounding like my grandfather. Love, love, love, have the courage to love, the courage to be, go down fighting. Whew! That's Chekhov's announcement, no doubt about it. There's never been another like him.

You think of the philosophical analogue of Anton Chekhov, who do you think of? Is there such a figure? I don't think there is. Wittgenstein probably could have been, but he was too cowardly in his life. He was courageous in his thought, but he couldn't live a life. I tell you, Ludwig Wittgenstein, the great genius of the twentieth century, enacted a philosophical dialogue within his life. He just couldn't muster the courage to love another. Brutal, cruel, beating his students and so forth. He didn't have enough courage in his life. And it's not his fault in any petty, personal way, he was shaped by a lot of different things, but he's just in no way comparable to someone like a Chekhov, who didn't just invest his genius in his work, his talent in his life as Oscar Wilde talked about; it was both. Almost meets the Nietzschean criteria of making his life a work of art, even as he's producing literary works of art, though he's primarily a doctor during the day. Unbelievable.

I think in the end, if there's something to aspire to, it's to be the philosophical analogue to Chekhov. This means that you have to be a kind of blues man, because Chekhov certainly had the blues, and his works in some ways sing the blues to hold the blues at bay. But he had a lot of other things going on in terms of his sheer curiosity, wonder, courage to go on, it's quite rare. Chekhov's really not taught in philosophy departments. You get some dialogues with Shakespeare, Sophocles, Aeschylus, and so forth, Chekhov not at all. It's very interesting. He deserves, really, to be thought about philosophically. φ

Stanley Cavell

A guiding theme in Stanley Cavell's work is Wittgenstein's commitment to replacing metaphysical or philosophical problems with our own ordinary needs. Finding a sense of liberation in this commitment, Cavell reads Wittgenstein as an engaging and personal philosopher who opens new conversations rather than as a deflationary thinker who brings philosophy to an end. Cavell outlines this reading of Wittgenstein in "The Availability of Wittgenstein's Later Philosophy," which is collected in his first book, *Must We Mean What We Say?*, and he develops it in the first part of his central work, *The Claim of Reason*. This is the part of Cavell's work that is best known in contemporary philosophy departments. It is a constitutive part of any study of Wittgenstein's work.

Besides recognizing the sense of liberation in Wittgenstein's work, Cavell also bears testimony to it in his other philosophical interests. Because he reads Wittgenstein as looking at our own philosophical needs, Cavell's starting point is an interrogation and articulation of his own philosophical concerns. He writes with an autobiographical voice and in a characteristic style that is attentive to his far-reaching interests. Cavell seeks to speak with and quarrel about these interests with prominent philosophers of the twentieth century—particularly John Austin—and with other thinkers whom Cavell sees as addressing his concerns. In particular, in *The Senses of Walden* and *This New Yet Unapproachable America*, Cavell engages with Thoreau and Emerson: he finds their interest in the "everyday" or the "common" as consonant with his interests in the twentieth century and as an American. By engaging with them in this way, he seeks to define the "literary" character of their thought as inherently philosophical and to identify their thought as characteristically American. Cavell couples his attempt to identify the particularly American in philosophy with an attempt to clarify what is shared in the Anglo-American and Continental traditions. His powerful readings of Heidegger are a part of this attempt.

Cavell is particularly interested in identifying the ways that skepticism manifests itself in our culture. This concern has been a shaping force in his thought since his early work, as the concluding essays of *Must We Mean What We Say?* (1969), "Knowing and Acknowledging" and "The Avoidance of Love: A Reading of King Lear," as well as his later work on Shakespeare, reveal. In *The Claim of Reason*, he shows how skepticism concerning other minds leads to, and becomes, tragedy. In his work on film, he interprets melodrama as an expression of skepticism (in *Contesting Tears: The Hollywood Melodrama of the Unknown Woman*) and explains early Hollywood comedies as an overcoming of the skeptical impulse (in *Pursuits of Happiness: The*

Hollywood Comedy of Remarriage). But his interest in film goes further and explores, especially in his early book *The World Viewed*, the ontology of film.

Cavell was born in 1926, received his A.B. in music from the University of California at Berkeley and took his Ph.D. from Harvard in philosophy. He taught at Berkeley for six years before returning to Harvard, where he became Walter M. Cabot Professor of Aesthetics and the General Theory of Value. He became Professor Emeritus in 1997. φ

Stanley Cavell
Reflections on a Life of Philosophy

Interview by
Charles Stang
in 1997

Through a series of miscommunications, the text of this interview that originally appeared in *The Harvard Review of Philosophy* was a raw sketch not intended for publication. The present version has retained what it could of the original and is meant to replace it.

HRP: I thought we might begin with a question on Wittgenstein. In 1996, you and Professor Richard Moran taught a course together on your book, *The Claim of Reason*. If I am not mistaken, this was your first serious and systematic rereading of that book since its publication. It also represents a return to your defining encounter with Wittgenstein. Why this return and how is this return significant?

Cavell: You are right, it is the first serious and systematic rereading of that book I have devoted to it (or participated in) since it was published. The why question is an interesting one for me, I've asked [it] myself. I don't want it to be swamped by the fact that there is a straight practical answer. I had been wanting for a while to offer this book as part of the offerings in the philosophy department at Harvard. If someone has written a big book in any department, it is very likely to get into their teaching. I never found a way to do that systematically. The presence of a young teacher new to the department, Richard Moran, whom I profited from and enjoyed talking to, struck me as a chance. I asked him if he might be interested. To hear a young, different voice from my own responding to this material seemed to me the context I had been looking for. It turned out to be a creative experience for me. I am greatly in my friend Richard Moran's debt.

With this book, or parts of it, more extremely than with anything else I have written, I felt I couldn't teach what I had written. It is not science, it is not logic; I don't want to be a policeman about whether somebody has got it right or not. From a teacher's point of view, of course, I care about correctness. But from a writer's point of view, any response gives me something to think about; why a particular response has been sparked in another human breast is something I want to understand. Beyond the chance to hear my words coming back, slightly alienated, there were two other, external features—are they external?—motivating me in returning to my book.

[In 1996] the French translation of *The Claim of Reason* came out. I had worked on this project, at various times over the past ten or twelve years as the translation was in progress, as it was halted and delayed. Thinking about these passages in another language is another source of the right sort of alienation, another way of experiencing what was going on in the text, as someone sometimes surprised, sometimes delighted, sometimes someone much less than delighted.

The other motivating feature was the wish to mark my last term of teaching before retiring. Saying goodbye to the official part of teaching seemed to me to suggest going back all over everything in my publishing life. Since *The Claim of Reason* reaches deeply back into my Ph.D. thesis and is still a part of the latest things that I do, if there were one text of mine that, in winding things down, I would go to, that would be it. I'm grateful it happened.

HRP: Your encounter with Wittgenstein is an encounter with his *Philosophical Investigations*. Why do you withhold comment on his other later writings, such as *On Certainty*, or *Lectures on Religious Belief*, or *Culture and Value*? Do you find them somehow inferior to the *Investigations*?

Cavell: I didn't respond to that part of your first question. I don't find that teaching the course on *The Claim of Reason*, for all the extent to which that text of mine is a commentary on passages from the *Investigations,* is taking me back to Wittgenstein. Probably the reason is that in a sense I've never really left Wittgenstein's writing. It is always close or always about to explode. So, why not other later work? That's a good question, it avoids the question of why not the early work as well. I take your point kindly.

So let me give you an exception to that withholding. I have specifically written on the miscellany of journal entries [in *Culture and Value*] on two occasions. A recent piece of mine ["The Investigations' Everyday Aesthetics of Itself," in *The Cavell Reader*] represents the first time that I have tried writing systematically about Wittgenstein's manner of writing. In that piece of mine, I relate Wittgenstein's taste, in part, directly to German romanticism. What might strike one as the oddity in placing importance on that connection may itself suggest why I do not feel compelled to go back or on with Wittgenstein. When a small piece of lightning strikes, I welcome it and I am glad to follow where it leads. Or when someone pushes me to do it, I am happy to. Or when someone tells me that Wittgenstein is a neo-pragmatist, or words to that effect, I may want, as I just did in a little paper that I gave at a pragmatist conference, [to] raise a question about that. I don't regard myself as a Wittgenstein scholar, and I don't continue to be fascinated by what he can do philosophically past the point that that life changing fascination came over me with respect to the *Investigations*.

I am sure that any one of those other texts could interest and inspire me, but I didn't find that about *On Certainty*, much as I liked some things in it. It seemed to me thin in comparison with the *Investigations* but why compare it to the *Investigations*? I compare it only because for me to become absorbed in it, it's going to have to suggest a new path. I am not interested, I find, in simply noting minor differences or minor advances in this way or that way. But I have friends whose philosophicality I respect and count on and any of them could get me into one of these texts if they wanted to. Nobody has really urged me to and, partly, I am so aware of how many other things I haven't read and thought about, that I usually let that sway me.

My interest in Shakespeare, for example, is exploding so fast again and in so many regions, some of which will come back to Wittgenstein. Since I have time, I am letting that take me that way. The connection with Wittgenstein's few explicit remarks about his reading of Shakespeare [in *Culture and Value*] came to attention in a piece of mine written at the invitation of the Shakespeare World Congress in 1996 ["Skepticism as Iconoclasm"]. There is another piece of mine, picking up what was for me an unexpected aspect of the project of the *Investigations* as a whole, on Wittgenstein as a philosopher of culture [part of *This New Yet Unapproachable America*], that dramatically showed me I had not exhausted my interest in that text that I thought I knew well. It was an assignment that I liked the sound of, given by a group of Wittgensteinians in Norway who asked if I had thought about Wittgenstein in that light. I hadn't, or not enough, and I wanted to. And when the idea dawned on me of how to go about thinking about the *Investigations* in terms putting it together with Spengler's work (a certain point of comparison with Heidegger as well) I was drawn to see it through. That is what it takes to bring me back, or forward, to Wittgenstein, being drawn to do it. To do it out of obligation, without passion, just to say that I have been complete, will not work, it is not my work. If I need an excuse for this stance, it could only be that I feel I have, as things stand, said more about Wittgenstein than, so far as I know, has been responded to. If that is not my fault, being more complete is not likely to balance the situation. If it is my fault, why not move on?

HRP: How do you feel about the appropriation of Wittgenstein as a philosopher of religion? Are you pleased by anything that you have seen in that area?

Cavell: It's a very hard question for me to answer. I haven't seen anything that I am exactly pleased by. I am not very up on most of the secondary literature about the later philosophy. I'm embarrassed to say that, but my writing about it began early; I'm stuck in my generation in this respect. My review of the *Blue and Brown Books* was quite early in the reception of Wittgenstein's later philosophy in this culture. It was, I don't know, forty years ago that I wrote "The Availability of Wittgenstein's Later Philosophy" and what I said there was something I haven't had to retract. It means that the path that I set out on heavily in my dissertation is the path that I've taken through Wittgenstein's work. And I haven't searched out further people to disagree with.

Of course, I think Wittgenstein should beckon someone with religious instincts or wishes or theological callings. Students of his have found it so; and one can read it in his texts. I don't mean to be overly fastidious. I feel such inclinations in the *Investigations*, and it is there that I have to test out on myself what bearing I think he might have on religious interests of my own. When he becomes comparatively casual but always interesting, explicitly on the topic of religion, I'm glad for people to respond to it. I don't feel puritanical about their having to earn every single syllable they say about the religious by having to work their way through the major texts of Wittgenstein. But, it's going to be hard for me to [be] much interested in it, if the advance doesn't come in that sort of way. (If a writer has a mind as powerful as Hilary Putnam's, than I am interested as much in what he says as in whether it is what Wittgenstein says.) Now I say this also in ignorance of a great deal of work that has been done. At my age you have to be specific with me, somebody has got to put a theological reading of Wittgenstein in my hands and say, "Here, you haven't thought of that, have you?" and then I hope I will happily look at it.

HRP: A question about Moral Perfectionism. Stephen Mulhall, who has taken a great interest in your work, says of the perfectionist thinking of such figures as Wittgenstein, Heidegger, Emerson, and Thoreau that it often shades into and is shadowed by religious thinking. Where does Moral Perfectionism encounter religion and what is the tone of that encounter? Is religion left behind or does perfectionism become a sort of religion?

Cavell: The idea of Emersonian Perfectionism, as I conceive it, is certainly one that invokes philosophy, not simply in connection with life as it is sometimes called for by people exasperated with academic philosophy, they want it to have some bearing, as they put it, on the way we live but even more stringently, philosophy itself as a way of life. Emerson picks up a very long, fascinating, honorable tradition of philosophical thinking. I don't know that I'd say quite that it is a substitute for religion, but it becomes a part of philosophy's quarrel with religion, a quarrel or competition with religion in forming some basis for human existence. Emerson, after all, left the pulpit when he was in his late twenties or early thirties. And the texts he produces in justifying this separation, the way he speaks of not believing in the Last Supper, the way he later denies the importance of the person of Jesus, and nevertheless, despite all, recommends a form of life that clearly has religious undertones, to say the least, in it, is, was, fascinating for me.

I have reported my difficulty in getting into Emerson, having written a little book on Thoreau. But once I found my way in, the wish or need to return to the Emersonian text has been recurrent. For example, the fact that it seemed to illuminate the writing of both Wittgenstein and Heidegger I found extraordinary. No doubt my interest in Emerson was equally some function of my interest in them. But it was Emerson that allowed me to see the connection between *Being and Time* and *Philosophical Investigations* that is rooted in their both being perfectionist works. What perfectionist means in this general connection is, it seems to me, chiefly two things: first, that the texts seem to reveal something about each of their writers as authors, placing a certain kind of demand on their readers that most philosophical texts don't place, I've called this a demand to respond to a marked fervor in the writing, something that calls out for a revelation from the reader; second, while both texts seem to bear upon religion and morality and aesthetics as well as epistemology and metaphysics, neither identifies itself with one of the traditional regions of philosophy. As if each is writing something I once called "philosophy as such." (I'm not suggesting that such a thing, said just like that, represents a clear or sensible aspiration. (Heaven knows it is not something that an academic program in philosophy could or should encourage.) I merely mark it as something I think it worth thinking about.) It is against such thoughts that I hear the question whether Emersonian Perfectionism has religious aspects, undertones, undersongs, overtones to it. You can see that I might wish to answer, initially, either yes or no. What is of critical importance, however, is that in Emerson's picture of the matter, in contrast to Plato's, the soul's journey has no necessary end state ("Around every circle another circle can be drawn"); that is, Emerson's is a perfectionism without perfectibility, distinctly without. It is his characterization of human finitude. (If one wished to speak of what I called the "demand" of these texts as "therapeutic," one must be careful not to suppose this suggests that we are offered a cure from philosophy, rather than by philosophy. And this should not itself distinguish the aspiration of these texts from, say, *The Critique of Pure Reason*.)

But while Wittgenstein was prepared explicitly to claim for the *Investigations* that it can, even should, be seen from a religious perspective, Heidegger, in contrast, over and over in *Being and Time* denies that it is an ethical or theological work. But he denies it so many times that you wonder why, and come to see why, he has to go on denying this, namely, because over and over again, one senses the moral or theological fervor in it. I would like to add that it is in *Conditions Handsome and Unhandsome* that I broach the issue of Emersonian Perfectionism and recognize (perhaps rather down-playing my astonishment in realizing this consciously only after the fact) that it is the region of the moral life explored in the genre of film I call remarriage comedy, to which I had devoted the book *Pursuits of Happiness*.

HRP: In your writing from the late '80s and early '90s, you take a serious interest in Heidegger's thought. For many philosophers, Heidegger is a taboo figure due to his involvement with the Nazi party. I was wondering if you could tell us how you make sense of Heidegger's philosophy in light of his politics. This problem seems to beckon a larger question: how do you understand the relationship between a philosopher's life and his writing?

Cavell: You're not expecting me to answer that whole question? Let me see if I can have some go at it. Even if I weren't as interested as I am in the texts of Heidegger's that I have read, given my commitment to understand the reach between philosophy as it's known in Europe and philosophy as it's known in the English-speaking world, I am bound to have tried to do something with Heidegger. No European philosopher (with so few exceptions that they become interesting in part for that reason) has failed to. Perhaps the most fascinating exception is that of Vladimir Jankelevich in France, a fearless, rich thinker, a wonderful writer and musician, who with the rise of Nazism refused to read anything further written in German, or to listen to German music. This sacrifice produced some forty books, but also somehow serves to keep them from being much read. He is, for example, extraordinary on the subject of French music (I have only read two of his many books on the subject).

I am not willing, though it costs me pain, not to read Heidegger, knowing his past, or knowing something of his past, not knowing what to make of his past. I know there are those who dismiss the pertinence of a philosopher's life to his/her philosophizing. It can be done. But at what cost is it done, I mean at what cost to one's conception of philosophy, to one's ambitions for philosophy? I do not mean to suggest that philosophers must take on the task of adumbrating the connections between a philosopher's work and life, nor that the knack of accomplishing the task, even in brief instances, is universally, or even widely, distributed. But in the case of Heidegger, not at least to acknowledge the task seems to be avoiding something. Here is an extreme, a lurid, case in which not only was a philosopher involved in malevolent politics, but his philosophy looks like, can be mistaken for, that malevolent politics. There are times when Heidegger's language approaches the language in which Nazism can be described making ultimate commitments to a destiny set by an encompassing political-metaphysical force. There are chilling, to use a pretty term for it, passages in Heidegger.

For example, as an American and as a Jew I am stuck with having to make what I can of Heidegger's Nietzsche lectures which set the standard for Nietzsche interpretation, the work of Nietzsche interpretation to which every European philosopher who is interested in Nietzsche, and there are few who are not, has had to respond. These are lectures in which Heidegger recommends especially the young Nietzsche to our attention, and that young Nietzsche is the Nietzsche most nakedly indebted to the writings of Emerson.

So in 1936, in Germany, Heidegger is giving endlessly influential interpretations of words, some of which, in effect, were Emerson's. I am stuck with having to make sense of that, as I am with the sense that Thoreau's *Walden* is interpreted by next to no philosophical work more intimately than by certain texts of Heidegger. I cite the essay "Building, Dwelling, Thinking," but there are related essays. Do such connections serve to taint the American's work or rather somewhat to redeem the German's? So far as Heidegger's cursed fate is concerned, and his damnation to have lived in a time when he was called forth by and associated with a tyrannical movement, philosophy is as such brought into question by Heidegger's fall. To the extent to which Heidegger inherited (Western) philosophy, not the only way of inheriting philosophy, but one genuine inheritance of a major part of Western philosophy, philosophy has bowed to tyranny.

HRP: Film has been at the center of your attention since the early '70s, but recently in *A Pitch of Philosophy* and some courses you've taught, you have turned your attention to opera. What do you find philosophically interesting in opera and how does this relate to your interest in film?

Cavell: What I have said before is that opera and film bear internal relations to one another in the fact that each was invented at datable times and places, in the level of emotion to which they both appeal, in the range of audiences to which they appeal. Film, I have said in the epigraph to my recent book on melodrama, is made for philosophy; it shifts or casts a different light on whatever philosophy has said about appearance and reality, about actors and characters, about skepticism and dogmatism, about presence and absence.

I don't quite believe that opera was, in that sense, made for philosophy, though I think it should fascinate philosophers more than it does. It has fascinated philosophers of the magnitude of Nietzsche and Kierkegaard that will do. But the fact of opera and the celebration of the human voice, so one could say, in the call for opera during the decade which saw the appearance of the great tragedies of Shakespeare, a generation before Descartes expressed his sense of ordinary language as falsifying our relation to the world, means that my own sense of philosophy, in tracing the exiling of the human voice in philosophy, is something I have thought that the fact of opera might bear on. Something I haven't talked about is, to adapt the first part of your question, why opera has so recently entered my intellectual life? Something it seems to mean is that music is reentering my intellectual life.

I suppose I should say that a direct consequence of having given a course on opera is a renewal of my interest in American musical comedy. And so again I am led, taking steps across invisible stones beneath the water, to raise questions about that: What kind of talent, what kind of culture, expresses itself in that way? What kind of people have the talent to perform in it? Who writes it? It's not just popular art. It's not high art. But it is a popular high art of a sort of high popularity that America is known for being able to create. To ask, therefore, what my interests in such things as musical comedy and jazz and film are is to ask what my interest in America is, and that question is really all over my work now. It is chapter of a confession that part of my commitment to philosophy has from the beginning been a commitment to finding a way to write that I cared about, in a way that I seemed always to know about. To use philosophy as a medium within which, or from which, to write, especially to write work that could remain within earshot of English-speaking analytical philosophy, might seem a last and perverse place to look for it. For me, for various reasons, in various ways, it has been inspiring.

HRP: You were here at Harvard in the '60s during the student movement. How did these times strike you? How do they strike you today? What has stayed with you from those years?

Cavell: Surely the '60s were formative times for many people whose lives were centered in the university. Virtually all of my young friends, virtually every student that I spoke to, whether they were in favor of student activity or not, were having their lives molded by this. One could not, to begin with, take the kind of interest which it is, after all, my business as a teacher to have in what the young are thinking, without immersing myself in that experience, partly through identification but partly, explicitly, through a certain distancing.

Part of my role in those years was to maintain precisely a shared imagination with the young and also some way of presenting a possible distance from what they were feeling as a way of remembering something America was supposed to be doing and still could do, that they had not in their lifetimes experienced. I have this image of hurling myself into the middle of any conversation to try to split the difference between the two sides. Sometimes, I got rather bruised in the effort, sometimes it worked. But the sense of closeness to what was tearing apart these young people and the pain it cost me that they did not know an America that I thought I knew and that that country was losing itself, was the painful mood in which I rediscovered Emerson and Thoreau for myself.

I didn't know then that this was somehow essential to my rediscovery of them. I wasn't interested in holding up Thoreau as a flower child. It hadn't occurred to me exactly that Thoreau was some favorite of the generation of the '60s until much later. I had assigned Walden among other works to a group of visiting scholars and intellectuals and artists from Europe, Asia, and Latin America for whom I was offering a summer seminar on classics of American thought in 1968 and 1969. This was the period when you could at any moment feel you might go crazy trying to imagine how anyone was conceiving an acceptable outcome to the mutual slaughter in Vietnam. The visitors' interest in Emerson and Thoreau was quite as avid as that expressed by younger American students. Everybody, it seemed, was trying to find an earlier or different American face from the one that America was showing the world in that moment, wanted to think better of America than, so to speak, America was forcing itself to think of itself in that awful period. Were the marvels of American thought we were discovering somehow related to the revelation of American capacity for folly? Was it the arrogance or ecstasy of innocence that felt it could do anything? Living through it with the students I cared about has permanently marked me. To say more about it we'd have to go on in detail. I think I do detect still a difference between those of my generation who went through it in closeness with the students as opposed to those who fairly consistently disapproved as I sometimes did of certain of their actions. I begin to think of too many stories that I have to put aside in beginning to talk about it. For better or worse, we are all changed by it. It did something to the culture, for better and worse, that nothing else could have done. I think that's by now a common view.

HRP: You have mentioned twice already this place called America. What is this America and what is its privileged position today? I mean not its position in academic philosophy per se, but its position in a tradition of thinking of which Emerson and Thoreau are exemplars.

Cavell: A minimum answer, I expect, is that America is the place where philosophy and literature exist in a different relation to one another than they do in any other contemporary culture that I know much about. If you consider that Emerson's necessity and possibility was to discover or invent an American difference in literature and in philosophy simultaneously, then you must be struck by the remoteness of literature, especially of American literature, from American philosophy since then. An institutional measure of this is the formation of American Studies with philosophy left out. (Of course the institutionalization of American philosophy is as much the cause of that as the American institutionalization of literary study.) Put this another way. For me it remains in some ways no more remarkable that America thinks of itself as being discovered, than that Emerson produced philosophy for these shores by calling for philosophy, resulting in an invention of a mode of writing that can sound like a parody of philosophy, anyway something that cannot be told from literature.

That's a quasi-professional aspect of an answer. A question seeking a different sort of answer is to what extent we can count on a continuing sense of social experimentation in America (the feature most plainly treasured by Emerson and Dewey) that is unlike the projects of other cultures. We're not still coming out of a colonial past. We're not coming out of a monarchical past. One feels that some possibility of further establishing the conditions of justice ought still to be motivating for us. The fact that we have an outstanding racial issue proposes a task that, at my most romantic, I feel will mark an unprecedentedly great social achievement if it can be made more tractable, or continue to be made I don't think that there have been no advances.

Somebody like me who comes from an immigrant family is apt to be fascinated by a thing I've actually called a part of the American difference in philosophy as registered in the writing of Thoreau and Emerson. Namely, their willingness for departure, for what they call abandonment, for what they call onwardness, in short, for an embracing of the condition of immigrancy in their lives. It struck me in my earliest thinking about Emerson and Thoreau that they reverse the Heideggerian emphasis on learning to dwell where you are, and insist on learning to leave where you are, which in part means becoming willing to allow it to change, willing to allow it to change you, allowing yourself to present yourself so that it changes. That is a remarkable aspiration for a culture and its guiding thinkers to set for themselves. φ

Alexander Nehamas

Even a brief summary of Alexander Nehamas's life and writings is a tricky task, since Nehamas has attended above all to the written lives of philosophers. This is not to say that Nehamas has been interested primarily in philosophers' biographies, or in their lives as writers. Rather, in his work he has attempted to understand the ways in which their writings create a life and a model for living. Nehamas's foremost concern is therefore not life or literature per se but what he calls, in the title of his first book, "life as literature." So, to steer by his own lights, it is through his writings that a philosophical biography of Nehamas needs to proceed.

Perhaps it is misleading to say that the figures who interest Nehamas are simply "philosophers," for Nehamas has often occupied himself with figures—like Montaigne and Foucault—who are sometimes thought to lie outside the philosophical tradition. In his writings on these figures, however, Nehamas has argued persuasively for their inclusion in that tradition, at least in one of its self-conceptions—while at the same time explicating why these figures have had a conflicted and equivocal relationship with philosophy proper. Foremost among these figures, for Nehamas, is Nietzsche. Nehamas's *Nietzsche: Life as Literature* (1985) represents an attempt to come to terms with Nietzsche's major writings (beginning with *Thus Spoke Zarathustra*) as a whole, rather than in the piecemeal fashion that his work has often seemed to invite. This whole consists, according to Nehamas, not in a unified style or set of assumptions but in a character, who is none other than the self-image Nietzsche fashions in his works, a "literary character who is a philosopher," a "creature of his own texts." A reader of the book cannot fail to note that Nehamas has in Nietzsche a kindred spirit (albeit one with whom he has deep disagreements about philosophy and life), not only as a classicist and literary philosopher but as a scholar of himself, whose *Ecce Homo* constitutes one of the few antecedents for Nehamas's own way of practicing philosophy.

One of the remarkable aspects of *Nietzsche: Life as Literature* is Nehamas's ability to show how a diverse hodgepodge of texts resonate with one another while at the same time recognize their insistent heteronomy. This is a way of reading that Nehamas carries out with a far wider and more varied range of texts in his *The Art of Living* (1998). *The Art of Living* courses from Plato to Foucault, and its ambitious scope is coupled with a still more ambitious aim: to sketch out a way of doing philosophy that is different from and in some ways prior to the conception of philosophy as a "theoretical" discipline. To this theoretical mode of philosophy Nehamas opposes (as an alternate, not a competitor) a "personal" mode, the readers of which "must never forget that the views that confront them are the views of a particular type of person and of no one else." This is the mode for the study (which is necessarily also the practice) of "the art of living," the process of self-fashioning in which many (but far from all) persons have engaged, and of which a few have left, for their successors, a record and a model.

Several of these few are the subjects of *The Art of Living*. The number of figures and texts with which the book deals may be misleading, for this book is, like *Nietzsche: Life as Literature*, in the end concerned with only one thinker: Socrates. Its subtitle is "Socratic Reflections from Plato to Foucault," and each of its chapters considers its subject—Plato, Montaigne, Nietzsche, Foucault—according to the terms set by Socrates, for "the art of living" is, for Nehamas, originally a Socratic art. But the structure of *The Art of Living* also manifests Nehamas's central quarrel with Socrates, over the question of whether there is one or many ways of life well worth living. In Socrates' view, there is only one such life, and to know it is to live it; for Nehamas, there are many such lives, and part of their praiseworthiness lies in their individuality. Indeed, one of Nehamas's central themes is the essential inimitability of the artful life. *The Art of Living* can thus be seen a book that must turn away from Socrates in order to be properly Socratic.

Most recently, Nehamas has published *Virtues of Authenticity: Essays on Plato and Socrates* (1999), the apparent focus of which—the book deals in detail and almost exclusively with the Platonic texts that have concerned philosophers since Aristotle—belies a wide-ranging web of themes and problems, many of which bring those texts in contact with the dilemmas of modernity, be they in logic or in mass media. Written over the preceding twenty-five years, these essays suggest that there is no one solution to their opening problem: how to come to understand Plato when so much time and writing lies between him and us. Rather, Nehamas suggests, the task calls for a range of intellectual efforts, which need to be as varied and urgent as the dialogues themselves. These essays are examples and exemplars for such efforts, implying that even the study of classical philosophy (perhaps especially such study) requires no less art and individuality than does the project of self-fashioning that Nehamas has made his theme. Nehamas is a professor of philosophy, humanities, and comparative literature at Princeton University. φ

Alexander Nehamas
On the Philosophical Life

Interview by
Nick Stang
in 2000

HRP: In your book *The Art of Living* you describe a tradition of philosophy whose practitioners concern themselves not only with advancing technically true theories but also with developing a unified and unique self through their work. You write, "The purpose of the art of living is, of course, living. But the life it requires is one in great part devoted to writing. The monument one leaves behind is in the end the permanent work, not the transient life." Socrates, of course, is the only of these philosophers who didn't write anything, and, so it can be said, left behind only a transient life. Why is the philosophy of the art of living so intimately connected with the art of writing and how does Socrates succeed as such a philosopher without writing anything?

Nehamas: The interesting thing about Socrates, of course, is that he never wrote anything, but Plato did it for him. He was extraordinarily lucky, if you like. In a very serious sense, Socrates and Plato are difficult to distinguish from one another, especially in the early dialogues, and in that sense we could almost say that Socrates did write. He wrote that which Plato wrote for him. And, as I said earlier in my book on Nietzsche, one of the reasons Nietzsche is so suspicious of Socrates—not suspicious, but jealous, I would say—is that Socrates didn't have to do any of the work of writing. Nietzsche attempts to become Plato to his own Socrates, Socrates to his own Plato—to play both roles. Socrates' transient life is not important at all. We know very little about it: people found him extraordinarily interesting, and he was executed. That would not be enough to make him a great figure. It is Plato's depiction of Socrates that starts off the tradition of philosophy as an art of living, not really Socrates' life itself. The actual events of Socrates' life, most of which we don't know, gave Plato the impetus to create that tradition. But I don't think it was just Plato's doing, as I may have suggested; a lot of other people were writing about Socrates at the time, and they were doing very similar things: they were all writing dialogues and they attributed to him the most varied views. So, clearly, there was something amazing about Socrates to begin with. He was, I think, incomprehensible to everyone around him, as incomprehensible then as he is now. And the tradition takes off once he is, so to speak, canonized—not just through his life.

HRP: In the introduction you write, "But his early works, in which Socrates is an unexplained mystery and simply leads a philosophical life, stand at the beginning of a different philosophical tradition"—that is, different from the tradition growing out of Plato's middle period in which philosophy becomes a purely theoretical activity. It would seem that philosophy as the art of living must constantly return to Socrates and reconsider and reencounter his irony. Do you think the art of living can be identified with or defined as the tradition of trying to make sense of Socratic irony?

Nehamas: I don't know that every philosopher who belongs to that tradition makes an explicit return to Socrates, but it's interesting that almost everyone who does belong to it exhibits what we might call Socratic features—particularly ambiguity. It's difficult to know when to take them seriously and when not. That applies not only to Montaigne or Nietzsche, but also to Wittgenstein—if you read Wittgenstein as a philosopher in that tradition. It's very difficult to know what exactly he's saying—when he's speaking in his own voice, when he is not. With Pascal, also, you have the sense of someone baring his soul, but you are never quite sure. How seriously are you going to take him? Many of those people are ironical. Montaigne is a highly ironical author, so is Nietzsche, and so is Foucault. The features we find in Socrates keep reappearing in the figures who belong to this tradition even when they don't write as Socratic scholars or interpreters.

HRP: I'm interested in what figures you would like to identify in the philosophy of the art of living who don't explicitly discuss Socrates.

Nehamas: I don't think Thoreau does, but I think Thoreau belongs to that tradition. (He does, of course, like Socrates, make a big issue of civil disobedience!) Emerson, who I also think belongs to it, talks a lot about Plato, though perhaps he is thinking of Socrates. Wittgenstein does not discuss him. Still, the *Philosophical Investigations*, perhaps even the *Tractatus*, can be thought of as a series of dialogues even more complex than Plato's, because we don't always know who's speaking—we don't even know how many interlocutors there are in the *Investigations*.

One feature of this tradition of philosophy is the direct examination of Socrates. Another is the presence of Socratic features. A third is an emphasis on literary style, or what we call literary style, because all philosophy is written in some style. By that I mean a personal style, an explicit interest in how you write. I think I see such an interest in Stanley Cavell; that's exactly what distinguishes him from many contemporary philosophers and why it's so difficult to create a school out of Cavell's thought—in the end, it's too personal, too "autobiographical" (to use his own term), for that purpose. Of course, many people created Socratic schools, but we have no idea how true to Socrates any one of them was; and no one has ever known exactly who Socrates was or what he believed.

HRP: I'd like to back away from philosophy as the art of living and concentrate on Plato and Socrates. In your work you consistently argue that some issue in their philosophy is directly relevant to contemporary debates. Sometimes you do so by overturning the standard interpretation. I'm thinking here specifically of your two essays in *Virtues of Authenticity* about Plato and the poets on the one hand and contemporary criticisms of popular culture on the other, as well as your reworking of the question about whether *arete* can be taught. To what extent do you think it is possible for someone of another time and culture to model his or her life on Socrates' project of self-creation? To what extent is the Socratic project singular and specific to fifth-century Athens?

Nehamas: I don't think Socrates' project is so specific to fifth-century Athens. It's something we find people doing all the time. What you can become, if you are involved in that project, is going to depend crucially on the situation and historical conditions in which you find yourself. But the idea of harnessing your energy, harnessing your personality, and making something worthwhile out of it is as basic and general as any human activity could possibly be. Of course, I don't think you could do it by going around and talking to people in the street any longer—if Socrates ever did that. So you would have to go about it in a very different way.

HRP: Might that have something to do with the fact that after Socrates, philosophy as the art of living has to be done through writing?

Nehamas: Philosophy is now a written discipline. It wasn't one for Socrates, but for him it wasn't even a discipline in the sense we use "discipline" today. The questions we ask can be too complicated to address for a culture that is no longer an oral culture unless it addresses them in writing. When I say that the art of living is an art practiced in writing, I don't mean that it is enough to just write about it. In some sense what you write must have an effect on your life and personality. That's why I think that ad hominem arguments, interestingly enough, are important and relevant to this kind of philosophy: you can criticize philosophers in that tradition if their lives do not reflect their thought—whereas, generally speaking, ad hominem arguments are irrelevant and fallacious when applied to theoretical philosophy. But to the extent that ad hominem arguments are relevant to it, there is more to philosophy as an art of living than just the writing. On the other hand, suppose that somebody who was living philosophically never wrote a word (and wasn't lucky enough to have a Plato do it instead!). That is possible, at least in principle. But could one then leave behind the kind of model that can make one part of that tradition? To me it seems pretty clear that this is impossible. No matter how influential you are on the people around you, unless either you or someone else writes about it, people will forget your effects, the changes your life produced. Like ripples made by a pebble in a pond, they will eventually die out. Writing remains; it keeps getting interpreted and reinterpreted, again and again, and so the ripples never die. Well, perhaps you might say, "I don't want to have an effect on other people. All I want to do is make sense of my own life and make a good person of myself." That's an admirable purpose. The trouble is that I wouldn't ever know anything about it, or about you, because I won't have any evidence. You disappear after you've done your job. And that's fine. But you can't have it both ways.

HRP: I'd like to return to a statement you make in *The Art of Living*: "The monument one leaves behind is in the end the permanent work, not the transient life." Earlier, you write: "Perhaps these people succeeded in applying their models to themselves, perhaps they did not; whether they did it is a matter of biography, and most likely it will remain a matter of contention as well. The image of life contained in their writings is a philosophical matter and, though it too will remain a matter of contention, the contention will be over whether that image is a coherent or admirable one." Remarkably, however, three of the figures you write about in *The Art of Living*—Socrates, Nietzsche, and Foucault—share one obvious distinguishing characteristic: the facts of their lives are common knowledge. Bearing in mind the extent to which these philosophers' lives have become common knowledge, I'd like to refer to another passage on this question, from Foucault's essay "What Is an Author?": "This relationship between writing and death is also manifested in the effacement of the writing subject's individual characteristics. Using all the contrivances that he sets up between himself and what he writes, the writing subject cancels out the signs of his particular individuality." How, despite what you and Foucault seem to say, have the lives of these philosophers become omnipresent in interpretations of their work?

Nehamas: We know very little about Socrates—I want to insist on that. We do, I must admit, have all those biographies of Nietzsche, but what we know about him "as a person" is so general and broad and, ultimately, useless for understanding the work that leaves you speechless. When people try to do the psychobiography of Nietzsche they say ridiculous things like, "He said that God is dead because his father died when he was a child and he couldn't get over it." That is an absurd simplification, reducing the significance of a view people hold to a single event in their life, thinking of the event (or events—it doesn't matter how many) as the cause of the view, of the view as the expression of the event.

The important question you raise here is this: what do we dispute about when we discuss philosophy? What I'm trying to say—and I'm not saying it very clearly either in the book or here—is that when you read people like Nietzsche or Socrates, Montaigne or Foucault you should not ask, "Were they right in the way they lived?" or "Did they themselves live the way they said life is to be lived?" but rather, "How does that affect me? What am I to do once I have read them?" The philosophical question is not about them, but about you and your own life. And what you do is whatever it is you're trying to do. You try to answer questions; you try to be good to your friends; you try to be generous to people—whatever it is that attracts you, whatever is part of your life. And, ideally, you try to impose some order and coherence on it all. So the question, again, is not whether Nietzsche produced an admirable model of life, although you may perhaps also want to answer that question. But somehow, ultimately, what you want to do is to make something of yourself—although not under that description: success is not itself a goal. My own goal is to get whatever interests me right, and to get it right in such a way that all its parts fit together. I don't want to have one view today and another one tomorrow, do one thing now and another later, and have them bear no relation to one another. It's important that our actions, our lives, manifest a consistent personality.

HRP: I would like to return to Foucault for a moment and recall the passage I read from "What Is an Author?" He seems an interesting exception to your view in *The Art of Living* that the author constructs for himself a consistent and unified literary self through certain literary styles. Foucault's writings seem characteristically impersonal, academic, and scholarly. And yet few interpretations of Foucault's writings fail to mention the details of his life, specifically his political activism, his sexuality, and his death from AIDS—facts you mention as well. What do you make of this conflict between Foucault's impersonal style and the predominance of biographical details in interpretations of his work?

Nehamas: Again, I don't think the biographical details are predominant. The biographies of Foucault contain the least interesting interpretations of his thought. As to his style, I think it undergoes the most radical changes during the course of his writing. If you start from the very early work you'll find the influence of Heidegger. You'll then detect in the middle works a shift toward Nietzschean ideas, although they are expressed in the most impersonal style—so impersonal that it has its own personality. The very late works, the second and third volumes of *The History of Sexuality*, for example, or the last lectures, which I discuss in the book, are written in a completely different style, completely personal. So I think the essay "What Is an Author?" vastly overstates the unimportance of the author that was in line with the impersonal style he was using at that time. I have actually written an article about that essay, and I argue that a writer inevitably constructs a persona, the voice of which is always heard through the text: that's what an author is: sometimes that voice can be very impersonal, but that very impersonality, as I said, can be a personal feature. There is, of course, another kind of impersonality—the impersonality you exhibit when you write in a style that is universally accepted in a certain discipline. That is an impersonality that does not distinguish you from other people—at least not from anyone else who writes in that disciplinary style. But when Foucault wrote impersonally he was creating the impression that he had seen a truth no one else had seen and was simply reporting on it—all the while asserting the most extravagant, sometimes almost outlandish, ideas. And that's a very personal style, after all, it's impossible to mistake it for anyone else's. So, I don't think he's an exception at all, and I believe that toward the end of his life, when he was writing *The History of Sexuality* and the lectures on Socrates and the Cynics, he was speaking in a self-revelatory tone. It's almost as if he was trying to say, "This is what I've been doing all along—this is what my life was all about." That's what I find fascinating about the lectures on Socrates: Foucault, at various points, cites a translation of the *Apology*, and then, without a break, he begins to paraphrase it and goes on to speak in his own person. When he says, for example, "I have been trying to treat you like a brother or a father," you don't know if it's Socrates or Foucault who is speaking: it's as if he is putting himself in Socrates' place. And that link, the revelation that all his work had this personal aspect, now allows me to go back and look at the early writing and see it as one part of a single protracted project, despite all the changes of direction, all the stylistic changes, all (to use his own term) the "ruptures."

HRP: Do you find that highly personal, revelatory style in, say, the second volume of *The History of Sexuality*, which for me is one of the keystones of what I have called Foucault's impersonal style? Even though he isn't writing within the recognized style or method of a discipline, he stills maintains this academic tone.

Nehamas: No, I don't find that self-revelatory style there. But I do find a great simplification of language in comparison to the first volume. All of a sudden the prose becomes much easier to read. In the introduction to the second volume, he says explicitly: "I've changed." He has had to "rework everything from top to bottom," and as to those who believe that such a change is a failure, he writes, "all I can say is that clearly we are not from the same planet." The language of the third volume is even simpler. It's important to realize that you don't need to be talking about yourself in order to reveal yourself. That is a major issue. Montaigne talks about himself. Nietzsche talks about himself in *Ecce Homo* and in his prefaces, but he doesn't do so very much in many of his other works. Of course, he always uses "I" and "we," but that's not the point. One reviewer of *The Art of Living* complained that the book says close to nothing about my personal life. That was silly. For, in this project to say who you are is to express your philosophical concerns, not how many children you have or what clothes you like to wear.

HRP: It's interesting that you've been saying that you can reveal yourself in your writing without talking about yourself, which seems to me one of the essential features of the way Nietzsche reads other philosophers.

Nehamas: Nietzsche has been horribly misunderstood in that respect. People think that when he writes in *Beyond Good and Evil* that every philosophy is an "unconscious memoir" of its author, he means we should treat philosophical texts as symptoms of an underlying psychological condition. But what he means is that most philosophies contain a picture of the life their authors espouse, admire, or want to avoid, and that seeing that picture is essential to understanding and evaluating a philosophy. When he says that every philosophy is an unconscious memoir, he isn't thinking of the philosopher's actual life, of a biography. He isn't saying that Kant believed this, that, or the other thing because he lived in Prussia, because he was a pietist, or because he liked to chew his meat, suck the juice out of it, and spit it out (someone has actually appealed to that to explain Kant's writing style!). He is saying that to understand Kant you must try to imagine what kind of life you would live if you accepted his views and lived according to them.

HRP: You frequently insist that the philosophical theses of Plato's dialogues should be interpreted in light of the literary techniques he uses to convey them, for instance, the Socratic *elenchus*, the other characters in the dialogue,

and so on. However, you rarely discuss one of the most transparently literary aspects of the dialogues, namely, the myths that Socrates tells in several
dialogues, especially the *Republic*. Do you think that the literary symbolism
of the Platonic myths has valid philosophical content?

Nehamas: One of the reasons I don't discuss the myths is that I don't really
understand their function. In general, I think, people don't talk about what
they don't understand. I have never been absolutely clear about the role
myths play in Plato's work. Actually, one of the first papers I wrote in
college was on Plato's myths, and I don't know anything more about
them now than I did then! In fact, it may be anachronistic to say that they
are the most self-consciously literary aspects of the dialogues. We think
of myth-telling as a literary device, and although the myths are clearly
a device of some sort for Plato to be distinguished from philosophical
argument, it doesn't follow that they are a literary device, since the distinction between literature and philosophy (which is not the same as the
distinction between poetry and philosophy) is not at all clearly marked in
the dialogues.

HRP: Then perhaps many of our contemporary interpretations of the style of
a philosophical treatise are anachronistic when applied to Plato.

Nehamas: There are features of the dialogues that are, so to speak, formal.
That's what I mean by irony or style. Those are the features I'm interested
in. I haven't really focused on the use of what we would explicitly consider
non-philosophical style to illustrate philosophical content. I actually do
have a theory about the myth of the *Phaedrus*. But I don't have a general
account of Plato's purpose in including these stories in the dialogues. They
do generally come in when an argument has reached its conclusion without
convincing everyone. Plato certainly thinks that stories have strong rhetorical powers, and perhaps he uses them when he knows his arguments are
for one reason or another inadequate. That suggests that Plato takes rhetoric more seriously and uses it more widely than many would expect, given
the criticism of rhetoric in the *Gorgias*. But we know from the *Phaedrus*
that he thinks that rhetoric is extremely important, and that one should
always tailor one's writing or speaking to the requirements of one's audience. So there's nothing wrong with Plato using rhetorical means for philosophical purposes. Personally, I find it difficult to think that he would write
the *Republic*, this immense book, and think that the myth that takes up its
last ten pages could ever replace what has preceded it. The myth is less
an alternative way to convince those who remain unmoved as it is a way
to give a memorable, lively, and moving summary of what he has accom-

plished. Still, I'm genuinely puzzled. I'd like to be able figure it out. So far, I have failed.

HRP: In *Nietzsche: Life as Literature* you discuss the various literary styles Nietzsche deploys, and the purposes for which he uses them. In this context you focus on two such styles, the aphorism and hyperbole. You suggest that the function of these styles is aristocratic, that the philosophical purpose of hyperbole is to present the view so forcefully that his readers cannot help but realize that it is explicitly Nietzsche's view. The desired effect, then, is that only people strong enough for perspectivism can read Nietzsche's hyperbole.

Nehamas: I'm not sure I would put any of this in terms of aristocracy or strength. I think once you realize Nietzsche's view is hyperbolic, that he is stating it in more extreme terms than he might have, you can't forget that it is his view. What you then go on to do is left open. You may decide that it's Nietzsche's view and also ridiculous; or you may decide that you will accept it precisely because it's Nietzsche's view (a silly reaction); you may decide, "Well, it is Nietzche's view: Do I agree with it? How shall I react to it? Is he right?" In the end, if you agree with him, you will be aware that you are agreeing with *him* and accepting part of his picture of life, and not just with some abstract truth that has no consequences for how you live. That, I think, is the rhetorical function of hyperbole; it is not particularly aristocratic.

HRP: Well, then, let's look at the aphorism. When Nietzsche talks about the aphorism at the beginning of *The Genealogy of Morals,* when he says that the aphorism always requires interpretation, he's not simply setting out his point. Also, hyperbole allows him to conceal the idea of perspectivism behind his literary method to such a point that you cannot help but realize how personal it is.

Nehamas: When you are faced with hyperbole, your first reaction is to find what it says silly. So, you ask, "Why is he shouting so much?" You need to interpret before you understand. It is the same with the aphorism: it doesn't wear its meaning on its face, and that's what Nietzsche is saying in the *Genealogy*: you need to do your own work in order to understand anything. But by doing your own work, you are, so to speak, changing yourself. So, again, the effect of both hyperbole and aphorism is to make you ask, not, "Does Nietzsche get it right?" but rather, "Who do I become as a result of trying to understand what he is saying?"

HRP: Aphorism and hyperbole seem to be two literary styles by which Nietzsche veils his precise philosophical meaning, in that he's not saying exactly what he means. In hyperbole, for instance, he says it so extravagantly that you can understand that it is his own view. With aphorism a certain level of interpretation is required on the reader's part. Do you find this interestingly similar to Socratic irony, at least in the early dialogues where Plato himself is trying to make out the riddle of Socrates? Given your interest in Nietzsche's lifelong relationship with Socrates, do you find any interesting similarities here?

Nehamas: Yes, there's a real connection here. There are so many ways in which Nietzsche and Socrates are mirror images of each other: hyperbole is for Nietzsche what understatement is to Socrates. Socrates is always putting himself down, admitting ignorance, saying, "I don't know, you tell me." Nietzsche, by contrast, is always, so to speak, "in your face:" he's always putting himself forward, always speaking as if he knows everything a little better than everyone else. But by using aphorisms, which, as he says, require a lot of interpretation, he makes it very difficult for you to know exactly what he's saying. Now, as I say in *The Art of Living*, it's never clear that ironists—and both aphorism and hyperbole have an element of irony in them—always know what they are saying. So, in a way, these literary strategies create a sense that Nietzsche himself is not that sure, that he himself is trying things out. On the one hand, you hear this voice of extraordinary certainty, and on the other, when you start listening carefully to its sound, you find that the mechanisms that express that great self-confidence also undermine it. In that way you realize that he is actually much less dogmatic a philosopher than he sounds! And since the content of his views is an attack on dogmatism, we have here once again a coalescence of style and substance. So, Nietzsche's strategies are Socratic because they are masks and because they are ironic and because they promote a tentativeness and a willingness to try out ideas that I find essential to the Socrates of the early dialogues. Also, they demand a personal response. Ideas shape life, because they are part of life, not something to be contrasted to it. Both Nietzsche and Socrates knew that, and make a central point of it.

HRP: In the *Nietzsche* book you consistently argue that, in Nietzsche's view, our relationship to the world can best be understood as the relationship of an interpreter to a text. As a particular instance of this, you write: "Nietzsche, I argue, looks at the world in general as a sort of artwork; in particular, he looks at it as if it were a literary text." Heidegger devotes the first volume of his lectures on Nietzsche to an interpretation of the will to power in terms of artistic creation: "Art is for us the most familiar and perspicuous configuration of the will to power.... But creation within art actually occurs in the productive activity of the artist." Do you think there are interesting conflicts between your desire to understand Nietzsche as thinking of our relationship to the world, and hence our will to power encountering the world, as bringing an interpretation to a text, and Heidegger's desire to understand will to power in terms of the act of artistic creation? Your model seems more one of spectatorship, though it could be argued that the interpretation is itself a creative act.

Nehamas: That's exactly what I was going to say. The most explicit and serious discussion we have of the will to power in Nietzsche is in the middle of *The Genealogy of Morals*, the very middle of the middle book, where he discusses punishment. He says that it is a universal law, even on the organic level, that in every event will to power operates. What does he use to illustrate that claim? Interpretation! For him, to create something is to interpret something else in a radically new way. There is no creation ex nihilo. That's in part what it is to be a historicist, something both he and Heidegger are. You are always faced with certain events, certain facts, certain objects, certain institutions that are given to you. What is it to be creative? It is to take these and, as we say, reinterpret them. What is it to reinterpret them? It is, so to speak, to put them to new uses. It is to see possibilities (now I speak in the language of the spectator) no one has seen before. But to see possibilities no one has seen before is, at the same time, to create something. "If a temple is to be erected, a temple must first be destroyed," as Nietzsche writes in the *Genealogy*. Nietzsche, I believe, would deny the distinction between spectatorship and creative ability. And although he often attacks Kant for looking at art, as he puts it, from the point of view of the spectator and not of the artist, he does not, in his own philosophy of art, leave the spectator behind. Instead, he tries to show that the spectator is a creative agent.

The big difference here (I don't know that Nietzsche would agree, I'm only stating my own view) is that, for Kant and a tradition that goes back to Cicero, our interaction with art involves a number of discrete stages. In Cicero there are four. In modern aesthetics, following Kant, there are two. First you interpret, that is, you understand; then you evaluate, that is, you judge. First you say, "This is what this poem is about," an activity we take to be mostly cognitive, with no creative aspect; then you decide whether the poem is or is not beautiful—nothing creative here, either. And then you're finished with it. For me, on the contrary, the judgment of beauty comes very early during our interaction with a work of art. Instead of thinking that the judgment of beauty is the culmination of criticism, I take it to be its origin. When you think that something is beautiful, you become interested in getting to know it better, to come to terms with it, to make it part of your life.

The judgment of taste, the statement, "this is beautiful," is not a conclusion we reach after we have interpreted a work of art; beauty, as Stendhal said, is "a promise of happiness"—a phrase that Nietzsche actually quotes in *The Genealogy of Morals*. To think that something is beautiful is to suspect, to guess, to have a sense that it has more to give you than you have been able to get out of it so far.

With Kant, you see, I think you do make your judgment at the end of your interaction with a work. When he says that the judgment of taste "is not governed by concepts," he means precisely that no description of an object implies that the object is beautiful (unless you beg the question and sneak in an evaluative term in your description). And although I agree with that, I think the reason the judgment doesn't follow is that it's not supposed to follow, because it's not a conclusion at all. When we see, read, hear, or are in any way exposed to something we find beautiful, we have a vague sense that there's something more we want to know about that thing, and that, whatever it is, it is valuable in some way we still don't know. The judgment of taste is prospective, not retrospective. It's a guess, a hypothesis. If it's a hypothesis, it goes behind the evidence; if it goes beyond the evidence, it can't follow from any of the features of the object we are already aware of. You find something beautiful as long as you feel you haven't exhausted it yet.

HRP: One of the most striking aspects of your writings on Nietzsche and Socrates is that you conclude that there runs through Nietzsche's writings an unresolved concern that his project is not so very different from Socrates', that he is not sure how original he is. Why does the similarity of their projects endanger the originality of Nietzsche's project?

Nehamas: It doesn't. I think he was afraid it did, because he wanted not only to, so to speak, appear different from other philosophers, he also wanted to be the first to have realized what philosophers were actually doing—but since I don't think there is one thing that all philosophers have always been doing, I don't think that's a problem. My sense is that the philosophical personality Nietzsche created and left behind was itself an immense accomplishment. That should have given him enough satisfaction. But perhaps it didn't; perhaps he wanted to accomplish even more.

That's not the same as saying that he was a miserable man, however. Another reviewer of *The Art of Living* objected that Nietzsche led a wretched life, and that he couldn't possibly set an example for us to follow: "I wouldn't wish that life on anyone," he wrote, "not even Rousseau." I was wondering what that could mean. Does it make sense to say, "I wouldn't wish that life on anyone"? That could mean you wouldn't wish anyone else to be Nietzsche. Well, of course no one else could be Nietzsche! That's trivial. But it could mean that it would have been better for Nietzsche if he had never lived. And that's clearly false—false for Nietzsche, and also false for us. People who believe that think of the "life" of philosophers as everything other than their work. But that's silly. Nietzsche's life is inextricably tied up with the writing of his books: the books are as central a part of his life as any—perhaps its most central part. The question is not, "Was Nietzsche's life apart from his work 'good', would you like to have had his migraines, and his near-sightedness, and his disappointments, and so on?" Well, of course not! Who in his right mind would want just the headaches and to vomit all the time and not to see where one is going? The question, really, is, "Were all the miseries justified and transformed through the work, does the whole constitute a worthwhile life, a life with significance?" And if that's what it took for him to have been able to write these great books, you might want to say that it wasn't such a bad life after all. Nietzsche flourished, even though he was unhealthy; he succeeded as a human being, even if his books didn't sell.

HRP: In *The Art of Living* you say that the philosophy of the art of living is still alive and worth pursuing again. This sounds a bit like a manifesto. What, in your opinion, is the state of the art of living today, and are there contemporary philosophers whom you consider in this light?

Nehamas: It's not an easy thing to live philosophically. Interestingly enough, most of the philosophers who belong to that tradition by and large did not belong to institutions. Socrates may have had a career—he may have been a stonemason—but by the time we meet him in Plato's early dialogues, he doesn't have a career—not even a job. Montaigne, famously, retired from his political career at thirty-eight and closeted himself in his library before he began writing the *Essays*. It turns out he was probably more active than he admits, but his life was very different from what it must have been when he was mayor of Bordeaux. Nietzsche was a professor, but most of his philosophical work appeared only after he resigned from the university and lived on his own small private income. Foucault always had a very ambivalent position toward, and relationship with, institutions. I don't think it's very easy to lead a life that's both philosophical and individualist inside an institution. So I find myself in a very difficult position, because I want to be able to say "Look, it's possible to combine individualism with life in an institution"—what am I doing teaching at a university, after all? And since the people I am writing about mostly stayed outside institutions, that makes me extremely uneasy. Then I think of Wittgenstein, who was Knight-bridge Professor of Philosophy of Cambridge—but he hated it!

Institutional obligations are generic, whereas the art of living, as I see it, imposes mostly individual requirements. What I would like to do is see if one could put the two together. What I'm trying to do, if you don't mind my being somewhat personal, is to bring together all the academic things I know—philosophy, criticism, the classics—and write in a way informed by all three, give them a kind of coherence, thematically and stylistically. Many philosophers are not interested in that sort of coherence, and I don't think they have to be. The question you asked goes to the heart of the matter: is it possible to do what I want to do and still belong to an institution? The answer is that I don't know and I probably never will. I am simply try-ing to do it.

HRP: What about an institution contributes to the art of living?

Nehamas: Not very much, I think. An institution, as I said, imposes generic obligations. Then, again, I think of Nietzsche, who wrote that every creation requires the existence of some kind of "tyranny," some institution, from which it emerges. Everyone is bound by constraints in one way or another. Historically, people who belong to the individualist tradition in the art of liv-ing generally avoid institutions. Dogmatic or universalist philosophers belong to schools and institutions—the Stoics, for example, often actually lived together, of course they were trying to formulate and follow a form of life common to all. The people I am interested in have tried to live different-ly from everyone else. It may be, after all, that I'm trying to have it both ways, and I can't. But that won't stop me from trying!

HRP: What are you working on now?

Nehamas: I am thinking about beauty. I am wondering why beauty and aes-thetics have come back to the center of intellectual discussion in the last few years. I'm not quite sure why. One thing I do know is that many people are trying to render these issues philosophically respectable by arguing that beauty leads to justice, goodness, or truth. I don't believe that. I'm interest-ed in a more independent justification of the importance of beauty, just as I believe we need an independent justification of the humanities: I don't think we should say to students that studying the humanities will make them more moral or get them a better job. Being moral or rich may be goods, but they are not the only goods. Studying the humanities, like admiring beauty, makes you a better person, but becoming more moral is not the only way of becoming better. Moral goodness does not exhaust human goodness. I believe we have neglected the domain of non-moral goodness. I believe aesthetic values are values in their own right—that beauty, complexity, style, elegance are virtues that need to be respected and loved for themselves, and counted among the components of a worthwhile human life. By making the arts, and the humanities, parts of our lives, we introduce such virtues into them; we make ourselves more complex, more interesting, more engaging people. That doesn't mean we become morally worse; it doesn't mean we become morally better, either. I believe there is an irreducible aesthetic element in life, and we need to pay much more attention to it than we have done so far. We should not disavow it simply because it's not identical with moral value or worldly success.

HRP: Isn't that tied in with a contemporary concern with the aestheticization of politics? That seems to be one of the ways the idea of beauty you're talking about is often criticized.

Nehamas: I don't want to "aestheticize" politics—that's both dangerous and inefficient. The aesthetic is more or less—I don't want to draw too strong a distinction here—a private rather than a public matter: "private" may even be too strong; perhaps I should say "personal," which involves a reference to other persons without involving one's whole political or social context.

HRP: How did you become interested in relating these issues of beauty to television and talking about television as an art form in a way that many philosophers of art and art critics are unwilling to do?

Nehamas: When I was writing *Nietzsche: Life as Literature* I was subletting an apartment with a color TV, which I had never had. Since I was too tired to read in the evenings, I would watch a lot of it, and eventually I said to myself, "Either I will have wasted a lot of my life watching TV, or I will have to make something of it"—actually, of course, it wasn't at all that explicit: that's how I came to see it somewhat later. I realized that a lot of TV was interesting and sophisticated. Some television shows were more satisfying than a lot of works in the more canonical genres and media: some television was better than some poetry; some television was better than some novels; some television was better than some sonatas. Our mistake is that we look down (or admire) a whole medium. That's a stupid thing to do. You have to look at individual works. But looking at individual works is always dangerous, because if their medium is in fact perverse and degrading, you may become perverse and degraded without realizing it, and even love what you have become. You change, and it's not always clear whether you've changed for the better or the worse—in this case, your very view of the character of those who watch TV changes: you can't look down on them in the way you might have before.

HRP: I take it you're referring to a view you once held?

Nehamas: I was a real snob about it. I grew up in a country with no TV. So, on one hand, it was really exciting for me to have it when I came to America; on the other, intellectuals were supposed to look down on it. Despite my contempt, however, I eventually found myself engaged by it. It's shocking and rather frightening to find yourself captured by something you had only contempt for. You wonder, what standards should I use? Those I had before I was captivated, which tell me that being captivated is bad for me, or those I have as a result of being captivated, which tell me that thinking that being captivated is bad for me is silly and ignorant? And you don't know.

I'm particularly interested in the connection between aesthetic and popular art forms. One of the most common developments in the history of art is that the popular art of one era, which is denounced and solidly excluded from proper social and intellectual life, becomes the fine art of the next. So when the novel first appeared in England, for example, it was taken to be an absolutely horrible genre. Coleridge attacked it: compared to Shakespeare, he said, reading novels is not "pass-time but kill-time." But in Elizabethan times, there was Henry Prynne, saying that Shakespeare attracts and creates only "ruffians and adulterers." Now Shakespeare is as close to the divine as any human being could ever be. The same thing happened with cinema, jazz, photography, rock-and-roll. What is popular, and there-fore pronounced harmful in one period is transformed into a standard of beauty a short while later.

You were talking of Plato's relevance earlier. Plato's attack on the poets in the *Republic* is the origin and the essence of all later attacks on popular cul-ture and entertainment. Plato, as usual, was much more honest than anyone else; unlike all those who say, for example, that television has no aesthetic value whatsoever, he admitted that despite his contempt he loved Homer but would stay away from him because he found him harmful. People today, either because they are ashamed or because they don't bother to look, will not admit that they are attracted to popular culture. But even television is gradually becoming acceptable: we can now blame everything on the Internet instead! In the eighteenth century they thought that reading kills. Literally! People wrote that reading—reading!—causes arthritis, epilepsy, pul-monary disease, and apoplexy! But if reading is bad for you, everything is bad for you. The right reaction is to realize that the difference is not in a genre or a medium, but in the way each one of us makes use of the individ-ual works a genre or medium offers.

Something similar is true of what we have been calling "the art of living." Each one of us, necessarily, confronts different situations, different choices, different circumstances from everyone else. They are bound to include both happiness and misfortune. What matters in the end is what we are able to make of them, whether through them we can live a life that is truly our own. φ

Cora Diamond

Cora Diamond has taught and written on Wittgenstein for over thirty years, and her work has exercised a decisive influence on the way Wittgenstein has come to be read by American philosophers. She has edited Wittgenstein's *Lectures on the Foundations of Mathematics* and has written over a dozen articles directly concerning Wittgenstein, the earliest of these "Secondary Sense" published in 1966 and, more recently, "How Old Are These Bones?" in 1999 and "How Long Is the Standard Meter in Paris?" 2001. She is widely regarded as one of the leading contemporary scholars of Wittgenstein. But to regard Diamond simply as a scholar of Wittgenstein is to miss the significance of her writings, and to misunderstand the influence of Wittgenstein's thought in contemporary American philosophy. For what is notable about Diamond's work is the relative rarity with which she engages in the explication of Wittgenstein's writings simply for the sake of scholarship. Rather, such explications are closely bound to her arguments about nettlesome problems in contemporary philosophy, even problems, such as animal ethics, of which Wittgenstein seems to have been unaware.

Diamond's route into professional philosophy bears a strong resemblance to Wittgenstein's own. Diamond took her undergraduate degree in mathematics, began graduate study in economics at MIT, and worked as a computer programmer for IBM before going to Oxford to take a B. Phil in philosophy (Wittgenstein worked as an engineer before going to Cambridge to take up philosophy). Like Wittgenstein, Diamond never went through a traditional doctoral program, a professional choice no doubt related to that aspect of her thought that most resembles Wittgenstein's: a wide-ranging sensibility characterized by a distinct lack of "churlishness" in the problems Diamond sets herself and the ways in which she unravels them. Diamond lectured in the United Kingdom for a decade (at the Universities of Swansea, Sussex, and Aberdeen), before taking a position in 1971 at the University of Virginia, where she still teaches.

Diamond is best known for her work *The Realistic Spirit: Wittgenstein, Philosophy, and the Mind*. Published in 1991, *The Realistic Spirit* is a collection of essays beginning with the aforementioned "Secondary Sense" of 1966. The book was one long in the making, and it reflects the diverse range of topics that have occupied Diamond in the course of her philosophical development, a development again like Wittgenstein's in its seemingly sudden shifts of focus that belie a set of deep and underlying concerns. The best example of that aspect of Diamond's thought is perhaps her treatment of the *Tractatus Logico-Philosophicus* and the *Philosophical Investigations*. The two books often look to be as different in their methods and themes as any two philosophical works could be, and they have generally been read by two quite separate groups of philosophers, each with radically different concerns. Diamond, on the other hand, has taken seriously Wittgenstein's dictum that the *Investigations* can be understood only in the light of the *Tractatus*. Thus Diamond writes, in a passage that is central to understanding her view of these two works as well as to her view of Wittgenstein's importance more generally:

> Whether one is reading Wittgenstein's *Tractatus* or his later writings, one must be struck by his insistence that he is not putting forward philosophical doctrines or theses; or by his suggestion that it cannot be done. . . . I think there is almost nothing in Wittgenstein which is of value and which can be grasped if it is pulled away from that view of philosophy. But that view of philosophy is itself something that has to be seen first in the *Tractatus* if it is to be understood in its later forms.

One of the consequences of Diamond's work, then, has been to convince many of her contemporaries of the inseparability of Wittgenstein's early and later work; another, no less significant, has been to bring Wittgensteinian ways of thinking to bear on ethical problems. Ethics is an area on which Wittgenstein seems to have had nothing to say, and in a post-*Tractatus* lecture he insists that there is nothing sayable about it at all. The last five essays of Diamond's *The Realistic Spirit*, however, are concerned explicitly with ethical problems, namely, with animal ethics, the relation between ethics and literature, and the role of argument in ethics. The last of these topics is the one where Diamond's Wittgensteinian bent shows itself most clearly, particularly in her view that argument is but *one* of the myriad means of persuasion by which one can convince another of one's views. But one of the lessons of *The Realistic Spirit* is that *all* of these essays are, in subtle ways, indebted to Wittgenstein (showing precisely *how* they are so related is one of the projects of the book). Understanding how this can be so requires a reader of Diamond to give up the idea that Wittgenstein sets forth certain topics to think about (and still less *limits* the scope of such topics) in favor of the view that what Wittgenstein's writings teach is, above all, a *way* of thinking about whatever problems philosophers, contemporary or future, come to encounter. φ

Cora Diamond
"What Time Is It on the Sun?"

Interview by
Simon Dedeo
in 1999

HRP: What I want to begin with is an aspect of your work I find particularly interesting: your notion of the riddle, and the idea that certain philosophical questions can be recast as riddles. At what point in time do we take a riddle to be nonsense? It seems that Wittgenstein would want to reject some riddles as nonsense in the *Investigations*. At what point in time is Wittgenstein, to take a term from one of your essays, Anselm's fool?

Diamond: Well I think—that's a difficult question, in some ways—we should begin, not with a philosophical question, but, rather, "what time is it on the sun?" Which is one of Wittgenstein's examples in the *Investigations*. I think he wants to suggest that we reject that riddle in the same way we might reject the philosophical questions we ask. Somebody might well want to reject the question "what time is it on the sun?" as a question we don't want to do anything with.

On the other hand, it's possible to imagine somebody picking up that question and doing something with it that we didn't see—so that when that person gives the answer, we say "Yes!"—as it were—"you've done something really wonderful with the phrase." So I think the suggestion is that with philosophical questions we're not laying down what you might not, ever, make something of, but that sometimes we say that this is not a question we want to do anything with at this point. It's just a phrase that we've put together by analogy with other phrases that we use. We don't know what to do with it, even though it attracts us; it doesn't fit in with any of the activities of our language that we're familiar with.

HRP: In your work you discuss the idea of the answer to the riddle having a "goodness of fit" that somehow seems correct—some clever thing comes up. It seems that the way we sense a "goodness of fit" is similar to the way, in reading Austin, one senses a rightness in what he's saying, a satisfaction with the way he's put it. Do you sense a connection there? In the satisfaction of reaching a—surprised—agreement?

Diamond: I think somehow Austin thought that the resources of the language deliver an answer. I'm not sure of that.

HRP: That there's no refashioning of the language?

Diamond: There's no, as it were, imaginative further step that we're taking.

HRP: When reading your article on Anselm about riddles, it seems as if you're dealing with a very particular kind of riddle. Whereas, one could pose a riddle such as "there's one man that always lies, one that always tells the truth. . . . "

Diamond: Yes.

HRP: And that would seem to me to be a very different kind of riddle from the one you deal with in the Anselm article, because it can be solved by logical means alone. There's no revisioning of the language that's needed there. What might the connections between these different riddles mean? What is the relation of this kind of riddle to the one you're holding up for examination?

Diamond: I don't think this is a matter of trying to find a definite line with things going one side, things going on the other. Wittgenstein somewhere says is it the case that the use of a word, the use of the same word, is significant in that it shows us how to play the game. In the case of some riddles, the familiarity of the word does not show us what to do with it.

I think here of a passage from the *Investigations*, section 563, where Wittgenstein asks, if we use the king in chess to draw lots to see who goes first, we will count that as part of the role of the piece in chess. The idea would be that if there's an essential connection, it has to do with the fact that you recognize from the fact that the piece is the king what you're going to do with it in this new context.

Whereas in Austin's case, say, the words "accident" and "mistake" I think are supposed to show you what you're supposed to do. The identity of the words is supposed to deliver the answer to the problem. Yet that's just what we don't have in the case of what we're more inclined to identify as riddles—we don't have the identity of the words delivering to us what we're trying to do.

One of the examples I used in that riddle paper was from the upbringing of my niece, when she was eighteen months or so, when my sister told her, "kiss your elbow." She struggled to do it—but it was clear what she was meant to do. And there the identity of the words kiss and elbow, which you're already familiar with, tell you what you're meant to do, only you can't do it. And then my sister said, "kiss your ear." Now what my niece did was kiss her hand and put it to her ear. There the identity of the piece does not tell her at all how to interpret the command. And so she invents a solution to the riddle.

HRP: In a sense, that solution wasn't invented for the elbow because the other was too close to being possible.

Diamond: It's so clear, one might say, what you're meant to do. Whereas in the other case the identity of the words doesn't tell you what you're meant to do at all. One of Wittgenstein's own examples is, "what color is the looking glass?" And again, you know the pieces, "looking glass" and "color." And yet the identity of the pieces doesn't tell you at all how to answer that question. And that's the one that's more analogous to the philosophical question.

HRP: Another question I find interesting in your work is the relation of skepticism in Wittgenstein, and skeptical treatments of Wittgenstein, to your criticism of Singer's argument for vegetarianism. Reading that criticism, it's as if you're dealing with a certain kind of moral skepticism. One person simply doesn't believe that there is any question of morality; it isn't even that she questions the degree. To make the analogy, it isn't the way in which the table is real, but rather that one person claims not to believe there's a table there at all. What do you see as the relation between morality and skepticism here?

Diamond: This is a complicated question because with skepticism in the senses in which we take it as central, skepticism about the external world, about other minds, and so on, there is, as Cavell has pointed out, a question of how we are with others and how we actually are responding to them. And we, as it were, mislocate that as a cognitive issue. So I do want to suggest that it's wrong to just take standard skeptical issues, if I can refer to them as such, as straightforwardly cognitive. They were presented as cognitive, but the cognitive issue is not necessarily the only one. This, I take it, is one of the things that Cavell points out.

On the other hand what I do want to suggest is that, within what goes wrong with philosophical treatments of ethics, we're beginning with those parts of ethical thinking that we take to be puzzlingly analogous (to a degree) to what we consider to be straightforwardly cognitive activities. And I'm going to regard those "cognitive" issues as straightforwardly cognitive although, if I were to focus on them, the whole issue of their being cognitive would have to be examined. So we look at questions of what ethical judgment someone is making as central, and, focusing on that in our philosophical puzzle, we ask whether it's objective, we ask what it is for it to be rational, we look for some kind of construction of what it is to be "rational," "unbiased." I think that this is central to Singer—it's partly derivative from Hare's work.

Anyway, we end up not looking at those elements of ethical thinking that are really at some distance from anything analogous to the cases of judgments about the world and about other people. What I have in mind is the way in which someone's ethical thinking can come out in the kind of factual description he gives.

A very obvious kind of example would be Primo Levi's descriptions of life in Auschwitz, where he, on the whole, does not use moral language very much. It's straightforward descriptive language. Then again, it's not such straightforward descriptive language, because there's moral passion in the way in which he is constructing that description. His moral passion is coming through in his use of "factual language." The idea that descriptions can have that kind of moral tension in them, and in that way reflect the kind of being that the speaker or writer is, doesn't quite match anything within the range of issues that we're looking at in, let's say, classical skeptical questions.

There's another example—I'm not sure exactly how to move from the example to the question, but let me develop the example and then try to move there. There's a recent book by the South African writer Coetzee about animals, and our lives in relation to animals. It was given as a series of lectures and among the people that responded was Peter Singer; the lectures and responses were published in a single volume later on. Coetzee's lectures are in the form of a fiction about a lecturer in English literature who is obsessed with the deep going evil that comes out in how we use animals and close our minds to it. Singer sees this simply as a peculiar way to state an argument. He cannot see this as ethical thinking. In his response he understands Coetzee's book to be as if someone thought: this is my argument—how shall I put it into words?—well, I might as well make it a fictional narrative.

What Coetzee is really doing is taking it that prior to, and in some degree independent of, our attempts to find the solutions to ethical problems, is the kind of being-in-the-world (if you want a phrase) that includes responsiveness to striking and puzzling and hurtful features of our lives. Someone can go through life with a wound—the wound being the question what can it mean, the way in which we relate to animals.

That's, I think, what I'm trying to get at in what Coetzee is doing. He's trying to ask questions about where we are coming from, what our life is from which we come, and asking us to forget about this whole business of should we do this, or should we do that. What Singer wants to do is see the rational, ethical creature as concerned with should we do this or should we do that, what are the arguments for this, what are the arguments for that. And in this way he isn't able to respond to Coetzee's work as anything else.

Now I don't know that there is something. Maybe that is analogous to things that Cavell is saying about our relationship to other human beings and the way in which it gets changed and distorted in the representations of skeptical questioning.

HRP: When I was reading about the idea of the escape from the thrall of metaphysics, I read that as an escape from the thrall of skepticism. That suddenly we don't have to be obsessed by the particular language in which we are asked to arrive at a proof of the table, if you like.

Diamond: Well I see the issues of philosophy often in terms of what the conditions are for our being able to speak about the table. This is really the same question from a different angle. I'm very interested in the kinds of ways in which people do what I take to be misreadings of Wittgenstein, seeing him as laying down conditions for sense. And so in that sense, in that kind of misreading, we're still looking at the skeptical issue, but from another direction. Instead of saying can we or can't we actually make claims about the table, we ask what the conditions are for which we can make true or false claims about the table, and we go on: we have to have agreement in judgment, we have to have this, we have to have that, we have to be playing a language game in which there are these features.

So I think what I want to resist there, what I see as metaphysical, is the notion of what has to be in order for us to do such and such, to see Wittgenstein as theorizing in that kind of way. Now to see him theorizing so is to see him in connection, in very close connection, with the kind of skeptical issues you're talking about.

HRP: In your treatment of Anselm's riddle you discuss Malcolm's argument that uses Wittgenstein to show that the fool's claim is incoherent, and you make the analogy with the pseudoargument that one can't regard the God of the Old Testament as a genocidal maniac because in this language game, "God is good." And therefore, the argument goes, you're "outside the game," you're "no longer playing." But then in your essay on eating meat, you write: "it is not morally wrong to eat our pets, people who ate their pets would have not have pets in the same sense of the term. If we call an animal we're fattening for the table a pet we're making a crude joke of a familiar nature." It seems to me that if we can have an evil God of the Old Testament, why can't we eat our pets?

Diamond: That's an interesting question. What I want to say here is that there's no short way with the kinds of clash that arise between people who think in different ways. In this case, I think Malcolm is making too short work of a genuine conflict. This actually comes up for me—it's a very, very interesting and, I think, important question—in a paper that I've just finished a draft of. There, I was asked to do a paper on Wittgenstein's lectures on religious belief. Which have been taken to contain Wittgenstein's stating that the believer and the unbeliever cannot contradict each other—it's very close to the Malcolm view that you refer to.

What Wittgenstein actually does in the lectures is imagines people who have a belief in the Last Judgment who ask him, "do you believe it to be right or wrong?" "I can't respond," he says, "I can't say this man is wrong." He, as I see it, is responding in a very personal way there. He's not saying nobody could say they're wrong. He's saying that's not the move that he sees himself as being in a position to make in response to them, that he's just nowhere with what they say.

I don't think you can move from that to any claim that if you're in one language game you cannot contradict people in another, that you cannot get a genuine clash. These clashes are interesting and hard to describe, and are often among the most poignant kinds of clashes.

For example, I've seen people claim that Jews and Christians are not genuinely contradicting each other about whether the Messiah has already come and whether Jesus was the Messiah. That the claim is that within the Jewish language game they have one way of talking about the Messiah; in the Christian language game they have another way. So for these people there is no genuine contradiction. This seems to me to really miss what's going on, just as, in the case of the view of the God of the Old Testament as a genocidal maniac, to say that you can't really say that is to miss the argument that the person is trying to make. It may be that because people are not using words in the same way, getting at the kind of conflict is difficult. Yet it's wrong to say, "O there's a kind of genuine contradiction, I have a logical insight into the nature of contradiction, and according to my logical insight, you can't have one of those if you're playing different language games."

Now in the case of if it's your pet, you can't eat it, I do certainly want to allow for genuine contradiction between different ways of thinking about animals. I think that in the case of trying to get clear what's going on in such a conflict, one should be aware of the problems in using the language. And indeed there could be—I don't think there is—a way of talking about animals where people actually used the word pet, the English word pet, and their language and lives had diverged from ours and there was a real clash between their mode of thought about animals and ours that emerged in their use of the word pet. Which we shared with them, but then we didn't share it, like the way Christians and Jews share and do not share the word Messiah.

I don't think that is the case with the word pet. I think that the conflicts that we have there don't focus on that word. And within the context of trying to think about this issue philosophically, probably that's not the word to focus on.

HRP: In these discussions, the question is pushed more toward that of how close two people have to be before they're "playing the same game."

Diamond: Yes—and I think that this issue of "playing the same game" has been taken up in philosophy and overused. One thing I would want to say is that in Wittgenstein's own use of it, often what he's calling "the same game" or "a different game" is spoken of with a view to the particular philosophical problem he has in mind. So why should we say—or why should he say, as he does in some lectures—that when you're talking about, "I remember X," this is one game if we're talking about, say, "I remember getting off the train at the station this morning" (where other people can bear you out, and so on), and it's another if you're saying, "I remember thinking of X just before I did so and so." That's a different game because there's no interpersonal, intersubjective complication there.

Why call it a "different game"? Because he's talking with people who think that memory is some one thing. That there's a sort of essence of memory. And within the context of thinking of memory as a particular mental process that you're trying to focus on, it might be useful to say "this is one game, this another." In a different context, why not just speak about the ways we speak about memory as a game?

To get back to the issue of "are we talking the same game, how close do we have to be," I think many of our disagreements involve complex disagreements in the ways in which we apply words. I don't think that we're going to get very far by trying to say that we're not playing the same game and so we're not genuinely disagreeing.

HRP: We're forcing an end to the argument prematurely, so to speak.

Diamond: Yes. There's a discussion that has been going on involving Hilary Putnam and a couple of papers this past summer, one of mine, one of Steve Gerard's, on issues that Putnam has raised partly in response to Dick Rorty.

You raised the question about when it is that people can disagree with each other if they're playing "different games." The issue we were involved with is the question of when can we say that people are agreeing with each other if "they're playing different games." The example that Putnam inherited from Rorty—or, rather, it's Putnam's example, but it's in response to a Rorty example where somebody utters in the tenth century the Latin sentence that later on Newton uses in stating one of the laws of motion. According to Rorty we can say he uttered a true sentence, but it would be better—that's to say we would be pragmatically in better shape—if we were to follow what he takes to be the Heideggerian view that we're not going to regard the sentence as either true or false if it's really just a sentence that has no role whatsoever within the context of the people who utter it.

So there's this tenth-century sentence: it's identical with the seventeenth-century sentence, but to call it true is simply to pay ourselves a queer kind of compliment. That's the Rorty line. Putnam's example is to suppose that in the seventeenth century some bones are dug up and someone there speculates "these bones, I wonder if they're possibly millions of years old." Now we know that these bones are millions of years old—we, now. Can we say that he was right without it being merely that we are again, as it were, paying ourselves this compliment?

What we don't want, if we're Putnam, is to say that what makes this an agreement, what makes it correct to say, "yes, he got it right" is that the person is in relation to some Platonic entity, namely, a proposition thought of as something that is timeless and independent of our existence altogether. He doesn't want to go down that route. But why should we not just take him to be saying something that connects up with what we are saying? In the sense that what he is saying, as a guess, is something that we now know to be correct. So that there's a use of a "what" clause—what he said, we now know to be correct. Without sort of reifying that into propositionality up in Platonic heaven.

So there you have the converse question of how close we have to be to disagree; and here we have the case of how close do we have to be to agree. This is connected up, for Putnam, with questions like this: suppose that in the seventeenth century the way in which people tell something is water is quite different from the way in which a chemist today would; that does not mean that we cannot take the word water, as they ordinarily use it, to be saying things that we can understand, that what they say is incommensurate with what we say. And I think the issues there of relationship across linguistic activities, across all these different language games—well, why not say that language games are different in many respects that we could list? I mean, they do do things that we don't do, they do have different criteria from ours. Okay, fine, but this doesn't mean we can't agree just as the difference in criteria doesn't mean that there isn't something we can well describe as disagreement.

This has been a very long-winded account! But I do want to say that agreement and disagreement are something we see and we don't have to postulate some kind of logical underpinnings in terms of language games or something else—propositions in Platonic heaven—to make sense of our relationship to others as agreement or disagreement.

HRP: In that same vein, I think about the example you take of Orwell, being unable to shoot a fascist running across the line of fire holding up his pants. You imagine his lieutenant saying, nonsense, just shoot him, he's a fascist. There you understand they're disagreeing without even getting to the question of, say, what propositions the lieutenant and Orwell hold in common.

Diamond: Peter Winch has a long and interesting discussion of an issue that is like this. Orwell has an essay where he's immensely critical of Gandhi—it begins with the wonderful sentence, "saints should be presumed guilty until proved innocent." Anyway, Orwell and Gandhi obviously, in many ways, think quite differently from each other. Their thoughts about social and political issues run in very different directions. What Winch wants to suggest is that you can't say because they're playing different language games there isn't a genuine conflict of view. You can't, as it were, set up boundaries in the kind of ways we try to do in philosophy.

HRP: To take up a different subject for the moment, your discussion of the *Tractatus*, and the "mythologizing" that goes on there: it seems as if one could make the case that, where Wittgenstein, in the *Investigations*, does suggest that words have a "home," a home from which they may be displaced, we might take this idea to be a new "myth"? That, again, we are placing limits on what language might be, might look like?

Diamond: Ah, well there you have another dangerous, complex word that crept in there: limit. Although, obviously, there is the notion of the limits of language in the *Tractatus*, there is also the very serious question of what, in particular, is going on with that notion. Because Wittgenstein isn't suggesting there that there's some limit to what we might do with words. What he is suggesting there is that we often take ourselves to be having intentions of doing something in language that is not thought through and that is self-defeating in a certain kind of way, such that pushing further on those intentions will lead us ultimately to see that we didn't want to say anything at all, to withdraw, to move backwards from that route.

In a sense the language itself is not limited in that, if there's something that you want to say, then you can say it. This is why I think that "what you can't speak of, you have to be silent about" reduces to "what you can't say, you can't say." And it's not that there's some content, there's the "what" that you can't say and you can't say that. I think ultimately that it's just, if you find out you're not saying anything, then you're not saying anything. There's not a genuine, peculiar kind of content that you cannot express. There is the notion of the limit as you get it in other thinkers, for example, in Russell, where you do have a notion of "what's out there," and we just can't get there; we are, in some sense, "back behind something." And I don't think that's the picture of the limits of language that you're getting in the *Tractatus*.

On the other hand, it is equally true that there are many uses of language that he is not considering as, in a sense, interesting—say, for example, the use of language in poetry. Obviously he himself is a reader of poetry, but he's saying nothing at all about those uses. And, in a sense, he's leaving them alone. There's a letter he wrote to the person he hoped would publish his book, and Wittgenstein writes there that the part of the book he didn't write was the most important. So there he isn't writing about many other uses of words that don't count, it's true, don't count as language in the sense in which the *Tractatus* takes language.

I want to go back and look at the original notion of mythology as it turns up, in Wittgenstein, as a term of criticism for what we invent when we won't look at the kinds of ways we do use words. Here I'm thinking in particular about the kinds of ways in which this shows up in a person like Kripke, in the idea that what we want, in our use of words, is to make certain kinds of connection with meanings that will enable us to have a clear answer to any question. That will give us clear answers to whether some term or other applies to some case, say. For Kripke, if we can't make contact with those things, then we're landed in some kind of skeptical situation: we don't have the fixity of meaning that we thought was necessary to make sense of what we say. What Kripke can't do is look at the kinds of ways in which, for example, to shift to another of his cases, we don't need to have to be making some kind of contact with a length, as it were, conceived as something independent of the footrule, in order to measure something.

You know the Wittgenstein remark where we see the signpost as a piece of wood, we see it as dead when we abstract it from some kind of life. It's as if, from Kripke's point of view, what we need is something that has it in it to indicate a direction. And a piece of wood does not have that, as we see it; it doesn't have it in it. Therefore, Kripke isn't looking at the fact that people respond, within this activity, to certain kinds of pieces of wood that are placed in some activity and that are used in certain ways. What he's laying down is that, in order for us genuinely to have a bit of information about where to go, we have to have a direction indicator—and a piece of wood cannot be that. Again, a piece of wood can only be, for us, a measure of a foot because it has a certain length—namely, a foot—and so it is, for us, a sample of something that is independent of it.

There is, as it were, "the length one foot," which is what we really need when making a measurement. We need to make contact with that length— the comparison with this particular dead piece of wood won't do. So Kripke isn't interested in the fact that we have games in which we make comparisons with pieces of wood, he isn't interested in how that game goes; what he is doing is saying that in order to measure we have to make connections with something that has it in it to tell us how long things are. In order to mean something, we must make contact with some meaning, which will tell us whether we're applying the word correctly or not. So in all these cases, what he's doing is laying down what we need in order to genuinely make sense of our activities rather than being able to turn his attention to the "home" of the words—to use this notion of home—to turn his attention to the notion of the everyday. So if you want to call this a kind of displacement—I'm not sure what's getting displaced, the words or the man—it's as if he got, somehow out of connections with his own activities, his own life.

HRP: I'd like to return to the notion of the riddle in philosophy for a moment, and to the example you take in an essay where Orwell cannot shoot the fascist—you can turn that into a riddle, it might go "when is a fascist not a fascist?" How far can one go here in making any question that seems philosophical into a riddle?

Diamond: I think that's interesting. One of the things that Wittgenstein does is to say at one point that what he's doing as a philosopher is trying to let you see certain things together and see certain things as distant. He's sort of changing the ways in which you see things. It's reported in Moore's notes of the 1933 lectures when he's talking about ethics and aesthetics. There, he notes that, in an aesthetic argument, one is putting things "here, rather than there," one is moving things: you are looking at it this way, let me invite you to look at it that way. And that's very close to your case, look at him as a fascist, look at him as a man. The way of seeing this man as a fascist, as enemy, is connected up with certain kinds of ways in which one does respond, and seeing this person as a fellow human being is then seeing the situation in a totally different way. We're reorganizing one's perception of the situation here, where one's perception connects up with the ways in which one understands which ways are right and appropriate responses.

Of course, there may be many notions we may use of shifts in our understanding of a situation, shifts in our understanding of, even, how we use language in a situation-riddle might be very good for some of those, but let's not necessarily group them all together.

HRP: What are you currently working on? What's occupying your mind right now?

Diamond: Well, there's what I'd like to get back to, and then there's what I'm in the position of having to work on at the moment. I mentioned a paper that I had to write for a conference on Wittgenstein and religious belief, and so that's something that's not quite finished, but that's not something that I myself would have chosen.

I'm supposed to be giving a paper for the APA in December [1999] and I must very soon decide what I want to do about that. One of the things I'd really like is to follow up on a notion of unfolding truth. Let me talk a little bit about that.

Frege has arguments against trying to give any kind of definition of what truth consists in. He says at one point that the concept of truth is unfolded by the laws of logic, and he says similar things later on. So there is this idea that we understand what truth is when we understand the normative structures of the thinking that is tied to truth. Now, that notion of unfolding truth is very, very interesting. You reject the idea of a theory of truth, of a correspondence theory, of a coherence theory, of a redundance theory. (Although there are elements of Frege that have been developed and led to the redundancy theory, I don't think that's really what you should ascribe to him.) Instead, you have this idea of unfolding truth by laying out what it is to be involved in thinking directed at truth, what are the norms of this activity.

HRP: What you're doing when you determine the truth of something.

Diamond: Right—what do you do when you give justification for your statements. That's subject to—if you're giving justifications—the laws of logic. And, in that way, if you are justifying what you say, what's internal to that is that you are seeking to establish a truth. So what it is to show that something is true is tied to what truth is, and you make clear what truth is, therefore, by showing the norms that we recognize when we try to establish truth.

I think that Wittgenstein in the *Tractatus* rejects the notion that you have laws of logic which play the role they do for Frege. For Wittgenstein, you can use them but they don't have the same status that they have for Frege. The propositions themselves are the only justification you need. So unfolding truth, so far as it has any kind of place as an idea that you can see as present in the *Tractatus*, would be unfolding what's involved in propositions and their relations to each other. If you can do that—which the *Tractatus*, in some sense, does—then you have "unfolded the concept of truth." So you have a transformation of the notion of unfolding truth. That naturally leads to the question, what would it be to "unfold truth" from the point of view of Wittgenstein's later philosophy?

So that's the question I would like to deal with, but it seems to me—it's not exactly a totally new question—that Peter Winch has said some things which lead into grave difficulties. Namely, if you start saying that you unfold truth by looking at the ways in which you establish what is true in various language games you lose any sense, it seems to me, of why we should make any connections among these sorts of activities, why we should think of truth as in any way, "one thing." And also I think you lose sight of, or can lose sight of, what might be involved in the Dummett idea of "that in virtue of which some proposition is true." This whole issue: if you're not putting forth a correspondence theory, you're not putting forth a Platonic understanding of a proposition, what kind of understanding of truth do you have?

Well, Winch pulls you back to the circumstances of the game in which you make the original assertion. But that seems to me again to be very peculiar because, to get back to the kinds of thing we were saying earlier, the circumstances in which the fundamentalists say that this animal came into existence may be that they read it in the Bible, let's say (to be fairly crude about it). The circumstances in which someone else says the animal, or the species of animal, came into existence, might be those he sees as those of modern biology. Now the fact that these two people have different circumstances in which they make their assertions does not mean that they are making statements that do not, in some sense or other, clash.

This is not a new question. It is, in a sense, a question that's been exercising Hilary Putnam, in another sense exercising John McDowell, and so it's a question I want to look at in connection with the notion of unfolding truth. Whether I can do that for this December conference I don't know. So that's one thing I'd like to do more with.

Truth interests me a great deal because it is, on the one hand, a moral notion, and I've written about it, not in *Realistic Spirit* but elsewhere, as a moral notion. Truth interests me as a notion as it turns up within contemporary theory of meaning where it often is totally abstracted from the kinds of circumstances in which it has moral significance. So what I would like, in a sense, is to be able to bring those strands together. I've done stuff on truth from the two different sides, and I would like to be able in some way or other to do more to bring those together. So that's one thing.

I'm interested also in the idea that there's this sentence—let's call this a riddle—"truth is one." What are you going to do with that sentence? Is it something you just want to drop? In a world of language games, does it just drop out of sight? Does it have any significance? Can I make any sense of it?

I have an essay I clipped some time ago by someone—I'm not sure what he's doing now—Peter Marin, who was writing about a criticism that had been published of an associate of Martin Luther King, Abercrombie, who had written about King's sex life. And Abercrombie has been criticized because, people have said, he was tarnishing a saint or, at least, the image of a saint, and this shouldn't be done. Marin was arguing that this was a wrong way to think, and that in fact it deepened our picture of King to see him as a human being who was like everybody else in having things that were not so wonderful about him. That it was very important to see that he could be a great man and that he was a human being, that this was very important. And he wanted to connect this at the end of this essay with the notion of truth being one. That in some sense we shouldn't shy away from seeing the whole truth of somebody.

Anyway, there's a moral understanding there of the notion of truth "as one," and there's another notion—a very, very important logical notion—that all truths, one thinks, are compatible with each other. And again the language game picture seems to make that a puzzle. Why should something said in one language game, why should that—or does it—have any relationship to what is said in other language games? Why shouldn't something count as assertible in one game, and something else assertible in another language game? What can be the relationships between them? So, again, we seem to lose this notion of, let's put a heavy philosophical word here, "objective reality"—the reason all truths are compatible is because of reality.

There are all these notions that Platonists emphasize and mythologize in a certain way; what is left of them for us? As it were, once the Platonistic misunderstandings are something we can see as misunderstandings, what can we do with notions of truth as one—or similar notions. I like Wittgenstein's remarks that he can't say anything "truer than he is" (though I think there's a difficulty in understanding that in translation; I don't think the distinction between true and truthful goes through in German in the way it does for us). But I think that his own understanding of what it meant to be committed to truth and the way in which he admired Frege's commitment to truth—well these are moral issues—how are they connected with the ways in which we see the logical issue? It's that range of topics that connects up, as you said, with notions of agreement and disagreement across language games.

I'd like to do more with ethics. As it happens, fairly recently, I've been asked to do this or that and it's been reasonably interesting but it's all been either about Wittgenstein or about early analytic or, in some ways, about both. The kinds of things I've found myself committed to in the last two years have not involved direct work on ethical issues. So I would like to get back to some of that. φ

Peter Unger

In 1979, as now, few agreed with the statement "I do not exist," but that was the title of a piece by Peter Unger in a book published that year. A professor of philosophy at New York University, Unger is best known for his penchant for provocation and for excursions to the extremes of philosophy. Long a skeptic and among the most demanding of ethicists, Unger has traced a philosophical career often at odds with conventional wisdom. But he has not always been perched out on a limb.

After majoring in philosophy at Swarthmore, Unger completed his D. Phil at Oxford with Strawson and Ayer. His thesis (completed under Ayer's supervision) did not foreshadow his controversial career. In it he defended a form of reliabilism, arguing that when certain of your beliefs don't merely happen to be true, but rather are sustained in ways that, over a wide enough range of situations, ensure that you will have correct beliefs, then those beliefs count as knowledge. Although he soon moved away from this reliabilism, his early papers in the late 1960s—published when Unger was an assistant professor at the University of Wisconsin at Madison—explored ideas similarly within the bounds of what he terms "respectable" philosophical discourse.

Ultimately, Unger did not just part ways with reliabilism—he found it utterly unreliable. With "A Defense of Skepticism," published by *The Philosophical Review* in 1971, Unger entered the almost uninhabited outer reaches of epistemology. Here, he laid the groundwork for his claim that it is impossible for humans to truly know anything. He continued to write about skepticism for the next four years, a period which produced his Guggenheim fellowship, his first book (*Ignorance: A Case for Scepticism*, in 1975), but few adherents in the world of philosophy. By this time, skeptics had been a rare breed for at least seventy years. This period also brought him to New York University, where he is still teaching.

Unger's reputation—for bold thinking and iconoclasm—grew. After five years of protracted skepticism, Unger moved even further from the philosophical mainstream: rather than merely doubting the existence of things, Unger promoted an extreme metaphysical nihilism, maintaining that almost everything thought to exist actually does not. Unger published papers like "There Are No Ordinary Things" and "Why There Are No People," as well as the previously mentioned "I Do Not Exist," denying the existence of rocks, chairs, planets, and plants. Perhaps to counterbalance this radicalism, he also published "Toward a Psychology of Common Sense" in 1982, exploring the mechanisms by which people convince themselves that almost all their concrete common nouns denote real things.

Soon thereafter, he examined the flipside of skepticism: rather than nothing existing, what if everything existed? Here Unger offered an extravagantly rich ontology, arguing for infinitely many worlds containing every possibility, including philosophizing fish. He held that any exclusion from the totality of things, including the exclusion of such fish, would be arbitrary.

Unger's 1990 book *Identity, Consciousness and Value* brought him closer to the realm of what he calls "socially acceptable" philosophy. Eight or nine years in the writing, the book returned to a more commonsensical metaphysics and embraced a form of physicalism. Taking the existence of most of physical reality for granted, he argued that what secures our survival as individual persons is the continuous-enough physical realization of our core psychology.

Looking back, Unger reflects that his next turn, a spin through ethics, reflected a desire to do something relevant to how we lead our lives and perhaps to contribute a little good to the world. The 1996 *Living High and Letting Die* was the result of this direction of his thought. Subtitled "our illusion of innocence," the book deployed an argumentation reminiscent of the life-or-death moral thought experiments of Judith Jarvis Thomson, Frances Kamm, and many others. It found no firm basis for the common assumption that it is morally acceptable to refrain from giving a huge portion of our income and wealth to save the lives of the poor in the third world. Inspired by Singer's "Famine, Affluence, and Morality," the book pitted one's moral intuitions in specific case studies against the general intuition that underpins our complacency toward easily preventable deaths in poor countries. To a much greater extent than that reached by most philosophers, Unger's argument leads its readers to precepts forbidding passive behavior toward distant misery. If we would think it wrong not to pick up a hitchhiker with a wounded leg, even if picking him up would damage the upholstery in our new car, why is it morally decent, Unger asks, to forego a similar expense and let a dozen children in Africa die of malaria? The book argued for a highly demanding morality, which, like his skepticism, sat outside the general discourse in ethics. That contradicted the far more lenient view endorsed by most recent writers on the subject. Nonetheless, the book proved popular. Written for a more general audience than his other books, *Living High and Letting Die* is in its sixth printing.

Unger's most recent work, in preparation for a book that he estimates is at least three years away, represents a return to somewhat mainstream metaphysical views. As he discusses in our interview, he is now examining "scientiphical" assumptions about the universe, asking about the implications of what is perceived as commonsense metaphysics. The course of his ideas has not exactly come full circle, but it has moved back toward philosophically polite society from the period of "Why There Are No Other People." Despite his reputation as a contrarian, he is, in conversation, self-effacing; having spent time intensely pursuing several different contradictory worldviews, he now finds himself a bit wary of total intellectual commitment to any particular conceptual scheme. "I think philosophy is too hard for human beings, or at least for this human being," he says. But as he pursues projects perhaps less ambitious than the denial of the possibility of knowledge, his reputation as a radical skeptic lives on. His early writings in defense of skepticism earned him his entry in Dennett's notorious *Philosophical Lexicon*:

unger, n. Extreme epistemic undernourishment, often developing into a sceptic ulcer. "The suggestion that no one knows what he had for breakfast this morning is strictly from unger." φ

Peter Unger
Science and the Possibility of Philosophy

Interview by
Alex Guerrero
in 2001

HRP: Five years ago you wrote *Living High and Letting Die*, a book that Peter Singer called "one of the most significant works of ethics published this decade." Since then, you've written mainly on metaphysics. Why the switch from ethics to metaphysics? What are you looking at in metaphysics now?

Unger: Well, first off, I should say that I've always thought of metaphysics as the most central part of philosophy. The nature of reality, the nature of me, how it is that I relate to the rest of reality (presuming solipsism is false), what of reality isn't me, what I am like, can I have much of an idea what the rest of it is like. What are the main relations between me and the rest of it, presumably only part of which is made up of other beings like me. You, for example. It's hard to be a Berkeleyan idealist. Most of what there is isn't much like us: thinking beings and our mere ideas. There is something called matter, whatever that is. Mere matter. Insensate, unthinking matter. Part of what I am doing is trying to see what the problems are, how good of a systematic understanding we can develop. That's what I've been working on for the last three or four years, and what I'm going to be working on for at least the next three or four years. I'm in the middle of writing this little book; at least I hope it's little. I don't want to impose on my friends a book that they're probably just going to skim around in a bit and then feel guilty about for not really having read their friend's book. [Laughs]

HRP: Some of this will have to do with what you are calling "Scientiphicalism"?

Unger: Yes, that's right. A lot of it will have to do in a way with Scientiphicalism. Scientiphicalism, of course, is the metaphysic that nearly all educated Westerners carry around in their heard. It takes off from whatever was going on with Galileo: most of the world being matter, and so on. You just concentrate on its clearly physical properties, and anything that seems mainly humanly interesting—like the colors and smells and so forth—gets backed up into the mind and ignored, given an almost epiphenomenalist, second-class status. We sort of carry that around in our heads. The real workings of the world are going on in the basic, or basic enough, physical "whatever-it-is." Quarks and leptons or whatever the next thing they will say it is—all of which is doing basically the same thing whether they are constituting anything interesting or not. Say, for example, you, or at least, your body. The only difference is that when these things are (as it seems to us) in interesting physical arrangements then they will serve to constitute these interesting complexes, like you. When they're in other arrangements, they're just boring, floating around in the air in interstellar space. They might constitute something semi-interesting, say, a rock. The only difference is in the spatio-temporal physical arrangement—and that's what's the epiphenomenal upshot of that? All the whip hand is in the basic physical whatevers. I think pretty much everyone carries that around in his or her head. At least all educated Westerners for the last couple of centuries or so. It has been the prevailing metaphysic in mainstream philosophy, which is sort of something like "analytic" philosophy, ever since doing metaphysics became somewhat respectable again.

HRP: When would you say that was?

Unger: Well, somewhere around 1960, 1965, when Wittgenstein's influence pretty much came to an end and he started to become a primarily historical figure, of primarily historical interest. Which he's certainly been for the last twenty years—merely an historical figure. The famous and highly regarded philosophers who have an interest in something that's supposed to be Wittgenstein now, mostly have an interest in Kripke's ideas in that book of his on Wittgenstein and rule-following. If it's really Kripke and he didn't get Wittgenstein right (and who knows what it is to get Wittgenstein right), then there's very little being done with Wittgenstein indeed.

HRP: Except for a lot of interpretive work.

Unger: Yes, just as is true for Nietzsche, and Kant, and Hume, and Descartes, and so forth. He's become a historical figure. Most philosophers don't take his questions as questions for us to work on. I mean, one of his main points was not to do metaphysics anymore. That was all supposed to be an illusion. Or, really, any systematic philosophical work of any sort. But that did fade out, some decades ago. Since then, a lot of work has been done in metaphysics, or in areas of philosophy that rely on metaphysics—philosophy of mind, even meta-ethics. And the metaphysics is basically this Scientiphical (as I spell it with a "ph," really for philosophical reasons) interpretation of whatever it is that science, mainly physics (presumably the most basic science), is supposed to deliver. We carry this around in our heads, and now the most influential people in the philosophical academy take it for granted and hardly even bother to espouse it, but it's there. The general idea is: whatever is real and isn't physical "supervenes" on the physical—whatever that means, and nobody really knows what it means. Each person has a slightly different interpretation, so that someone who looks carefully at the other guy's interpretation finding something wrong with it, but something else that is right. Whatever it is, it's not very different from the old epiphenomenalism. It's a classier way of looking at things that is supposed to avoid certain things that were taken to be mistakes of the old epiphenomenalism.

So, that's the prevalent view. There are many problems with it, once you start thinking about it hard. First, there's a difficulty in getting to an understanding of what the "physical" is. Most people think, "oh, that's fine, it's just this 'Supervenience' thing that we need to get clear on." Goodness knows, I don't have any clue *about* what the Supervenience thing is. But, the more basic issue is this: people had better get clearer on what the physical is—on what is this more basic reality that all else, everything else that's "concrete," anyway, is supposed to supervene on. We need to get clearer on its nature—well, its "intrinsic nature," to use a fancy expression. And, nowadays, hardly anyone in metaphysics works on that at all. It's a very bad situation, I think. Here's part of why I think it's so bad, which should give you a feeling for what I mean. Well, we can't really be clear about what's physical once we've moved "qualities"—something like phenomenal color, roughly, away from the physical world. That's what Galileo did, and everyone since—Descartes, Locke, and so forth. We can't really get a conception that adequately distinguishes between a world of, on the one hand, Newtonian particles, little material spheres colliding with one another, attracting and repelling one another within space and, on the other hand, a sort of "Swiss-cheesy" material plenum or field with little spherical vacuums, perfectly empty bubbles. In this world the bubbles' trajectories are said to be timed perfectly parallel to trajectories of particles in the Newtonian world. The bubbles' trajectories are supposed to be determined by the undulation propensities of the plenum. The upshot of this is that the bubbles go up and down, left and right, wherever they go. So have we really conceived two different worlds? Or do we just have two different vocabularies, a plenum-style vocabulary and a particle-style vocabulary? What's the real difference? Both are somehow too abstract, too devoid of quality, for us to have in mind anything definite at all. In a way, even in the simplest cases of having physical worlds, we really don't have any idea of what we are talking about. The alternative, of course, is to reverse what Galileo, Descartes, and Locke have foisted on us and get back to a picture that gets some "quality" back into what is supposed to be physical—and run with that for a while. That's the first thing to do.

HRP: You have a paper, "Free Will and Scientiphicalism," that addresses some of the issues that arise with the adoption of a Scientiphicalist worldview. How do you think your work will fit into the general debate over whether reasons explanations can and/or should be reduced to causal explanations? Do you see your work addressing this question directly?

Unger: I think that, if we have any choice in the matter, (as we better, if we are to make any sense of most of human life, and not just ethics—including that but other things as well), we better have, within our mental power, a power to choose among the alternatives. And this looks as if it can't possibly be understood as any sort of physical power, however "physical" is construed. There has to be something beyond what most philosophers think of as causation, which they think of as event causation. They think that this "event causation" is somehow more in line with everything being basically physical or other stuff supervening on the physical, and so forth. Actually, it is something dubious that event causation has much more to do with physical goings on. Many people have noticed this, going back at least to Bertrand Russell, who wrote extensively in support of the view that, in anything like physics as it had been developing, the notion of causation really has no place. We often think that we understand cause and effect by looking at science. In science, there is supposed to be a directionality from cause to effect; there is supposed to be an asymmetry. The cause is supposed to be prior to and productive of an event. What does this have to do with science? In science you have Newtonian particles mutually attracting one another through the evolvement of time. Or an electron and a proton repelling each other over time. What is going on here? So we say that 'the cause' of this electron's going toward this proton is the proton's "pulling it" or something? None of it really makes much sense. We can talk that way, but we feel that it is really a kind of nonsense. It's a projection of some other thing onto what really doesn't have much to do with cause or effect at all. I think Russell was right. But more than that, I think that the very root idea of cause that we best understand is pretty much the way that Berkeley said it was. Everybody now thinks that Berkeley was this great figure but no one takes anything he said too seriously—he's read just for historical interest, unlike Hume, who is said to have set the agenda. But actually Berkeley should be taken as having set part of the agenda too. This is the idea: the real idea of causation that we understand best is that of an intentional agent doing something that exercises its will and intelligence. That is what we really understand. My casing it to be the case that I imagine a red disk, or a blue disk, or whatever. There you have something that you can really understand as someone bringing about a change—maybe in this case being just a change in his own mind. The other thing, the physical, is just these inert 'whatevers' bouncing around in the world. There is supposed to be some event. Well, is the event really *productive* of some other event? It doesn't really make much sense. We start treating the ones that are called causes as little "semi-agents" or something like that. Now, it may be dubious how often this root notion of causation, agent causation, really is instantiated in the real world. Maybe the real world is a kind of sad place, which is all just illusion, and that there is just a sort of flow of the physical. We hope not, and it seems reasonable to think not. We really believe that we make a difference: we believe that we do make changes, that we cause there to be certain changes. I used the word "make"—in most instances it will work just as well as the verb "cause." Cause to happen, make happen.

HRP: Often "make" is tied up with purposeful action. To speak of particles in that way often seems inappropriate or at least metaphorical.

Unger: Sure, purposeful action. Someone making a dinner, making a bowl—causing the bowl to be. And, though I'm not a believer, God making the world, God making people. The root understanding of cause, I feel, has to do with this idea of an agent making something happen. Looking at the problem the other way seems to start off getting the problem backwards.

HRP: It's interesting, because people generally take causal explanation to be the better understood case, with reason explanations being somehow more complicated.

Unger: I think we generally understand reasons explanations better. It's just that we have a very hard time understanding how reasons are going to fit in with what we take the world really to be at bottom, which is this Scientiphical business, the physical goings on. How are reasons explanations supposed to fit into this picture, on their own terms? That is the question that is hard to answer.

HRP: We've discussed some apparent problems with Scientiphicalism or a bottom-level scientific understanding. One question I have is how do you understand the "successes of science," the way it seems to do many things well? How do you understand its coming to reign as the predominant metaphysic? It seems to have quite a bit going for it, in that it allows us to manipulate our environment and allows us to do things that previously no one would have thought possible.

Unger: Well, I think it has to do with two things. I do think that scientists are talking about a reality, most of which is beyond them and us and our ideas. There's *something* right about the Scientiphical metaphysic; I am what is called a "realist" about a lot of things physical. It's hard to know what I'm then a realist about. Let me say on the other side, though, that while it's very much out of fashion now, if you ask philosophically inclined physicists what their conception of what they're doing is, a fair number of them *won't* be realists. Even Einstein thought that pretty much most of science was just setting up equations that were incredibly useful tools for predicting experiences and manipulating the world. To a large degree, that was very often Bertrand Russell's position. Einstein read Russell, and I think he seconded Russell's notions. Now, I don't agree with Russell. I'm not a Phenomenalist, which Russell was then, but I'm not exactly sure what I am when I say I'm a realist about the physical world. And how it is that I'm supposed to differ from these Phenomenalists.

HRP: About what do you disagree when you say that you disagree with the Phenomenalists?

Unger: I don't think that all the physical world is, is some sort of construction out of our experiences, or sense data, or perceptions. I *also* don't think that the physical reality that the physicists are saying something about is a "construction" out of perceptible objects, that is, out of only those things, like tables and chairs, and electron microscopes, and the pictures these microscopes take—the things we can perceive directly, or directly enough. So I also disagree with Instrumentalism—a less extreme, less mentalistic cousin of Phenomenalism. Here's something interesting that's very, very different from what I believe: A very distinguished philosopher of science at Princeton, Bas van Fraassen, believes in God and *doesn't* believe in electrons. Yes, I believe in electrons, but I don't really believe in God. Still, I'm not exactly sure what it is that I believe in when I believe in electrons. I'm trying to get a better idea; that's what I'm doing now.

HRP: Somewhat of a general question now. You've said that metaphysics is more central to philosophy than ethics. I guess one question that seems fair is: why study philosophy at all? Is it just interesting? If it is just interesting, then why is it okay to study it before we deal with other ostensibly pressing problem in the world, such as those raised in your book *Living High and Letting Die*?

Unger: Without getting too tricky about the whole business, I think it is much more important (let's suppose that some things are more important than others), to do what we can for people in direst need than to pursue art or metaphysics. Thus, during the last three of four year and probably during the next three or four years I'll be doing something that is less important than what I should be doing, than helping the people in direst need, which each of us can do a lot about. In this way, I'm not very surprising. People aren't that good. When it's conspicuously pushed in our face about what there really is to be done, what the world is really like, then we tend to be more responsive to what really is important. If I were thrown down in the middle of the worse sorts of preventable African horror shows, and I were unable to leave, given a choice between spending a few hours a day working on metaphysics or spending a few hours doing something about it, in that situation I'd probably spend a few hours a day doing something about it. But that is, as I bring out in my book, very pale and removed form me here. I'm not there. It's hard for me to be very impressed with it most of the time, and it is extremely easy for me to be much more taken with other things, most of the time.

HRP: That's the situation most of us are in most of the time.

Unger: Sure. One of the things that is important to remember is that if you are living in a country where most of the people are committed to these sorts of things all around you, then it is a lot easier too. But if everybody around you is involved with getting a nice apartment set up, having people over to dinner, and so forth, then it's harder. People on the whole do pretty much the same thing and live pretty much the same lives as other people in their society. Pretty much most of my life is like most college professors and other professional people living in nice urban neighborhoods, and so forth.

HRP: Liam Murphy has just written a book, *Moral Demands in Non-Ideal Theory*, in which he addresses some of these concerns. I was wondering if you had any thoughts about his approach to these issues and whether or not you think his position might be a way out of the predicament, so to speak.

Unger: Well, first off, I must admit I haven't carefully gone through the whole of the book. I plan to teach a course on it next spring, but I haven't gone through the finished product completely. That said, I can certainly see a lot of good things in it, even just from having looked at the draft chapters. Still, I can't believe that his position is right. I think that my position is closer to the truth. His position feels nicer, because it is not demanding, and so in a way I'd like his position to be right. Look, here's Liam's view—its main thrust anyway: each of us should do her "fair share" to lessen the suffering and loss of the worst off folks—the malnourished, sickly, "third-world" kids, for instance. So, each of us should do only as much would be needed from her *given that* everyone else who's well off were doing what's needed from *them.* So, if you guy's *don't* give through UNICEF, OXFAM, and so on, the pretty big amount needed from you—and it's pretty big—that doesn't mean that I then have to give them almost everything I've got. On my view, of course, it does mean I've got to go "all out." So, what he "wants" from each of us is much more approachable. The thing now puzzling me with what I take, or took, to be the right position is this: up to the point where we can say that's really true that you *can* do things to help, it's really wrong not to do as much as you can to alleviate the serious suffering that is going on. But, it could be that, to a much greater extend than I allowed, just implicitly, well, it could be psychologically impossible for most well-off people to do very much. It could be that for most people, given the actual situation that they're in and given the actual mind that they have, they really can't do much more than what they are doing. Maybe most of them can't even do as much Liam's system would require.

HRP: That would be an empirical question, I suppose.

Unger: Yes, that's an empirical question, and I don't really know what the answer is. It's largely empirical, but it's also partly philosophical, in terms of determining what really is meant by what people can and cannot do. But a large part is an empirical question, the answer to which I really don't know.

HRP: On a slightly different topic, returning to what you are working on now, you have a recent paper "The Survival of the Sentient," in which you write "to better understand ourselves, we must continue to think of ourselves as being, most essentially, thinking and feeling individuals." Could you speak a little about the ideas behind this quote and in general how this relates to what we were discussing earlier regarding Scientiphicalism?

Unger: Well, the main opponent here, in that paper anyhow is the biological approach, which may go back to Aristotle. I just took on the contemporary guys, who argue that we are more basically or essentially biological beings than that we are psychological, thinking or feeling beings. On my view, and lots of others too, of course, the psychological is essential and biological is really secondary. Suppose that you could replace my biological parts, particularly those of my brain insofar as it supports thinking, with some non-organic gut causally just as effective little bits—tiny bit by tiny bit, gradually. Each week, maybe each day, replace one percent of my brain with an inorganic fancy material that would continue to interact with the rest of my brain so that altogether the bits would support the kind of thinking that I regularly engage in, that I enjoy and suffer and so forth. This would go on for one hundred days or so. In the end, you have a being that thinks, with a biological shell. Take the inorganic matter, now functioning as my brain did before, out of the biological shell and hook it up to the appropriate sort of vat. Then have a steam roller or something go over the body. I would then exist as a non-biological being. I would be the self-same entity that always had *my* power to think and *my* powers of experience. If my life would be worth anything, then I would on occasion manifest these powers, so that I would sometimes think and would sometimes experience.

HRP: It seems something like a functionalist interpretation?

Unger: Well no, I mean it doesn't say anything about *why* it is—I'm just saying that suppose it is right that you *could* do this sort of operation. But at least in terms of the concepts, it seems that it would still be me. It would just be good therapy of a certain sort. to overcome certain kinds of degenerative disease, or whatever.

HRP: I guess that's what I mean by a functionalist interpretation, in that what is preserved through time, what is you now as opposed to earlier, really is this system, or something of that sort.

Unger: Whatever it is that has *your* power to think and experience. I'm not sure that the world does work that way, but if this sort of thing would keep waking up and experiencing, it really would exhibit the same categorical disposition to think. It would be you. This is a partly empirical question, whether you could replace the biology by the non-biology. But as far as the concepts go, it seems that the psychological powers are the important ones, not the biological powers.

HRP: This example raises a general question about philosophy and particularly the use of examples in philosophy—deadly trolley cars, brains in vats, and the like. You rely on them heavily in *Living High and Letting Die* and in your more recent work as well. I guess I would be interested if you could speak on the general practice of using examples: What type of information do these sorts of examples provide, how should they enter into philosophical argument, and so forth? What do we learn from examples of this sort?

Unger: I think there are very few rule of thumb that are very useful regarding the use of examples. One should evaluate each case on its own merits. Here's one rule: when you have cases that seem ingenious and philosophically very interesting, very often something else is going on than what you think the example is supposed to be showing. In very boring cases, very clear cases, you can trust your response to the cases. The boring ones you can trust. A business man kills his main competitor because he wants to succeed at all costs. Did he do something wrong? Of course. It is a boring case. The same holds for other branches of philosophy as well. Here's a case of a ball sitting on a table. Is this also a case of a table being under or supporting a ball? Yes, seems so. Fine; boring. There is not much going on. When the cases are more interesting. It is hard to know where it is doing something of philosophical interest, or when it is doing something else.

HRP: So knowing that, how do you proceed? In a couple of your more recent papers you offer many of what must be called "ingenious" examples, such as the one in which your pet is slowly made non-organic, and we are asked to consider our attitudes toward the pet. How do you deal with this problem?

Unger: You can't trust them very much. It really is the best I can do. The cases seem to be examples that may be illuminating rather than distorting, but you can't be that sure. And thus you can't be that sure of your argument, insofar as it rests on them. You shouldn't be all that confident, and so I'm not. [Laughs]

HRP: On something of a different topic, but a topic that is raised by our earlier discussion of current work done on Wittgenstein, what are your thoughts on the historical study of philosophy in relation to what is more like looking at particular problems somewhat apart from the historical context that might surround them. One question that relates to this: How should departments prepare students?

Unger: I think you can learn enormous amounts from and should continuously go back to the generally recognized canonical philosopher. For me, and I think for most people nowadays, I get more out of and find more accessible people in the modern area—Descartes and so forth—than the ancients and medievalists. Their whole outlook is *so* different from ours that it is so hard to know what they are getting at, at least at times. A brilliant colleague of mine, Kit Fine, seems to find a lot in Aristotle that is metaphysically very interesting and very important. Personally, I get more from the more modern writers, even from Locke, who is a terrible writer. I think that you have to go back to these guys: they really have got the big problems. A bad thing professionally is that nowadays, there has been a split between people on the one hand who take on historical scholarship, and they get *very* scholarly, into the nuances of textural interpretation and so forth, and those on the other hand who are trying to do philosophy on their own bottom. You don't get enough of a mesh. The older generation had people who were doing work on the canonical figures—maybe it wasn't the greatest and most texturally pure—but it was interesting and it was stimulating. One of my teachers, Peter Strawson, was good at this. For the most part, though, there's been this division. The scholars are completely involved in this very close textural work, and the others don't get enough from the canonical figures. It seems like a bad trend. When the old generation goes out, for the most part you will just have the very scholarly scholars just talking to each other, and the other people who try to always start from square one. It seems like a bad trend.

HRP: It does seem a shame, reinventing the wheel.

Unger: Well, if you're doing really *serious* philosophy, you really need to go back to the historical figures. You want to be informed by people who know what is going on; you can stand on their shoulders in order to see more. I am trying to do this in my work because, let's face it, these historical figures are far greater thinkers than I could ever hope to be. So, I'm trying to go back into the history, to learn from those long dead guys what are the really central issues. I do some of that in, say, my paper "The Mystery of the Physical."

There is another sad trend: the sameness of what is considered serious by dominant philosophical groups. Everybody is something like a Scientiphicalist. What does that mean? One thing it means is that you have virtually nothing in the way of Idealism of any sort, virtually nothing in the way of serious dualism, nothing different at all. It's pretty much all the same; there are only little wrinkles of difference. Everyone is accepting the same sort of basic world outlook, where the physical is pretty much all that there is, maybe all there is, at least all that is really serious. And what is that? Well, it's not essentially mental, sometimes it gets together and constitutes something mental—but whatever it is, that's it. There's no real diversity of viewpoints. And that's unfortunate. Here's something a little interesting: I have been invited to a conference on the metaphysics of human beings, which is going to meet this summer. Most of the senior people who will be there are theists. I might be the only atheist among these senior people, maybe even the only non-theist. Now, this *is* a group where there is some real diversity of viewpoint. They really do have some of these other views as their metaphysical outlook. Bob Adams from Yale is going to be there, and I've heard that he really is an idealist like Berkeley. Unfortunately he hasn't published on this, at least not to date. There are a few British theists who have actually published on these different ways of looking at the world. And, some of them are at Oxford, like John Foster, who's a sort of Berkeleyan idealist, and Richard Swineburn, who's a substantial Dualist, somewhat like Descartes. But it really is mainly just the theists who are articulating these views. And, though they're at Oxford, these guys are very much outsiders. Their work has virtually no influence. In fact, it's not their theism that does them in. No: it's much more the fact that they're trying to advance views that disagree in a basic and wholesale way, with the dominant Scientiphicalism, with that, for the last fifty years or so, has been the well-entrenched same-old, same-old. And that's *very* unfortunate.

Anyhow, there should also be plenty of non-theists developing deeply diverse views. And, these deeply alternative non-theists—well, a few of them at least—should be taken seriously, very seriously, by the dominant Scientiphical guys. Then present-day philosophy would be more interesting.

HRP: Why do you think that these views are so unpopular? Do you think that it is just that people feel that the views—idealism, dualism, and so forth— have been (or are in the process of being) defeated? Is it just that people think they are false?

Unger: I just think it's the times. Different things are popular at different times. Different things become popular; we get in a groove and roll for a half-century or more. One thing about the current trend, one part that has been in force since Moore and Russell revolted against Bradley and Hegel's absolute idealism—the whole world as an immaterial one, a single, immaterial entity—is the development of this "common sense" thing. More and more, in the last fifty years, there is the working assumption prevalent in the dominant groups of academic philosophy, that common sense has to be right 99 percent of the time. we make a few little adjustments, but we have to get our philosophy set up so that propositions of common sense fall out as theorems.

HRP: Not too unlike the use of examples, where what we appeal to is our "intuitive" response to cases.

Unger: Sure. Since Moore, everyone has to care a lot about common sense or is just considered a nut case. That's been an unfortunate thing. A second thing is that we take science to really tell us what the world is like. Science delivers the goods; we'll just say a few secondary things about what things are. But our priority is to agree with common sense. This is a relatively new thing for philosophy.

HRP: Definitely a more limited role for philosophy.

Unger: We can't let philosophy win too much, because common sense has to win. And you can't tell too much about what the world is like, because you are not a scientist. You are backed into a corner. You can do ethics, because there is no science of ethics. But it's hard to know what you are really doing, because *maybe* there are no facts there. *Anyway,* if you're trying to do metaphysics, you really can't try to do too much. You really are backed into a corner. φ